CompTIA Project+ Certification Guide

Learn project management best practices and successfully pass the CompTIA Project+ PK0-004 exam

J. Ashley Hunt

BIRMINGHAM - MUMBAI

CompTIA Project+ Certification Guide

Commissioning Editor: Vijin Boricha
Acquisition Editor: Rahul Nair
Content Development Editor: Dattatraya More
Technical Editor: Nirbhaya Shaji
Copy Editor: Safis Editing
Project Coordinator: Kinjal Bari
Proofreader: Safis Editing
Indexer: Mariammal Chettiyar
Graphics: Jisha Chirayil
Production Coordinator: Shraddha Falebhai

First published: September 2018

Production reference: 1270918

Published by Packt Publishing Ltd.
Livery Place
35 Livery Street
Birmingham
B3 2PB, UK.

ISBN 978-1-78953-449-8

www.packtpub.com

To my husband, Chris Lambert. Without you, nothing is possible; and with you, the impossible becomes reality. Thank you for all you do for us and for inspiring me always. I love you!

– J. Ashley Hunt

`mapt.io`

Mapt is an online digital library that gives you full access to over 5,000 books and videos, as well as industry leading tools to help you plan your personal development and advance your career. For more information, please visit our website.

Why subscribe?

- Spend less time learning and more time coding with practical eBooks and Videos from over 4,000 industry professionals

- Improve your learning with Skill Plans built especially for you

- Get a free eBook or video every month

- Mapt is fully searchable

- Copy and paste, print, and bookmark content

Packt.com

Did you know that Packt offers eBook versions of every book published, with PDF and ePub files available? You can upgrade to the eBook version at `www.packt.com` and as a print book customer, you are entitled to a discount on the eBook copy. Get in touch with us at `customercare@packtpub.com` for more details.

At `www.packt.com`, you can also read a collection of free technical articles, sign up for a range of free newsletters, and receive exclusive discounts and offers on Packt books and eBooks.

Foreword

Hello, readers.

There is a reason you are reading this student guide right now. Maybe you are looking to get certified, or to learn about formal project management for career advancement, or perhaps you are looking to make a career switch. I applaud all of those triggers for embarking on this journey. But how will this undertaking in project management certification affect you? That is what I'd like to share. You'll see the world with a different lens. A project management lens will help you interact with those around you, predict success or failure, mitigate major risk events, and exploit opportunities.

It is the little things that you'll learn through this journey that will change you. Take, for instance, the discussion of how organizations operate. As a project manager, you'll interact with teams that are already slammed with work. How will you get the resources you need if they don't report to you? How will you get the most out of the individuals that are involved in your project? You'll be more likely to get the team you need if you know how to negotiate for them, motivate them, get them through tough times, and then stand back when they are on a pathway to success.

You will learn how to look at metrics and detect whether you'll have cost overruns, miss a schedule milestone, or deliver as planned. Ultimately, a good project manager is a coach, a firefighter, a referee, and a mathematician all rolled into one. The role of project manager is multifaceted, challenging, and rarely the same day to day. A good project manager can completely change the dynamics of an organization for the better. I'm hoping this all sounds exciting to you! It is a rewarding profession, and we need more good project managers in this world.

If you've picked up this book, you are in good hands. J. Ashley Hunt and I have known each other and worked together for a long time. I met Ashley in 2002, in what is the infancy of the group that I run at StormWind Studios now. Ashley was a great project management instructor back then and is even better now. She is the quintessential PMP®, Project+, CAPM®, and PMI-ACP® instructor. She'll help you learn the formal information, apply that information, and not bore you to tears or force something on you that is impractical.

She is an authority you can trust, and in doing so, you can give yourself up to her as she shepherds you through this journey. As I say to all my own students, I wish you the best of luck to you in all your pursuits. Exploit this opportunity. Project management knowledge and certification can make a world of difference for your career and your organization.

Dan Young, CCIE & PMP
Vice President of Operations
StormWind Studios

Contributors

About the author

J. Ashley Hunt is currently the senior project management instructor at StormWind Studios for Waterfall and Agile project management. A nationally and internationally known subject-matter expert in the areas of Project Management and Professional Development, she has created training offerings for and delivered project management training to more than 10 thousand people working for enterprise clientele around the world. Ashley has developed an admirable reputation as a consultative trainer and engaging speaker in several disciplines, consistently receiving exemplary evaluations from her students and clientele. This is her second published study guide. Relevant technical experience: PMP®, Project+, PMI-ACP®, CSM, MCAS, LSSGBC certified.

Thanks go to Dattatraya More and Nirbhaya Shaji, for excellent guidance as my editors; Rahul Nair, who reached out to me to start this venture and Bob Simpson for the technical edits. Dan Young, for being the best leader I have ever worked for and with – thank you for writing the foreword! Thanks to all at Packt Publishing. Lastly, thank you to StormWind Studios for being an incredible place to work and grow professionally.

About the reviewer

Bobby Simpson is the creator of GhostSentry.com, an access control and compliance firewall, and CIO for the accounting firm Finley & Cook. Bobby has 20 years of experience managing technical projects and infrastructure, along with policies and procedures compliant with HIPAA, PCI, and NIST. Bobby holds several technical certifications, including CISSP, CompTIA Project+, SANS GPEN, GCIA, GCIH, and Cisco+Security. He is a SANS mentor instructor and a member of InfraGard.

Packt is searching for authors like you

If you're interested in becoming an author for Packt, please visit `authors.packtpub.com` and apply today. We have worked with thousands of developers and tech professionals, just like you, to help them share their insight with the global tech community. You can make a general application, apply for a specific hot topic that we are recruiting an author for, or submit your own idea.

Table of Contents

Preface

Congratulations on your decision to become CompTIA Project+ certified!

Because you are preparing to take the CompTIA Project+ (PK0-004) exam, you'll undoubtedly want to find out as much information as you can about the variety of best practices found in IT and other types of project management. The more information you have at your disposal, and the more hands-on experience you gain, the better off you'll be when attempting the exam.

The goal is to provide you with enough information to prepare you for the exam, but my hope for you is – aside from having letters after your name (which is great!) – that you'll learn new best practices that you can bring into your current or future projects.

You may find that some of the best practices don't align with your day-to-day projects, and that's okay! I like to think of this information as *perfect-world project management.* We don't live in a perfect world, so if you read through something and think to yourself *that will never work in my organization,* or *we would never use this,* that is totally okay and expected.

There will, however, be tons of great information and best practices that you *can* use in your projects. Talking the talk is great, but walking the walk is even better. The more you learn and implement, the smoother your projects will run. Plus, that makes it all the easier to pass your exam.

I've included review questions at the end of each chapter to give you an idea of what to expect in your exams. If you're already working in an IT project environment, I recommend that you check out these questions first to gauge your level of expertise. You can then use the book primarily to fill in the gaps in your current knowledge. This study guide will help you round out your knowledge base before tackling the exam.

If you can answer 90 percent or more of the review questions correctly for each chapter, you can feel safe moving on to the next chapter. If you're unable to answer that percentage of questions correctly, re-read the chapter and try the questions again. Your score should improve as you continue your studies.

You may also find that many of the best practices come from the **Project Management Body of Knowledge (PMBOK® Guide)**. If you are not familiar with the PMBOK® Guide, it is published by the **Project Management Institute (PMI®)**, who developed the **Certified Associate in Project Management (CAPM®)** exam, the **Project Management Professional (PMP®)** exam, and the **Project Management Institute Agile Certified Practitioner (PMI-ACP®)** exam, as well as many other certification-based exams for project managers.

There is more information following on where to find other certifications if you are ever interested in obtaining more in future.

For now, let's focus on your Project+ and its correlation to the PMBOK Guide®. The PMBOK Guide® contains all the best practices for *predictive* project management, meaning fully plan-driven. CompTIA acknowledges the guide and all the best practices but narrows everything to more of an introductory level and targets the IT industry specifically.

The material is presented from a beginner to intermediate technical level. Experience with and knowledge of different types of roles and responsibilities in small- to medium-sized projects is helpful but not necessary for the CompTIA Project+ (PK0-004) exam, which is the most up-to-date exam at the time of writing.

Getting your foot in the door

CompTIA's goal in putting together the Project+ (PK0-004) exam is to call attention to the multiple methodologies and best practices involved in project management.

There are many other certification types that are proprietary, such as the following:

- The CAPM through the PMI, www.pmi.org

- The **Project Management Professional (PMP)** through the PMI, www.pmi.org

- Axelos PRINCE2 Foundational exam, https://www.axelos.com/certifications/prince2

Although many of these certifications have numerous experience requirements to sit the exam, CompTIA Project+ does not. However, it is a great jumping-off point and shows you are working toward your goals. The content itself is not company-specific or partial to any one set of processes over another.

After passing the exam, you can take your new knowledge and apply it based on your organizational best practices and processes as needed.

Who this book is for

In a world that is becoming more focused on technology, understanding project management across multiple industries is an essential career skill. CompTIA Project+ certification proves that you have the knowledge and skills to solve business problems in virtually any business environment running small- to medium-sized IT projects on a regular basis. If you are a new project manager or a seasoned project manager in the field of IT, certification can help you become more competitive and employable.

Certification also shows dedication to your organization and your career trajectory. Research shows that people who study project management best practices get hired or promoted more often than those who do not. Job applicants with high school diplomas or college degrees who included project management coursework or certifications on their resumes fared consistently better in job interviews and were hired or promoted more often.

Testing for certification can be an invaluable competitive advantage for IT project management professionals.

What this book covers

Chapter 1, *Introduction to the CompTIA Project+ Exam (PK0-004)*, is an overview of what to expect from the CompTIA Project+ certification process and the steps to help you with certification. It also provides a practice exam to test your knowledge.

Chapter 2, *Project Initiation*, will help readers learn about how projects are defined based on different organizational structures and introduce the different project selection techniques that are used to charter a project.

Chapter 3, *Project Roles and Responsibilities*, will describe the variety of stakeholders who could be involved in any type of project and will define the responsibilities they may undertake.

Chapter 4, *Developing a Project Charter*, will describe the different process groups found on projects or phases and provide information on how key deliverables and high-level requirements are determined based on a business case and stakeholder engagement.

Chapter 5, *Creating a Work Breakdown Structure (WBS)*, will provide the ability to accurately plan other areas such as the schedule, budget, and procurement.

Chapter 6, *Developing a Project Schedule*, will review defining and sequencing tasks to best determine durations. Once the schedule is put together, the critical path can be determined and a schedule baseline can be set.

Chapter 7, *Resource Management Planning and Communication Considerations*, will cover the best practices for selecting team members and advice on how to create a cohesive team.

Chapter 8, *Budget and Contingency Plans for Risk*, will review how project budgets are created and why setting a baseline is so important. It is also necessary for most projects to understand how risk events can help or hurt your project financially.

Chapter 9, *Monitoring and Controlling Project Work*, will cover how to monitor your project work and make changes to bring performance back in line with the plan and provide best practices to help you keep an eye on your projects and close them out successfully.

Chapter 10, *Formal Project or Phase Closure and Agile Project Management*, talks about how closing out a project or phase in a formal manner is important for the tracking of lessons learned and for finalizing anything left of project work or deliverable transition. It is also important to know that project management isn't a *one-size-fits-all* situation, therefore there may be a need to tailor best practices using a more agile approach.

To get the most out of this book

Answer the chapter review questions at the end of each chapter. Check your score and review the items you missed before moving on to the next chapter. It may take two times through to truly be ready for the exam. This guide is more than an exam prep book; it is an overview of all best practices that may be necessary in any given project at any given time. To get the most out of this book, be sure to place yourself in a variety of different situations that may occur on your projects and ask yourself whether you could use the recommended best practices or even tailor them to suit your unique project needs. While having a certification is excellent for your career, it is also important to be able to walk the walk.

Read and re-read the chapters you find the most difficult and look online for other practice exams you can study from.

No study guide is designed to mimic the exact questions on the exam and you will not see the exact questions from this guide on your exam. It is merely a way to test and solidify knowledge.

I hope you enjoy the content and I wish you the best of luck in your studies and all future endeavors!

Download the color images

We also provide a PDF file that has color images of the screenshots/diagrams used in this book. You can download it here: https://www.packtpub.com/sites/default/files/downloads/9781789534498_ColorImages.pdf.

Conventions used

Bold: Indicates a new term, an important word, or words that you see onscreen. For example, words in menus or dialog boxes appear in the text like this. Here is an example: "Typically, there are two types of milestones: **mandatory** and **discretionary**."

 Warnings or important notes appear like this.

 Tips and tricks appear like this.

Get in touch

Feedback from our readers is always welcome.

General feedback: If you have questions about any aspect of this book, mention the book title in the subject of your message and email us at customercare@packtpub.com.

Errata: Although we have taken every care to ensure the accuracy of our content, mistakes do happen. If you have found a mistake in this book, we would be grateful if you would report this to us. Please visit www.packt.com/submit-errata, selecting your book, clicking on the Errata Submission Form link, and entering the details.

Piracy: If you come across any illegal copies of our works in any form on the Internet, we would be grateful if you would provide us with the location address or website name. Please contact us at copyright@packt.com with a link to the material.

If you are interested in becoming an author: If there is a topic that you have expertise in and you are interested in either writing or contributing to a book, please visit authors.packtpub.com.

Reviews

Please leave a review. Once you have read and used this book, why not leave a review on the site that you purchased it from? Potential readers can then see and use your unbiased opinion to make purchase decisions, we at Packt can understand what you think about our products, and our authors can see your feedback on their book. Thank you!

For more information about Packt, please visit packt.com.

Introduction to the CompTIA Project+ Exam (PK0-004)

In this chapter, we'll provide an overview of the CompTIA Project+ exam (PK0-004), how to apply for the exam, and some study tips to get you started. You'll also have an assessment test at the end of this chapter to see where your knowledge lies and areas to target for further study. While this information is readily available online in a variety of places, this overview will provide you with all of the information you need to know in one place.

This chapter covers the following:

- The CompTIA Project+ exam
- How to apply for the exam
- What to expect on exam day
- Study tips
- Assessment test

Why project management certification?

Project management has been around since the dawn of time. Imagine trying to figure out the best way to build a fire for the very first time or how to catch a dinosaur without getting hurt! Humans have always found ways to improve how things are done. Think of ancient Greece and Rome, and imagine the artistic creations and the building of incredible architecture; in a lot of cases, people were creating better ways of doing battle and organizing their troops. All of those are projects.

In the industrial age, project management was applicable to building tall edifices, ships, and trains and utilizing new machinery to improve commerce and quality of life. Now, we are in the technological age and even though we are still building tall edifices, trains, planes, and automobiles, we are finding new types of projects that need their own best practices.

Many project management best practices have stood the test of time, such as **scheduling, budgeting, resourcing,** and **determining what the result will be**. The reason they have stood the test of time is because they work.

Our use of tools and best practices will need to be adapted so they work for technological projects, such as protecting your organization with cyber security, installing servers or software development, and help-desk management. There isn't a one-size-fits-all approach to project management in any industry, and most of the time our organizational processes and enterprise environment influence our projects the most.

But what if you had multiple tools and knowledge at your disposal to adapt and adjust as needed to meet the demands of your projects? What if you could adapt those best practices to conform to your organizational processes and industry? Then it wouldn't matter whether you were trying to catch dinosaurs, building the Colosseum, or building a data center. You could pick and choose what would work. That is the beauty of learning best practices. On top of that, if you can prove you know those best practices through certification, now you have some project management clout in your back pocket!

The CompTIA Project+ exam is designed for people like you: professional people who have set best practices based on their organization but are looking for a common language to use, those who need tools and best practices that have been proven over and over again to work but are adaptable to your environment.

Having one or multiple project management certifications shows your willingness to learn, try new things, and improve your organization's projects, which in turn provides value to the organization. Congratulations for taking the first step to career improvement!

Project management is in high demand globally. Project managers make anywhere from $70,000 to $150,000 based on their location and what types of projects they work on. Every organization has an IT department and even if you don't have a lot of experience yet, going into the career of project management without a lot of bad habits is greatly appreciated by organizations. So, don't worry if you're just starting out, because the CompTIA Project+ exam was designed for you.

Everything you will cover in this guide will prepare you for not just certification and passing an exam, but my hope is that it will also give you the tools you can use right away on your current or future projects.

You may see some things in this guide and on your exam that don't necessarily align with your organization's best practices or simply *won't work* in your current environment. That is totally okay! You will need that information to answer questions correctly on your exam, and maybe as you progress in your career you'll find a need for some of those skills.

What will you learn?

Everything we will cover can be found on CompTIA's exam content outline overview on the CompTIA website (https://www.comptia.org/).

You'll want to review the topics that are tested on and how each topic weighs as far as your score is concerned. The following is an overview of the skills you will learn in this guide and an overview of the exam information. All chapters have review questions to help target your exam studies, plus you'll gain an understanding of the best study tips to pass the exam the first time. When you review the exam content outline on the CompTIA website, you'll see it is broken down into several categories:

- Project basics
- Project constraints
- Communication and change management
- Project tools and documentation

All exam questions fall under these *domains* or categories. The following section shows everything we will cover in this guide, along with the correlating domains found on the CompTIA website.

The CompTIA website walks you through everything you will need to know for your exam: https://certification.comptia.org/certifications/project.

Exam objectives (domains)

Here are the list of things that we will cover in this guide:

Domain	% of Exam
1.0 Project Basics	36%
2.0 Project Constraints	17%
3.0 Communication and Change Management	26%
4.0 Project Tools and Documentation	21%
Total	100%

Chapters and corresponding domains

Here the details of the chapters and the corresponding domains that they cover:

Chapter 1: *Introduction to the CompTIA Project+ Exam (PK0-004)*

Understanding what CompTIA is and the value of Project+ certification

- How to apply for the Project+ exam
- Having a good understanding of the best study tips and tricks to pass the exam the first time
- Review question types pertaining to the chapters to help target your studies

Chapter 2: *Project Initiation*

Project basics

- Defining organizational structures and influencing factors on projects
- Recognizing the different knowledge areas that can be utilized on projects
- Understanding the role of the project manager including skills like communication and problem solving

Project constraints

- Understanding the development of a business case and how projects are selected

- Developing a scope statement
- Developing a work breakdown structure and WBS dictionary

Chapter 6: *Developing a Project Schedule*

Project Basics and Project Constraints

- Creating and navigating a network diagram
- Understanding different techniques to estimate duration

Project Basics

- Identifying the different types of resources that can affect duration
- Review the importance of a schedule baseline

Project Basics, Project Tools, and Documentation

- Navigate critical path methods and how schedule-compression works

Chapter 7: *Resource Management Planning and Communication Considerations*

Project Tools and Documentation

- Using matrix, hierarchical, and text-based documentation to determine resource needs

Project Basics

- Recognizing different conflict-management techniques and when they are appropriate
- Reviewing team-building and motivation techniques

Project Basics, Project Tools, and Documentation

- Determine ways to monitor team performance throughout the project

Chapter 8: *Budget and Contingency Plans for Risk*

Project Basics

- Demonstrating different ways to estimate costs based on the situation

Project Constraints, Project Tools, and Documentation

- List the typical information found in a cost baseline

Project Basics, Project Tools, and Documentation

- Using earned value formulas to track performance

Project Constraints

- Best practices for identifying, analyzing, and responding to risk

Chapter 9: *Monitoring and Controlling Project Work*

Communication and Change Management

- Understanding the change-control system and how to process changes through formal change-control systems

Project Tools and Documentation

- Understanding the procurement process and the different types of contracts
- Reviewing how sellers are selected and the project manager's role in procurement

Chapter 10: *Formal Project or Phase Closure and Agile Project Management*

Project Basics

- Identifying best practices for closing out a project
- Understanding different project-ending types
- Understanding the basics of Agile project management
- Hybrid project management

Project Tools and Documentation

- Learning how to create *lessons learned*
- Preparing a final project report

About the CompTIA Project+ exam (PK0-004)

The CompTIA Project+ exam will rotate through different questions across multiple test takers, however the number of questions and the basics of a passing score are the same globally, as are the domains and the scoring weight. Here is some information about the test:

- **Number of questions**: Maximum of 95
- **Type of questions**: Multiple choice
- **Length of test**: 90 minutes
- **Recommended experience**: Minimum of one year of managing, directing, or participating in small- to medium-scale projects
- **Passing score**: 710 (on a scale from 100–900)

How to apply for the CompTIA Project+ exam

While the steps for gaining your Project+ certification may seem fairly easy, it's important to know what those steps are, so you can begin to prepare for your exam. The following steps will help guide you through the process:

- Review the exam objectives
- Practice for the exam by answering the practice questions at the end of every chapter
- After you have studied for the exam, review and answer as many sample questions as you can to prepare for exam day

 Review the certification objectives to make sure you know what is covered on the exam: https://certification.comptia.org/certifications/project.

Ready for your exam?

There are several steps involved in preparing to take your exam. The following information will walk you through the process:

- Purchase your voucher from the CompTIA website and then find a testing center and schedule your exam at a nearby location. It's possible there will be an in-home remotely-proctored exam if a location can't be found near you.
- Pearson VUE are the proctors for in-person exams, so you will need to create an account on their site as well. Visit `https://home.pearsonvue.com` to do that.
- Once you have an account, you will be able to buy a voucher (if you haven't obtained one through the CompTIA website already); choose a testing center near you and schedule your exam.
- Pearson VUE also offers scheduling via phone if you are having trouble scheduling online.

 The CompTIA website: `https://certification.comptia.org/certifications/project`.

From the CompTIA Project+ page, you can navigate to all of the information to pay for and schedule your exam.

What to expect on exam day

Here is what you can expect on exam day:

- Show up a few minutes early so that you can sign in. You will be asked to provide two forms of identification, and to leave your belongings in a locker provided by Pearson VUE. The proctor will give you something to write on and something to write with, and then walk you to your computer station.
- The exam will be computer-based with one question presented on the screen at a time. You will easily be able to navigate the exam by using the **Next** and **Back** buttons.
- You also have the ability to mark questions for later review in case there's a question you're not sure of or that you cannot answer.
- You may have a short tutorial on how to navigate and mark questions before you begin your exam.

I marked about twenty questions on my exam and had plenty of time to complete all of the questions and cycle back through the exam to double-check my answers.

- For any questions that involve formulas, you will have access to a calculator built into the question, so you don't have to do any math in your head. Yay!
- The exam will present you with situational questions and will ask you to put yourself in the shoes of a variety of positions on a project team. The majority of the questions are written from the project manager's perspective, but be prepared to understand all of the roles on the project team.
- You may find that some questions have two or more correct answers. Do your best to select all that apply. It is also likely that you will get questions that contain extraneous information that doesn't pertain to the correct answer.
- Once you submit your exam, you will find out within a minute whether you have passed your exam, and Pearson VUE will give you a certificate proving you have passed. Your certification is good for life without the need for continuing education credits or future retakes of newer versions of the exam.
- CompTIA will mail you your certification shortly after. You may want to buy a frame for it. It's a big accomplishment and you should be very proud!

You will be in a room with other test takers. These test takers will be taking different types of exams, some of which will include typing. Try not to get too distracted by what everyone else is doing so you are able to focus on your exam. You may be offered headphones to use during your exam but this may depend on the testing location.

Study tips

Here are some study tips to help you prepare for the exam:

- Take and retake practice exams until you score approximately 85-90% several times in a row. Be aware that the practice questions in your student guide will not be the same questions you will get on your exam as there is a test pool of thousands of questions.
- You never know which questions you will get on your exam. You could be sitting next to someone taking their Project+ exam and they would have a different pool of questions to answer. The content is aligned to the domains and exam content outline, but it is presented in different ways.

- The exam itself is not adaptive, so the pool of questions you get when you sit down will not change based on your knowledge of one topic over another.
- I highly recommend that you use these practice questions as a way to solidify the information rather than to rote memorize it, as you will find the actual exam questions will differ.

 I'll let you know when there is anything you need to memorize for exam purposes as you move through this book.

- If you find yourself memorizing the answers to the questions in this guide without actually knowing why an answer is correct or incorrect, it may be helpful to test yourself with additional practice exams that present the information in a different way.
- CompTIA can also provide you with a couple of free questions via request from their website, and they offer a paid service called **CertMaster Practice**.
- Be careful about old or incorrect brain dumps on the internet as there are multiple websites that have exam information. Do your research before selecting sites that provide additional practice questions.

 Make sure any practice questions you find outside of the student guide refer to this latest version of the Project+ exam (PK0-004). With the amount of questions that you have in this guide, you should not need to look elsewhere unless you deem it necessary for your own success.

- Make sure that you read everything carefully! If you don't read carefully, you may miss a better answer or the nuance of the question itself.
- Use this study guide to review all pertinent information, best practices, and suggested processes. You may find if you are already working on projects that you do not need to utilize what is suggested as a best practice in a student guide and on the exam. The reason for this may be because of your organizational processes and your enterprise environment.
- Remember project management is not a one-size-fits-all situation. You may learn some new best practices that you want to incorporate in your day-to-day, and you may learn some best practices that are not relevant in your day-to-day. The best advice is to learn the content as it's presented to pass your exam and then determine ways where you can incorporate the recommended best practices into your current or future projects.

Don't forget to breathe! The exam is comprehensive but not impossible. Cramming won't help you, so my best advice is to get into the mindset of the best practices, take and re-take practice exams, and read through this guide as much as needed to solidify the concepts.

Summary

In this chapter, you reviewed all the necessary information about the CompTIA Project+ exam as well as study tips, and why certification is beneficial to your career. It's never a bad idea to reread this chapter after you finish your studies to remind yourself what to expect. Use the domain review as a guide to focus your studies prior to your exam. It's a great checklist for a knowledge review. The assessment test is a great overall gauge of current knowledge and where you should focus as you move forward.

In Chapter 2, *Project Initiation*, we will cover project initiation, review the definition of a project, program, and portfolio. Then, we will cover different organizational structures that will impact how a project is managed. We will also review different project selection techniques, development of a business case, and your role as a project manager.

Questions

Below you will find a baseline assessment test to see what areas to focus on while studying. Don't worry if your score is lower than you might like. You are just starting this journey! It's less about your score and more about areas to focus on, or even to observe what best practices are different from your day-to-day. These questions are a good cross-section of what you can expect on your exam. You can find the answers to these questions at the *Back Matter* section of the book under *Assessments*. Good luck!

1. While controlling quality on your projects you will monitor repetitive activities and plot sample variance measurements to determine if the product is in control (which is defined by being plus or minus three standard deviations of the mean). Which tool and technique does this describe?
   - Scatter diagram
   - Statistical sampling
   - Pareto chart
   - Control charts

2. You've prepared the following analysis for two different projects for review by the selection committee. Project A's payback period is 8 months and its NPV is -27,000. Project B's payback period is 10 months and its NPV is 150,000. Which project should the selection committee pick?
   - Project A, because its NPV is lower than Project B's
   - Project B, because its NPV is highest and there is more than six months difference between payback periods
   - Project B, because its NPV is a positive value
   - Project A, because its payback period is shorter than Project B's payback period

3. Who should always issue the project charter?
   - A person internal to the project's organization
   - A project initiator or sponsor
   - A low-level manager of the performing organization
   - A high-level manager of the performing organization

4. Standards and regulations concerning the work of the project should be taken into consideration during the planning process. All of the following are true regarding standards and regulations except:
   - Standards and regulations are one of the elements included in the enterprise environmental factors and are part of planning for quality
   - Regulations are approved by a recognized body and employ rules and guidelines that should be followed
   - Regulations are typically imposed by governments
   - Standards are not mandatory

5. Which of the following is the best description of a project charter?
   - It describes both the project scope and the product scope at detail level.
   - It authorizes the project and the use of organizational resources to meet project requirements.
   - It breaks down the project scope over several steps to describe the project on work package level.
   - It describes all activities which are necessary to create the project deliverables.

6. At the beginning of project execution, you notice there are different opinions between team members relating to project work and deliverables, and to the level of overall complexity. What should you do first?
   - Give your team members some time to develop a common understanding of the project scope and product scope. Upcoming interface problems may be resolved later.
   - Use the risk management processes to identify and assess risks caused by misunderstandings and develop a plan with measures in order to respond to them.
   - Organize meetings to identify and resolve misunderstandings between team members in order to avoid interface problems, disintegration, and costly rework early in the project.
   - Use interviews in private with each individual team member to inform them of your expectations and your requirements in an atmosphere of confidence.

7. During execution of your project, you have observed that a team member is being isolated by other team members. Which is a wrong approach in such a situation?
   - The interpersonal relationships between team members are their private issue. You should not interfere.
   - You should apply team-building measures to improve the team's effectiveness.
   - You should try to get feedback from the isolated team member to understand the situation.
   - You should try to get feedback from the other team members to understand the situation.

8. Change-control systems serve all of the following purposes except?
   - Track the status of change requests
   - Define the level of authority needed to approve changes
   - Control scope-creep completely
   - Document the procedures that describe how to submit and manage change requests

9. A project has undergone a major scope change, which increased cost and work levels. What does this mean for earned value data?
   - The cost baseline will be updated, and the new baseline will be the basis for future earned-value analysis.
   - As baselines should generally not be adjusted, the project is due to exceed its budget from now on.

- There are several reasons to change a baseline, but not scope changes. The project will exceed its budget.
- Earned-value analysis becomes useless after a scope change, the technique should not be used any more.

10. During your project planning, you have determined that you will need to compress your schedule to meet a customer's schedule constraints. You have moved some activities to be performed in parallel instead of sequentially to compress the critical path. What technique have you used?
    - Crashing
    - Fast -Tracking
    - Schedule Compression
    - Resource Leveling

2
Project Initiation

In this chapter, you will learn about how projects are defined based on different organizational structures, as well as different project-selection techniques that are used to initiate a project.

This chapter will also cover how different knowledge areas influence unique projects and define the role of the project manager. This information is important to understand so you can begin a project effectively based on the circumstances of the organization and your own leadership abilities.

In this chapter, we will cover the following topics:

- Defining a project
- Understanding organizational structures
- Project-selection techniques
- Project management knowledge areas
- The role of the project manager

Defining a project

What exactly is a project? A project is something that is temporary and unique, which could literally mean anything from the building of the Colosseum in Rome all the way to building a new data center or upgrading hardware or software for your organization. A project doesn't necessarily have to produce anything that's tangible. It could be a product, service, or result. You may very well be updating a process in your organization or perhaps reorganizing your help desk. These would be considered projects as well.

Businesses are concerned with making money and often projects are undertaken for that very reason, whether it's to develop a new product, service, or result or to simply improve business practices to save the organization some money.

There are two phrases that define a project:

1. Temporary
2. Unique

Temporary

It may not always feel like it, but all projects have a beginning and an end. Some projects last a couple of weeks, while others could be considered mega projects and last for years in a global environment. No matter what, a project will always end. It may have been completed successfully or not. Some projects are even canceled due to budgetary constraints, a change in the market, or because the business need no longer exists

Because projects are temporary, they are not to be confused with **operations**, which are ongoing. An example of operations may be the day-to-day work necessary to keep an organization running smoothly. That could be anything from an automated payroll system in the human resource department or other functional departments, such as sales or marketing, that go about their daily work with very few changes.

Occasionally departments in an organization will run projects based on the internal needs of the department. For example, if your human resource department decides to upgrade their payroll system, that would be outside of normal business operations, and therefore it is a project. They may even assign someone from within their department to help manage the project.

 We'll review organizational dynamics and how they impact projects a little bit later in this chapter.

In our example, it makes sense that once the payroll system is up and running and utilized regularly, it is then considered a part of operations because the project life cycle has ended.

Unique

Projects produce a product, service, or result that can be considered unique. You may be thinking that you run multiple similar IT projects all the time-an install on Monday, patches on Tuesday, a data center upgrade here, and a help desk revamp there. It all seems like there isn't anything unique about it. Trust me, there is! We'll review different stakeholders and team roles in `Chapter 3`, *Project Roles and Responsibilities*, but until then I would imagine that you are working on multiple projects with different people who have different wants and needs.

Upgrading to the next version of an operating system is a project because even though it's one Windows system over another, different departments may be scheduled differently in a roll-out and therefore there are different unique stakeholders with a unique result: from the old operating system to a new operating system. It may seem that there is nothing unique about your organization's projects and your day-to-day work. But if you think of it this way, everything is based on a specific scope of work, differing schedules, possible risk events, budgeting for materials and equipment, managing a team of people, and so on.

There is always a reason why an organization takes on a project. Sometimes it's due to a customer request, a demand in the market, updates to meet regulatory compliance, or even for the social welfare of a group or groups. The ability to manage stakeholder needs and produce the result for which the project is being undertaken is what projects and project management is all about.

You may get questions asking about the definition of a project. Just remember, *temporary* and *unique*.

Another term describing projects is **progressive elaboration.** This is a fancy term for planning for what you know today and updating it as you learn more information. Elaborating in a progressive manner. All projects evolve this way; even if you know what the result is supposed to be, you may not have all of the information needed to plan everything out in the beginning.

If you are planning a vacation, you may know your destination, how many days you will stay, and your budget. What you can't predict are risk events, such as bad weather. You also may not know what restaurant you will choose on day four of your vacation. You have a known scope of work, schedule, and budget, but you'll have to wait until you arrive to see the other aspects clearly.

What is a program?

A program is a group of related projects managed in a coordinated way. Lots of organizations run programs because they can accomplish multiple deliverables or output and have a set group of best practices that can be applied to all of them. Think about it this way. If you were building data centers at 15 locations, there are some standard approaches you would use at every location. This may include the process by which you order or transport materials, similar (if not the same) types of resources, and how you create your process flow charts. Even if you had 15 project managers working at each location, there are some best practices that are applicable across all projects.

You might be wondering how these projects could be considered unique since everything sounds the same, but remember you are at different locations.

Different stakeholders have different needs for their data storage, different thoughts about the final result, different risk events, and even different scopes of work. One data center could be much larger than another and have different configurations. All these items make each project unique, but similar enough that best practices and processes can be shared and implemented across the program.

What is a portfolio?

A portfolio is a group of unrelated projects or programs. Organizations that run portfolios are typically large organizations with multiple products or services, or a rapidly-growing organization needing large updates or process-integration in their departments. You could have one department creating the latest, greatest software, while another could be improving the sales process, and still another installing a data center at every global location. Some are temporary and unique projects, while others may be part of a program. It isn't outside the realm of possibility to assume that organizations that run portfolios are typically multi billion-dollar global corporations.

Another way to look at portfolios is to imagine a stock portfolio. It could be a variety of different items, such as a 401k, annuity stocks, and tiered bond structures. You would have a portfolio manager who understands everything in the portfolio, even though everything is different for each client. Some can be managed as a one-off, such as a 401k (project), some are managed in a coordinated fashion, such as a group of related tech stocks (program), but either way you need the portfolio manager to keep an eye on the entire thing to manage your money correctly.

Another way to identify a portfolio is in an organization that would like to achieve a strategic objective such as reducing its carbon footprint, or improving its brand recognition.

The portfolio manager would have a dashboard across multiple unrelated projects or programs that contribute to meeting the strategic objective.

What is project management?

Project management can mean different things to different people based on your organizational dynamic and whether you are managing projects, programs, or portfolios. In general, it is the project manager's job to utilize a set of best practices, tools and techniques, and good communication and to coordinate of all the moving parts to bring the result to a successful completion. It takes a lot of skill and knowledge to manage a project effectively, which is why the majority of what we will focus on are best practices that are specific to certain categories, such as scope, time, or cost. The goal is to create an integrated plan that allows for effective coordination.

Effective project managers will have multiple skill sets in different areas.

The following isn't an exhaustive list but an overview of some of the many skills great project managers have:

- Leadership
- Communication
- Requirements-gathering
- Risk management
- Team-building
- Time management
- Effective planning skills
- Problem-solving
- Negotiation

If you are looking at that list and thinking you don't have experience in one area or another, don't worry! Even seasoned project managers are consistently working to achieve new skills in an ever-changing project landscape. For example, I'm not the greatest negotiator. I know this because I have a twenty-year-old daughter who never fails to negotiate her way out of why her credit card bills are so high! All kidding aside, for me, negotiation improvement is an aspirational skill. I have to learn and practice. That is why having a road map of best practices you can follow enables you to learn or improve upon current or future skills. This is also why certifications such as this are so important. It shows you are focused on knowledge and improvement.

Other aspects of project management have to do with the life cycles of a project, which we will cover in depth in Chapter 4, *Developing a Project Charter*. For now, it is important to know that the *PMBOK® Guide* and *CompTIA view the Project + exam* content as *mostly* predictive project management, or as it is sometimes known **waterfall project management**.

As a bit of a history buff, I'm always curious about where some of the labels, vocabulary, and best practices come from. You won't see this on the exam, but it's still interesting. Winston W. Royce was one of the founders of project management. He began his career working on spacecraft projects as an aeronautical engineer. In 1970, he published a very influential article called *Managing the development of large software systems* in which he presented several project management models, including what are now known as waterfall, iterative, and agile.

The best practices you will learn mostly fall under the category of waterfall or predictive project management, but you will see in Chapter 10, *Formal Project or Phase Closure and Agile Project Management*, that we cover some agile best practices, specifically a framework called Scrum. Why?

These days it is very important to be able to designate what best practices will work on your unique projects. The ability to tailor your best practices to your projects is a highly in-demand skill to acquire. In Chapter 10, *Formal Project or Phase Closure and Agile Project Management*, I mentioned that not everything you learn will be applicable to your day-to-day. That is why the Project Management Institute and CompTIA have determined that some knowledge of agile is necessary. That is also why you will see some questions on the Project + exam relating to Scrum as a **framework rather than a project-management process**.

I think it's realistic to cover what the differences are at a high level and then review agile more in depth in Chapter 10, *Formal Project or Phase Closure and Agile Project Management*.

Waterfall project management

You may see other terms used interchangeably with waterfall, such as predictive, plan-driven, or traditional. **Predictive project management** as the name implies, means you can predict what the result will be. If you are building a data center, you will end up with a data center. That doesn't mean everything will run perfectly or it's in some way easier. It isn't except in the respect that everyone knows what the result is *supposed* to be.

It is very typical for waterfall projects to have a formal change-control system because, in order to change the project plan in any way, it is necessary to assess all of the impacts of that change and create a solution that will probably work. The plan and any changes along the way need to be communicated and approved by the powers-that-be *before* they can be implemented.

Because **waterfall projects** are predictive, you wouldn't ever see a change request that changed the scope of work exponentially from the original scope of work. If your customer wanted a bicycle and now wants a motorcycle halfway through the project, that isn't a change request. It's a brand new project.

The other nuance of waterfall is that plans are made in advance because we can *predict* the result. Baselines are created, and all work revolves around the plans until or if they change through formal change-control.

Agile project management

In an agile environment, you would typically be working on highly technical projects such as developing software programs, although many organizations see the value in utilizing some of the best practices outside of software design.

Think of the word **agility,** which is the ability to think or move quickly. Agile projects are not predictive at all. We may only know in the beginning that our HR department wants a new payroll system. We have no idea what features they want yet, how they imagine the software working, or what the final result will be. Instead, we plan at the last responsible moment, and we work closely with the customer to collect requirements. If those requirements change it's okay because we are only running in very short sprints or iterations. The team is only a week to four weeks into work at any given moment. Change is okay and is expected. Front-loaded planning isn't an aspect of agile and, in fact, documentation without working products, service, or software is a colossal waste of time and provides no value to the organization. This is due to the rapid changes occurring regularly. In Chapter 10, *Formal Project or Phase Closure and Agile Project Management*, we will cover sprint cycles and key aspects of agile frameworks.

Understanding organizational structures

Much of your day-to-day lives running projects will be significantly impacted by your organizational processes and the culture of your organization. That could be based on your industry, what regulatory compliance is necessary, or simply because of how your organization chooses to run things.

The biggest impact on how these processes evolve is based mostly on how your organization is structured. Some structures are better than others for projects and sometimes trying to implement new best practices can be a bit painful due to your organizational influences.

I often look at organizational processes as the handbook of how they do things at an organization. The rules, best practices, and set processes. The enterprise environment is when you go to lunch with someone and they tell you how it *really* is! The organizational culture, the software you use, how assigning your resources works, and the political system within your organization are good examples of an enterprise environmental influence. In a perfect world, both the organizational processes and the enterprise environment need to work in harmony to get anything done. However, in general, harmony is the last thing that is occurring.

In order to get closer to the perfect world, it may be necessary to restructure the organizational dynamics to accommodate projects. Some organizations began as a siloed functional organization and then expand and grow into something more effective in the project-management space. This takes time and effort though, which is why many organizations avoid change. Change is painful and let's face it, change doesn't always work.

In my experience, when organizations attempt to massively change their structure to something more conducive to their current business needs, the entire organization goes from status quo to chaos. Unfortunately, organizations often blame the new set of processes as not working instead of understanding that change causes chaos and it takes time to reach the new normal. As a project management consultant, I've seen organizations try too many new things at once and put their staff into a tailspin. I always recommend they try a few new things until they are proficient, and then add new skills as needed. There is still chaos, but it is minimized.

You might be asking yourself, *Where are these magical organizations that try new things to improve best practices?* Trust me, I get it. Lots of organizations are like a squeaky wheel that never gets fixed; they are so set in their organizational processes that change isn't an option. So, what is a project manager to do?

Without proof something works, the wheel will always squeak. That is why it is so awesome that you are learning this information and preparing for your exams. Once you begin trying new best practices to improve your projects and you can see it is working, you now have the proof to back it up, and the respect that comes from your position and your certification.

Change is painful and chaotic, and we have enough going on every day, so I give you the same advice I give my clients. Outside of exam preparation (because you'll need to know all the information), try one to three new best practices you learn in this guide on your next project. If it doesn't work out so well, try again in a different way that better matches your system in the real world. Before you know it, you'll have the proof you need to show your organization the value of doing things a bit differently. Trust me if it saves them time or money or improves the quality of the result, they will listen and change will come.

One more thing to consider is how your organization is structured. Different structures and dynamics can help, or they can make your lives more challenging as IT project managers or as project managers in any industry. Once you know your structure, you can adapt the implementation of best practices accordingly. Some structures are designed for project management and may be more open to better best practices, and some are more focused on departmental operations and may be less enthused about changes.

Let's review the descriptions of each organizational structure, and as you go through, try to identify the one you are currently working in.

 You will get questions on your CompTIA Project + exam based on these descriptions. Be prepared to read a situational question and identify which project organizational structure the question is describing.

Three organizational structures and their elements

There are three core structures to know for your CompTIA Project + exam. *The PMBOK®️ Guide* addresses several other types of structures but, for your exams, you will only need to recognize the three main types of organizational structures:

- Functional
- Matrix
- Projectized

Functional organizations

Functional organizations are a bit dysfunctional for project managers in the respect that all work is done in a siloed approach to business. The functional organizational dynamic has been around for hundreds of years and was very effective during the industrial revolution. Since functional organizations have been around so long, many businesses are still structured that way, making it difficult for project management to truly be a part of day-to-day life. If a functional department takes on a project, generally the functional manager runs it, rather than a project manager.

Some of the key aspects of functional organizations include the following:

- The manager of each department is in charge, rather than a project manager.
- If a project is managed in the department, someone may be assigned to help with the project but may not be given the title of project manager. They may instead function as an expeditor who helps move work along and supports the functional manager on a part-time basis. In some cases, it may be a coordinator who has a bit more responsibility but still reports to the functional manager.
- If there is a project manager, they may be part-time and have very little authority over project work or project team members.

It may sound like this type of dynamic is impossible for project managers to work with and the project is automatically set up for failure. That isn't the case at all. If you are working on a project in a functional department, you know you have your *real job* to do but you are also helping your department get something new accomplished. This helps the department become more successful. This is also where a lot of newer project managers get their start, either coordinating or, in part, managing a functional project.

There may also be a large project in a department that would best be executed with a full-time project manager who would then return to their day job once the project has ended. In short, functional departments may not be the best place to manage projects but it is done successfully every day. Often, jumping in to help run a project that involves a smaller base of similar stakeholders allows for better best practices to evolve organically. Team collaboration and communication are important aspects for success in any project environment, but highly necessary in a functional dynamic.

In *Figure 2.1*, you can see a functional organization based on individual departments:

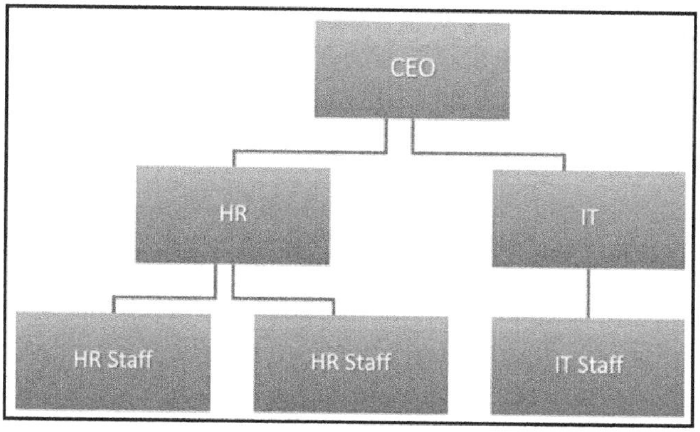

Figure 2.1: Functional organizations

Matrix organizations

Matrix organizations are typically developed in one of three ways depending on the organizational processes and how integral projects are to the organization. In fact, the three types could also represent the progression that organizations would have to take to get to the point where project work is as important as functional or operational work:

- Weak matrix
- Balanced matrix
- Strong matrix

Weak matrix

In a lot of ways, a weak matrix is similar to functional organizations because the organization itself is more focused on operational, functional work versus project work.

Some of the key aspects of weak matrix organizations include the following:

- They operates in a functional, hierarchical design.
- The project manager has low to moderate authority and may work with some full-time and some dedicated part-time resources. Typically, resources are dedicated part-time to project work.

- The functional manager is in charge and the project manager's role may be that of an expeditor or coordinator who works part-time on project work, and has a position on the functional team as well.

In *Figure 2.2*, the diagram shows a weak matrix organization and some of the challenges it presents:

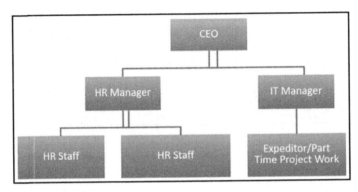

Figure 2.2 Weak matrix organizations

Balanced matrix

Balanced matrix organizations put equal emphasis on functional work and project work. That means power is shared between functional managers and project managers. Even though it may appear that the project manager has low to moderate authority, the chances are higher that they will have more power over project tasks and project work.

Some of the key aspects of balanced matrix organizations include the following:

- They emphasize equal focus on operational, functional work and project work
- The functional manager still is in control of the resources, so they may be the ones to assign resources to the project, but the project manager may be the one assigning those resources to project tasks and managing those tasks accordingly
- The resources could be loyal to the functional manager, which can cause some power struggles on the project
- Improved interdepartmental communication is an important aspect of a balanced matrix dynamic

In *Figure 2.3,* you can see a balanced matrix is becoming more workable for a project manager:

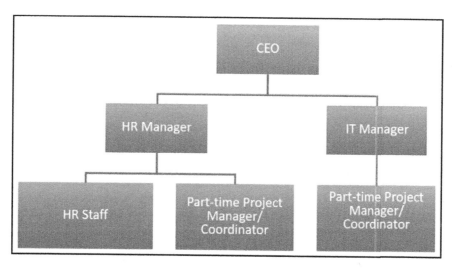

Figure 2.3 Balanced matrix organizations

Strong matrix organizations

Now project managers are getting somewhere! In a strong matrix dynamic project, work is emphasized over functional work. That doesn't mean you don't have functional departments working their operational work. The difference is that project managers have full-time authority over their project team, project scheduling, and budgeting, and are accountable for the requirements being met. There may actually be a department called a **project management office (PMO)** that oversees projects, programs, or portfolios depending on the size of the organization and their products and services. We'll cover the PMO and its role more in depth in Chapter 3, *Project Roles and Responsibilities.* For now, imagine the PMO as a functional department for project managers.

Some of the key aspects of strong matrix organizations include the following:

- Core project teams help the project manager plan and execute the work.
- The project manager is in full control but may borrow resources from functional departments or via procurement staffing as needed.
- Borrowed resources are loyal to the functional manager but focused on project work. They answer to the project manager during their role on the project, and are released back to their functional departments when their work ends.
- The project manager and project team are full-time.

In *Figure 2.4*, the strong matrix organization is represented and is one of the best dynamics for project managers:

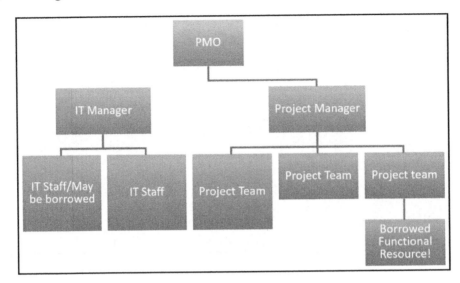

Figure 2.4 Strong matrix organizations

 Many questions on the CompTIA Project + exam assume a strong matrix is the organizational dynamic unless otherwise stated in the questions.

Projectized or project-based organizations

Just as the name of these organizations suggests, it is projects all day, every day. This type of organizational dynamic is the best for project managers for many reasons, but it is difficult for organizations to attain unless they were set up that way from the beginning. Many large organizations, such as Apple, Amazon, and Microsoft, could be considered project-based organizations because there are so many products, services, and processes happening all the time. It would be impossible to produce all of that in a functional environment.

Some of the key aspects of project-based organizations include the following:

- Most, if not all, of the team is co-located.
- The project manager has full authority.

- Support staff reports to the project manager, including borrowed resources as needed.
- The core project team doesn't report to anyone else, so their loyalty is to the project manager and the project.
- Often, the core team is released after the project ends to work on other projects. This means they may not totally belong to the project manager on every single project. The downside to that could be that the team members don't actually have a home department they return to after projects end.
- Most have a PMO and could also have a **change-control board (CCB)** whose job it is to approve or deny change requests.

In *Figure 2.5*, the project-based organization is shown and is considered the very best dynamic for project managers, however it is difficult for organizations to create if they were set up in a different dynamic originally:

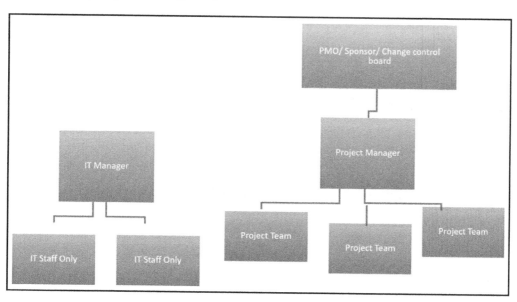

Figure 2.5 Projectized or project-based organizations

Were you able to identify your type of organization from the descriptions? Sometimes people see aspects of all of these in their current organization. This could be considered a **composite organization**, which is a combination of two or more organizational structures. This can be done for simplicity on a project or because the organization itself runs different projects with different needs.

Because you will get questions on the different dynamics and be asked to recognize them in situational questions, the following is a quick reference of the three major types you could see on your exams:

Functional	Weak matrix	Balanced matrix	Strong matrix	Projectized
No power	Limited power	Some power	In charge of the project	Complete control
Functional manager in charge	Functional manager in charge	Functional manager	The **project manager (PM)** is in charge but borrows resources from functional managers	The PM is in charge and has a dedicated team
Your role is an expeditor	Your role is a coordinator	Your role is a coordinator	Your role is a PM	Your role is a Project Manager
Part-time project work	Part-time	Could be full-time	Full-time	Full-time *Best dynamic

Project selection techniques

There are many reasons why an organization would decide to undertake a project. As mentioned earlier, businesses are concerned with making money, but they are also known to run projects for the greater good.

The categories of why projects may occur include the following:

- Market demand
- Business need or opportunity
- Requests from customers
- Advances in technology
- Legal or regulatory compliance
- Environmental considerations
- Social need

Regardless of the reason why a project may occur, businesses need to validate their reasoning for taking on a project and determine whether it is feasible and fiscally healthy to do so. Usually in the first few stages of determining what project to undertake and how it can help align to the organization's strategic plan, there are numerous decisions to make about which project to select and how much to spend.

Creating a case for business

It is not unusual for a business analyst to be involved in the validation of a project and be involved in project selection. After all, organizations need to make sure that whatever they spend their money on aligns with the intended **return on investment** (**ROI**) or the outcome they were hoping for.

Because the global economy fluctuates so much, a business analyst will look at several different financial models and make an educated guess on expenditures and ROI. Although a business case isn't completely money-oriented, the majority of project decisions rest on financial considerations. This can help executive management and key stakeholders understand the initiative from a financial perspective and weigh in the results from a scope perspective, and decide whether it's actually worth it to charter the project.

The business need and justification can also come in the form of high-level estimates of an overall project budget, a predicted result for the scope of work, and possible timelines that would be acceptable, given the expected return on financial investments. This helps the prospective project manager understand project work from the business perspective.

Trust me when I say that even after all the financial analysis that goes into developing a business case, that analysis can be very wrong when all is said and done. This is why the project manager will gather scope requirements and build a schedule and a budget around what is actually going to occur at a fine-grained level. Even then, they could be wrong. There is a better chance at getting close to the right numbers once the project is planned and understood. It's the project manager's job to determine whether the crunched numbers are feasible in the beginning of the project. That is why, in some cases, the project manager is a contributor to the process of project selection and may be part of the selection committee. Still other times, all this analysis is being done in spite of us as we happily go about our day, unknowing that a new project is being considered.

The range of possibilities could be unacceptably wide. To narrow the gap, more work is needed. There are several categories of techniques that are used to analyze the costs versus the benefits:

- Decision models
    - Constrained optimization
    - Benefit measurement
- Economic models
- Expert judgment

Decision models

Most organizations use decision models to determine which projects to select for charter. The reasoning behind this is that there is a set, fixed criteria that is pre-approved or agreed upon by the selection committee. Decision model is more of an umbrella term that covers multiple methods. Most decision models are a combination of **constrained optimization methods** and **benefit measurement methods**.

Constrained optimization methods

In the very simplest of terms, constrained optimization methods are mathematical models that can be used in very large projects. One would use constrained optimization methods if they need comprehensive calculations and they can leave it to computers to figure out.

There are several techniques that can be utilized in constrained optimization and they are as follows:

- Linear programming
- Nonlinear programming
- Integer programming
- Dynamic programming
- Multiple objective programming

The good news is that you don't need to know or even understand the constrained optimization methods for your Project + exam, but what you may have to identify is **constrained optimization** when the question is asking about computer models and programming for project selection.

Benefit measurement methods

There are three main categories of benefit measurement methods that are used to measure the potential benefits of one project versus another. All three may be used to determine the fiscal health of potential projects and most include considerations for the current market. The categories show decision-makers what the potential project costs will be versus the benefit or return *could* be. Those categories fall into three distinct areas:

- Cost-benefit analysis
- Scoring models
- Payback period

Cost-benefit analysis

An easy way to think of a cost-benefit analysis is to look at both what the project will cost and whether it's worth it to undertake said project with limited information. Predicted costs versus the benefits to the organization will be analyzed. In this case, it is mostly money-oriented. A **benefit-cost ratio (BCR)** takes into consideration the **benefit/cost** formula. Keep in mind that the numbers that are being analyzed are based on expert judgment, historical information from similar projects, and projections in the current market.

You will not be asked to calculate benefit-cost ratios on the exam, but you may be asked to determine which is the best project to select based on its benefit-cost ratio.

The result of a benefit-cost analysis will be represented as a ratio. For example, if we assume that our organization will receive a **return on investment (ROI)** of $500,000 and we will have to spend $300,000 to make that happen, our BCR = 1.67 which could be construed as an ROI of 167% return. Conversely, if we spend $500,000 and get $300,000 back we would have a BCR of 0.6 or a 60% ROI, which isn't a good result. That project would be considered too financially risky to take on.

Always choose the highest BCR on exam questions. The higher the better.

Scoring models

Scoring models are utilized by organizations when they are attempting to consider multiple variables when making project-selection decisions. Typically, the model has a scoring structure and a weighting structure so that each potential project can be analyzed based on a variety of information. Because this type of decision method contains both financial and other considerations for project selection, it allows key stakeholders to determine which variables are the most important or carry the most weight. Stakeholders will then use their current knowledge of the project to begin to score each prospective project accordingly. Certainly, financial considerations are part of that process but there may also be categories for industry growth, increased product value in the market, or a key opportunity that may or may not be realized.

Because the scoring model is a **standard organizational model,** there may be some project potentials that don't even make the cut due to a low score or missing key aspects on the list. This allows everyone to view a variety of both objective and subjective categories and make the best decisions they can, based on what they know today. Similar scoring models are used in vendor selection for procurement decisions, which may be part of project selection as well.

Payback period

Value can be different things to different people. The **payback period** is exactly what it sounds like. How long will it take before we recoup the money spent on a project before we realize its value? Typically, the payback period determines how quickly the money will be paid back over time, but it doesn't have to be. On some projects, spending money to improve a process or product may cost money to complete, but that money won't be returned. The value is a leaner process flow, better quality management, and so on, which can help the organization save or gain money in the future.

For exam purposes, the majority of questions will be based on the premise of how much the project will cost and how quickly the invested money will be paid back before the organization begins to make a profit. Some payback periods are faster than others, which is the best-case scenario for organizations because today's money isn't going to be worth the same tomorrow. The faster the payback period, the faster the organization profits.

Payback period is the *least precise* of the selection techniques, and in some cases longer-term projects take more time to recoup costs but may end up with the higher ROI in the long run. That is why the payback period is combined with other methods. Other methods help organizations have a well-rounded assessment.

Think about the biggest blockbuster movie you have seen recently that made millions on the opening weekend. It may have taken two years and $8,000,000 to get to opening night, but the studio made $27,000,000 opening weekend and continues to make money in theaters. The payback period was fast and profitable. A cult classic may take years to become popular and take a longer time to recoup the initial investment. Both are profitable, but the blockbuster's payback period is much better. We can't always know though. There are studios that make a huge flop and never get their original investment back. This is typically why organizations gather as much information as they can in the business case in an attempt to make educated guesses based on historical information and expert judgment.

Always choose the fastest payback period if it is the only variable in the question. For example, project A has a payback period of five years and project B has a payback period of three years. Which project do you select? Project B. When you review the economic models in the following section, you'll see why the payback period on its own is the least influential selection method when combined with other methods.

Remember, the payback period is the least precise project-selection method and would need to be combined with other methods.

Economic models

Different economic models can provide more in-depth data on the overall financial potential of any given project under consideration. There are three core economic models that can be used to develop a business case:

- Discounted cash flow
- **Net present value (NPV)**
- **Internal rate of return (IRR)**

Discounted cash-flow analysis

Because businesses are concerned with making money, it makes sense that they would want to know what the future financial return will be worth. Determining discounted cash flow involves three very specific variables that help to determine the present value of today's money (in today's market) and apply that to a potential future return on investment:

- The first thing that is necessary is to determine the payback period or the time that is projected to take to recover the initial investment.
- Then, the analysis will focus on determining what's going on in the market and figure out the applicable discount rates, which are typically the current interest rates. Some consideration for inflation could be involved as well.
- The third consideration is the assumed amount of money the organization will recover in the future.

Even though the discounted cash-flow analysis could be considered a subjective analysis, it actually is more objective because we are looking at the assumed payback period as well as the present value of today's money and potential return on investment in the future. Remember, some projects are chartered because of a customer request so the analysis could be based on promised returns that have already been discussed, hence making the analysis more predictable.

Net present value

If more specific details are needed, then **net present value** (**NPV**) can be used to see potential net gain or net loss that your organization will incur in each period or timeframe, which is then discounted to today's values. This allows organizations to see the fiscal health plotted out over time and determine which costs and/or revenues will be realized. The payback period strongly influences net present values when trying to determine what today's money will look like in the future. NPV is an extension of the discounted cash-flow analysis and can provide more specific information that can be used to make decisions. Basically, NPV analysis is the process of taking expenditures, net gains, and net losses for each potential year in an attempt to determine whether the project will return enough net revenue to keep up with the cost of capital over time.

Always choose the **highest net present value** as the correct answer on your exam. Even if the payback period is documented in the question, that information has already been processed in the formula and should not be considered when choosing the correct answer.

Even though organizations would prefer to make more money than they put on a project, upon occasion that is not the case, either by accident or for a very specific reason. That specific reason could be regulatory compliance. An organization would have to spend money now to update a process to become compliant that can become profitable later or improve business overall. Some organizations need to make investments into new equipment where the value is not necessarily profitable.

Business analysts and the organization would still most likely do an NPV analysis to determine whether the expenditures could be realistic but since there isn't a payback period to consider, it might just be a forecasted return on investment. In general, organizations aren't in the habit of taking on financial losers and more than likely selected projects will have the highest NPV possible.

Internal rate of return

Internal rates of return (IRR) are also considered during product selection, because the process allows the calculation of the rate of return on the project without any external factors to consider, such as inflation or the cost of capital. IRR also considers the time value of money and is really designed to look at returns on investments and what they are worth today versus what they might be worth in the future.

A return on investment that occurs tomorrow is worth more than the same return two years from now. The longer the return on investment takes, the lower the internal rate of return becomes. In general, organizations can use IRR as a litmus test for profitability, and using NPV, the organization can attempt to prove net value if an investment is made.

An easy way to think about the internal rate of return is to consider walking into a bank and asking about opening up a savings account. The financial adviser at bank A states that if you keep your money with them, you will get a 1.0% return on your investments. The financial adviser at bank B states they will give you a 3.5% return on your investment. Which one would you choose? I'm betting you would choose the latter. Organizations are no different.

 Always choose the **highest IRR**, which is represented in percentages.

It is the job of the business analysts to crunch the numbers and look to the future to determine the best decisions to make financially. Those considerations can help organizations select the best projects. There are also big, scary formulas involved with all of these, but the good news is you don't need to know them for the exam!

A good way to keep these all straight is to always choose the highest number except in the payback period where you would want to choose the lowest. If the question has all three variables, review each project and determine which would be most profitable for the organization. Typically, in the exam situation, the NPV is the key indicator of a profitable project.

Expert judgment

If there's one tool that is utilized more than any other in project management, it would be expert judgment. Whether it's the beginning, the middle, or the end of the project, utilizing expertise from a variety of stakeholders, subject matter experts, consultants, and business analysts makes good sense. In project selection, there will be numerous key stakeholders involved who have a variety of historical information, lessons learned, and even opinions as to which projects should be selected.

The downside to using only expert judgment to select projects is the potential for **groupthink**. Groupthink is when a group of people are trying to make decisions they all agree on and the stronger personalities believe they are correct and convince others to go along with their ideas. The problem arises when the group is closed to outside ideas and alternatives, and the decision-making becomes irrational or counter-productive.

Unfortunately, some organizational politics are key influencing factors in project selection. This is why CompTIA recommends knowing other project-selection techniques, such as those you just covered (at a high level at least), so if you are providing expert judgment on the development of the business case, you know what you're looking for and how to make the best decisions.

Feasibility analysis

All of these specific project-selection techniques are designed to help the organization determine whether the project is feasible and is fiscally healthy enough to meet the needs of the business. Much of the analysis of feasibility will depend on expert judgment and will be based on your organizational processes and your enterprise environment, not just the financial ROI.

The business case

In order to make a case for the business to take on a project, there are multiple variables to be considered outside of just the financial considerations. Because the business case is the very first document to be created for a potential project, it is an important piece of a go/no-go decision. There are typical headers found in most business cases that describe a variety of items for consideration by the selection committee.

The executive summary is first on the list, but usually the last to be written and it describes what the selection committee believes are the key points for consideration.

Other headers may include the following:

- Issues that the project is addressing
- The anticipated outcomes
- Any recommendations from the selection committee
- The business case analysis team
- The problem definition and statement, which describes why the project is under consideration
- The organizational impact of the project
- Technology implementations
- Project overview and description
- Goals and objectives
- Expected project performance
- Any assumptions or constraints
- Major milestones
- Strategic alignment
- Cost-benefit analysis
- Alternatives analysis
- Approval signatures

As you can see, a business case can be very comprehensive even given the fact that not much is really known about the true breakdown of project scope, actual costs, schedules, and the need for resources at this point. Remember, in a predictive environment, it is easier to see the finish line at the beginning of the race because everyone knows where the finish line should be, hence pre-project initiation decisions are a bit easier to make.

Project management knowledge areas

There are 10 areas of expertise or knowledge that can be utilized on most, if not all, projects. The 10 project-management knowledge areas each contain specific processes, input, tools and techniques, and output that relate to specific areas of the project. These knowledge areas come from the *Project Management Body of Knowledge or the PMBOK® Guide – 6th edition*.

You will cover a variety of best practices and processes from their related knowledge areas as you move through this guide. This is just an overview of each knowledge area and its role in project management. As you go through the overview, ask yourself which of these knowledge areas are part of your day-to-day projects that would need to be planned for, executed, monitored, and controlled.

Some project managers only work with the core constraints of scope, time, and cost, on a regular basis and may not be involved in procurement activities for example, and each project manager determines what is necessary to utilize in their unique projects. In one project, you may need a comprehensive quality-management plan and in others you may not. It is part of the project manager's responsibility to understand the knowledge areas, best practices, and the processes well enough to determine what is needed and what is not:

- **Project-integration management**: It involves determining what is necessary to create a comprehensive project-management plan to properly manage the project. This is also where the project charter and deliverables are created, where project work is monitored and controlled, and where formal project or phase closure occurs.
- **Project-scope management**: It coordinates the collection of requirements for both product and project scope of work, plans how that work will be completed, and includes formal signoff on the deliverable by the customer. The scope of work is a key constraint that could very well be the main influencing factor on your schedules, budgets, and resource assignments.
- **Project time/schedule management**: It is the knowledge area that deals with scheduling. It's important to correctly determine activities or tasks and sequence them in a logical fashion. Once we know the order in which things occur, we can then begin to estimate resources and durations to come up with a schedule that we can probably meet.
- **Project-cost management**: It deals with estimating costs, budgeting costs, and controlling costs. Not all project managers manage budgets, but somebody is paying attention to the money based on the business case. It's important to understand the best practices in case you are asked to manage a budget for people, equipment, or materials at some point in your career.
- **Project-quality management**: It deals with best practices to produce a deliverable or result that is fit for use and that works the way it's designed to work. Part of quality management involves planning for how to meet requirements and to document your quality process, as well as making sure that you're managing quality during project-execution and controlling quality to prevent defects. This may be another knowledge area that is not a part of your day-to-day work, but everybody is concerned with the quality of the results and therefore may be part of your responsibilities.

- **Project-resource management**: It involves people on your team and how you acquire, develop, and manage them. Much of the CompTIA Project + exam is focused on your ability as a project manager to team build as well as manage the allocation of resources across project work. Resources also include materials and equipment that are aligned with other areas, such as cost and procurement.

- **Project-communications management**: It is designed to determine how you will distribute information and communicate on the project. Project managers spend 90% of their time communicating, so it is important to create a communications-management plan and distribute information accordingly. Communications-management is about making sure that you get the right information to the right people, at the right time, and in the right format.

- **Project-risk management**: It is perhaps one of the knowledge areas that is not attended to as frequently as needed, but is necessary in order to protect project work. Risk can be compartmentalized into two categories: threats and opportunities. It's important to identify your risks and analyze and create responses for them on a regular basis, as a risk can impact all knowledge areas.

- **Project-procurement management:** It is concerned with contracts and agreements that may be necessary to complete the deliverables. There are some project managers who are not involved in procurement, or the organization has a procurement department that sets the process for all things procurement-related. You may be asked to determine what may be needed from an external seller or vendor and you also may be asked to create a procurement statement of work. That could lead to analyzing vendor responses and contributing to seller selection. Even if you're not involved in project-procurement specifically, the project may begin with a contract agreement and you would need to protect your organization from future costs or litigation by not breaching the contract.

- **Project-stakeholder management**: It concerns those who have a stake in the outcome of the project. They are typically individuals or groups that have requirements that need to be met, or they could be end users. Either way, stakeholders are involved in the project life cycle and as a project manager you will need to manage their expectations, which could change throughout the project. Good communication is one way of effectively managing stakeholders on your project.

Now that we have covered a high-level overview of all of the knowledge areas, it's important to understand your role as a project manager.

The role of the project manager

It's probably pretty easy to tell that there is a lot involved in being a project manager. I can tell you after many years as a project manager, there are days when I question the sanity of my stakeholders and, quite frankly, my own. However, the beauty of being a project manager is that we have the ability to work with different kinds of people, produce results, and essentially keep the entire ship sailing straight. It doesn't always work out like that of course, but in a perfect world, we have all the best practices, tools and techniques, and the right attitude to get to the finish line.

The role of the project manager includes the following:

- Managing the project team
- Solving problems
- Managing communications across multiple stakeholders
- Identifying and analyzing the right requirements for scope
- Creating and managing a budget and a schedule
- Identifying, analyzing, and removing threats and taking advantage of opportunities
- Understanding quality assurance and quality control as needed
- Planning effectively across multiple knowledge areas
- Utilizing effective organizational skills

Some of the soft skills that are necessary include the following:

- Leadership
- Team-building
- Communication
- Active listening
- Consensus-building
- Problem-solving
- Conflict-resolution
- Negotiation

Most of the soft skills in this list could be considered aspirational skills and it is not expected that every project manager should be an expert in all of these. As I mentioned before, there are always going to be areas where we can seek to improve our skill sets and utilize those improved skills on projects.

Even though the list of soft skills seems pretty self-explanatory, it's important to look at the skills through the eyes of a project manager in order to answer questions correctly on your exam and to implement in your day-to-day life. Let's start:

- **Leadership**: It involves goal-setting in a strategic manner and having the ability to lead, direct, inspire, and motivate your team of individuals. Project management exists in a global environment and it's important to be culturally aware and to be able to work with a variety of people. The leadership category is an important one because project managers need to lead by example. Just like parenting children or helping a younger sibling, leading by example helps everyone understand the rules and the processes that are acceptable within your project. Leading by example is also the ability to have a passion for your work, which will allow you to become trusted by others and interact with people from all walks of life.

- **Team-building**: It is an important part of project management. Trust me when I say nothing will ruin a project faster than people! If you're lucky enough to have worked with the same people for a long period of time, chances are your team is built and performing. There may be an occasional conflict or flare-up, but for the most part the team works well together already. Your job at that point is to maintain the momentum. But what if you have a brand-new team? At this point, they may be more concerned with the expectations of the project and be dependent upon the project manager to present that information. Over time, there may be some conflict before the team settles into a routine. Team-building is important during those points, to help align everyone to the goals of the project and also to develop trust in their teammates and in their project manager.

- **Communication**: It is another skill that is necessary to be effective in project management. That doesn't mean you have to be a chatty extrovert. It simply means that you have the ability to know and understand what you will communicate, how often you communicate information, who will receive the information, and the method by which they will receive it. You might not know it, but body language makes up 55% of face-to-face communication, 38% represents your tone of voice, and only 7% are the words you are source. When you remove the face-to-face communication, as when communicating via emails or text messages, tone becomes the prominent factor over the words that are written. If you are like me and read and re-read your emails or texts before sending them out, you are checking for tone. How people perceive you is how they will receive you. Even though you can't control others' thoughts and perceptions, you can present the message in a way that ensures the tone is considered and reviewed before pushing send.

Fun fact: this is why emoticons were created. They step in for the lack of body language and make sure that the tone of the message was not misunderstood. Not all organizations find emoticons business-appropriate, so be sure to check your tone more often if that is the case. :-)

Active listening is a skill we can all work on. Trying not to think of what you are going to say next or about other things, or being distracted by your cell phone when someone is talking is difficult in this day and age. True active listening is focusing on the message that the other person is communicating, asking questions for understanding as needed, and then responding appropriately to the message.

In summary, reaching a consensus, solving problems, reducing conflict, and being an effective negotiator are also skills to either acquire or improve upon throughout your career. I don't know a lot of people who actually enjoy conflicts, although there are those who enjoy drama. I bet somebody's name just popped into your head, didn't it? For the most part though, we are talking about functional conflict and we will cover different resolution strategies for conflict in Chapter 7, *Resource Management Planning and Communication Considerations*.

Summary

In this chapter, you learned about how projects are defined based on different organizational structures as well as different project-selection techniques that are used to initiate a project.

Then you reviewed the 10 different knowledge areas that influence unique projects as well as the role of the project manager. This information is important as a stepping stone or baseline that can lead to managing a project effectively based on the circumstances of the organization and your leadership skills as a project manager. In Chapter 3, *Project Roles and Responsibilities*, you will review the different roles and responsibilities of a variety of stakeholders. This is necessary information for exam considerations as well as your real-world projects.

Questions

1. What is the definition of a project? Choose all that apply.
   - A group of related programs
   - A temporary endeavor

  - Managed in a coordinated fashion
  - Produces a unique product service or result
  - Managed by a project manager

2. What is the definition of a program?
  - A group of unrelated projects
  - Temporary and unique
  - A type of organizational structure
  - A group of projects managed in a coordinated fashion

3. Which of the following represents a portfolio?
  - A group of unrelated projects and programs
  - A group of related projects and portfolios
  - A program and multiple projects
  - None of the above

4. You are helping your manager expedite a project in your department while still working on your day-to-day work. What type of organizational dynamic are you working in?
  - Matrix
  - Project-based
  - Functional
  - Composite

5. Which of the following are considered the best organizational structures for project managers? Choose all that apply.
  - Project-based
  - Weak matrix
  - Strong matrix
  - Functional
  - Composite
  - Balanced matrix

6. The selection committee is trying to determine which project to charter and has several options to choose from. Which project is the best for the committee to choose based on the information given?
  - Project A has a payback period of 1 year
  - Project B has a payback period of 2 years and an NPV of $350,000
  - Project C has an internal rate of return of 0.6
  - Project D has a payback period of 1 year and an NPV of $350,000

7. The project-selection committee is working with a business analyst who is predicting that the project the organization is considering has an internal rate of return of 1.3%. Based on this information alone, this is a project the committee should consider. True or false?
   - True
   - False

8. How many knowledge areas are there in the project management body of knowledge?
   - 12
   - 10
   - 8
   - 15

9. A strong matrix is a good organization dynamic for project managers because:
   - The project manager reports to the functional manager
   - The project manager is not in charge of the project and the team
   - The project manager is in charge of the project and the team
   - The project manager shares resources with functional departments but is still in charge of the project

10. Which of the following knowledge areas manages the project-management plan and the production of deliverables?
    - Scope-management
    - Schedule-management
    - Procurement-management
    - Integration-management

11. During project-selection, the business analysts use integer programming. Which of the following categories of project-selection techniques is this part of?
    - Expert judgment
    - Economic models
    - Scoring models
    - Constrained optimization

12. In a balanced matrix, which of the following situations could be considered true?
    - Project work is valued over operational work
    - There is an equal amount of focus on project and functional/operational work
    - There is more focus on functional work
    - The project manager and the PMO have equal power

13. All of the following describe the soft skills that are important to project management except:
    - Leadership
    - Team-building
    - Scope-management
    - Communication

14. During project-selection, the selection committee decides to take on a project with a negative NPV. Which of the following is the reason why an organization would make this decision?
    - The organization needs to change a process or product for regulatory compliance
    - The organization knows that the lower the NPV is, the better
    - The organization is only concerned with the payback period
    - The organization needs to produce a new product or service

15. Which of the following knowledge areas best represents relationship building through good communication?
    - Communication management
    - Human resource management
    - Procurement management
    - Stakeholder management

3
Project Roles and Responsibilities

In order to be considered a stakeholder on a project, you need to be involved in the project life cycle and have a vested interest in how the project is going, as well as whether its requirements are being met.

There are many different types of stakeholders involved in a project. In this chapter, you will review the key stakeholder roles and responsibilities.

This chapter will cover the following:

- An overview of stakeholder roles and responsibilities
- Key stakeholders' requirements and interests
- Project team roles and responsibilities
- The **Project Management Office (PMO)**
- Creating a stakeholder matrix

An overview of stakeholder roles and responsibilities

Stakeholder management is one of the key knowledge areas for project managers to consider. It is an iterative, everyday interaction with a variety of different roles, responsibilities, and requirements. Some stakeholders will be on the project from the second it begins until they sign off on its completion. Others may come and go as project needs dictate.

When a business case is created, there are already multiple key stakeholders involved. Once the project request has begun, it is typical for the project manager to begin to identify the project stakeholders and begin crafting a plan to engage, communicate, and work on the requirements necessary for the project to be successful.

At this point in the project, there may only be a business case completed and a project selected, so the list of stakeholders may include the project sponsor, the customer, and the business analysts who crunched the financial numbers. It is important for you, as the project manager, to be able to understand or even explain the major characteristics of the project well enough to identify which stakeholders may be involved now or in the future.

In order to do so, it's important to understand the business need the project is addressing, to clarify the goals and objectives as much as possible, and describe the correlation between the business need and the product service or result.

That sounds like a lot of information to assemble when you don't really have a lot of information yet. The good news is you will not be doing this in a vacuum. As you'll see in the next section, there are a variety of stakeholders that you can communicate with to gather the information that you need. In some cases, you are a contributor to the business case or considered a subject matter expert utilizing your expert judgment and may already have a good understanding of the scope of work and the stakeholders currently involved.

In Chapter 4, *Developing a Project Charter*, you'll delve more into the kick-off of a project and where to find the information you need once you are formally assigned to begin project work. For now, you will review the different roles of project stakeholders and create a stakeholder matrix to keep track of the information you'll need to collect requirements and engage stakeholders.

One thing to keep in mind is that stakeholders encompass a lot of different roles and responsibilities, and there could be numerous people and organizations you will work with to try to figure out what the project requirements should be. Some stakeholders will have more influence or power on the project to make changes or adapt the scope of work or even cancel the project. Other stakeholders may have more interest in how the project is progressing. Still others will have a high level of influence and a high level of interest in the day-to-day from the beginning of the project until the end. Managing stakeholder expectations is a delicate balance and is one of the more important skills a project manager can have.

 On the exam, some stakeholders may be described as end users, but keep in mind these end users are not consumers who purchase a product after it has entered the product life cycle. End users would be people who have requirements and would be involved in the project life cycle.

Key stakeholders' requirements and interests

Different stakeholders have different interests and different requirements. For example, your customer might want certain features or functions in the result, but the sponsor may want to make sure that you're keeping to the budget. Sometimes not everybody gets what they want. If you're diligent in collecting requirements and are transparent in your communication and reporting, you will be able to engage your stakeholders and work with them effectively to determine project requirements and decide what can and can't be done.

The title of stakeholder is really just a label for anybody involved in the project life cycle and who may be interested in the result once the project ends. There are often a variety of priorities, needs, and requirements from stakeholder to stakeholder, and it will be important to reach a consensus prior to the actual execution of project work.

I mentioned in the exam tip that stakeholders are involved in the project life cycle and have needs and requirements during the life of the project. But what exactly is meant by the project life cycle versus the product life cycle?

If the definition of a project is temporary and unique, it stands to reason that when the project is over, the deliverable has a life cycle of its own. If I decide that I'm going to a big box electronics store to purchase a new computer monitor, I have the option of choosing from multiple types of monitors with a variety of features and functions. If I walk out with one of those monitors, I'm not a stakeholder—I'm a consumer. You might be thinking, *Aren't you an end user?* I am an end user but, in this case, I am not a stakeholder.

The reason I'm not a stakeholder is because I did not provide any requirements to the project team to create the monitor I was looking for. I simply walked in and bought it once it had been mass-produced. The monitor that I bought is currently in the product life cycle. Until that product is retired and upgraded to the latest and greatest, that product life cycle continues. Once that product is retired, the project life cycle for the upgrade begins.

Now let's look at this through the eyes of an actual stakeholder rather than a consumer. If I went to the organization that can build monitors and ask them to custom-build something just for me that included the size of the monitor I needed, the pixel specification of the monitor, in the price range that I was looking for, and so on, I would then be a stakeholder and an end user.

In reality, it would be very difficult for organizations to identify all of their consumer end users. Typically, when a project is being selected, an average end user will be kept in mind in order to produce the features and functions that the market is asking for. Consumer end users are there in spirit but are not part of the project.

At the beginning of a project, we have a high-level description of the scope of the work that explains why the organization determined the project is necessary. Your job is to clearly understand why the project is being undertaken, what problem the result will solve, and be able to communicate those variables clearly enough to help determine whether the project is realistic.

Just because a project is considered doesn't mean it is the best idea. Since you will be responsible for the success of the project or, in the worst scenario the project's failure, you will want to make sure you have all of the information you need to clearly communicate the high-level scope description. That will help you to evaluate the project request and begin determining who the stakeholders are that you will be collecting requirements from when the time comes. In the next chapter, Chapter 4, *Developing a Project Charter*, we will review the process of taking a project request through formal authorization, therefore we will be able to begin project work. At that point, there will already be stakeholders involved and those stakeholders will lead you to still others who will have a stake in the project and its result. Many of the categories of roles and responsibilities on projects can be found in the next section. Even if you don't have every single type of stakeholder on your current projects, in the future, you have many or all of them.

Project team roles and responsibilities

While this is not an exhaustive list of different roles and responsibilities that can be found on a project, it is a generic list of the most common project roles and responsibilities that stakeholders hold:

- Sponsor
- Champion
- Customer
- Project manager
- Project coordinator
- Scheduler
- Project team
- PMO
- **Change-Control Board (CCB)**
- Functional managers
- Sellers, vendors, and suppliers
- Procurement managers

Project sponsor

Typically, the project sponsor is the **check writer** and a supporter of the project manager throughout the life of the project. It is not unusual for the project sponsor to be internal to your organization, but just like anything else in project management, it depends on your situation.

Unless otherwise stated, the exam assumes that the project sponsor is an executive in your organization who provides the money and potentially provides additional resources to the project.

The project sponsor's role is greater than just writing checks though; this is the key stakeholder who contributes to the project charter and is also the one that needs to approve the project charter. You will review the project charter in depth in Chapter 4, *Developing a Project Charter*, but for our purposes now, the project charter gives the project manager formal authority to begin project work. The charter also provides high-level requirements.

As the project manager on the project, it will be your job to work closely with the project sponsor and to keep them up to date on the project deliverables as well as any potentially major risk events. The sponsor may have the last word and be the decision maker on any project issues.

The main responsibilities of the project sponsor are as follows:

- They work to help define the business case and justify the project is necessary.
- They contribute to and approve the project charter which, in part, assigns the project manager and defines their level of authority on the project. The charter also gives formal authorization for project work to begin.
- They provide the financial resources necessary for project work dependent upon the business case or possible contracts in place.
- They define and approve high-level requirements.
- They approve the project baselines after planning and before execution of the project. If updates to the baselines are necessary during project-execution, the sponsor would be part of the change approvals process.
- They help the project manager resource their projects and in general are supportive of the project manager and project work.

The project champion

The project champion can sometimes be and, in many cases, is the project sponsor. Either way, the champion is considered a crucial stakeholder because they generate support for the project by explaining the benefits to the organization and other stakeholders. They will champion the cause!

The customer

The customer can be internal or external, groups or individuals, and is typically the stakeholder with the most requirements. It's not unusual for project managers in certain industries to have both internal and external customers on a variety of different projects.

It's safe to say that the customer is going to drive the scope of work, drive whether or not the deliverable is accepted, and probably drive you a little crazy as well. That is why it is so important to identify the customer's requirements, keep them informed of your progress in a transparent manner, and identify any impacts on project work if the customer requests any changes.

One of the biggest challenges to project managers is keeping up with the scope requirements when the customer keeps changing what they want. Because the customer will have a high amount of power and interest in the project, it will be crucial to communicate effectively, set expectations, understand expectations, be crystal clear in what success looks like, and manage changes in a formal manner.

The project manager

You are the person that keeps it all running smoothly, hopefully! You have a lot of responsibilities as a project manager which is why it's great that you're reading this guide and pursuing your certification. There are a lot of hats to wear, and a lot to juggle but you can do it. I promise!

The following is in no way, shape, or form the entire list of things you will be doing on any given project, but it is the crux of project management. Your organizational processes and enterprise environments may impact your ability or inability to do all of these things successfully, which is why I am hopeful that some of the best practices you learn in further chapters will help you in your day-to-day project work.

Much of what your responsibilities are will be covered in the rest of the guide. For now, let's look at an overview. Get ready:

- Create a **comprehensive project-management plan** that will help you manage the entire project successfully. In order to do that, there are multiple knowledge areas, best practices, and tools and techniques that will need to be addressed prior to creating an integrated plan. But don't worry. By the end of the guide, you'll know what goes into it.
- Create a **project baseline** during planning that will allow you to track planned versus actual performance throughout the project. A typical project baseline could include a **formally-approved schedule, budget, and scope of work**. Some baselines will also include quality-management considerations in order to meet requirements and produce a deliverable that is fit for use.

In order to have a comprehensive project-management plan with its included project baselines, you will have to put together some formal plans. These plans can include (but are not limited to) the following:

- Human-resource management plan
- Communications management plan
- Scope management plan and the scope baseline
- Stakeholder management plan
- Schedule management plan and the schedule baseline
- Cost management plan and the cost baseline
- Risk management plan and documentation on the risks that have been identified
- Quality management plan that describes your assurance and inspection process
- Procurement management plan
- A variety of documents templates and other additional project artifacts

There are some key points to make regarding an integrated project management plan:

- The plan, once approved, can only be changed through formal change-control. This includes the management plans and baselines.
- The project management plan will include all of the necessary subsidiary plans you need for your unique project.
- Key stakeholders will need to understand your strategy for the project and give final approval on the project-management plan.

- Any changes or updates to the project management plan will need to be validated to make sure that those adjustments work the way that they're supposed to.
- It is not necessary to include every knowledge area's management plans or baselines if they are not needed for the project. That would be considered excessive documentation, and it's up to the project manager to determine what is necessary to effectively run the project.

What exactly is the project management plan?

It makes sense that the entire project team, project manager, and stakeholders would need to be on the same page about how things will go on the project. I like to think of the project-management plan as your GPS navigation of project work. Essentially, the project-management plan is a **how-to guide** that is compartmentalized by specific knowledge areas and provides direction on how to execute, monitor, and control the project.

For example, if there's ever any question about how risk will be managed, the risk-management plan will describe the process.

I like to explain it to my classes like this: what is the last thing that you looked up how to do on YouTube? Many times, the answer is installation of some kind of equipment, how to change the oil in your car, how to use certain functions in Excel, and one person even looked up how to swing dance!

There are multiple channels and instructional videos that can be found there. YouTube is a wealth of **how to** information. Let's say you need to figure out how to use a certain function in Excel, so you go out to YouTube to choose a video that you think will work for you. You watch the video, and then try to duplicate what you just learned; you might watch it multiple times until you have conquered that function.

The project-management plan is a channel of YouTube videos that are compartmentalized by things such as the how-to for scope management, the how-to for cost management, the how-to for schedule management, and so on. If the video works and you are able to duplicate the function in Excel, you can revisit that video over and over again as needed. It is unnecessary to change the video because it provided you with what you needed. Conversely, if the video did **not** provide you what you needed, you would have to change the video.

If a management plan is not working for the project, you would need to change that management plan to something that does work. That can take some time and discussion with stakeholders. Once the direction is determined, the necessary change would incorporate formal change-control. Why? Because you need to take specific actions to change the plan in order to get the information that you need and everyone needs to agree on the direction in which you are now headed. Otherwise, if everything is working perfectly, there's no need to change anything in the project management plan, and its channels of knowledge areas would remain static and maintain its usefulness throughout the project. Though that sounds a bit like perfect-world project management, doesn't it?

The bottom line is you will probably have to change direction at some point in the project as you progressively elaborate on the information. This is especially significant because your customer will probably change their mind fairly often. That would then lead to updates to at least your baselines if not your management plans (how-to guides) through formal change-control. If it isn't broken, don't fix it. If it is, initiate formal change-control.

You will be reviewing significant management plans that are fairly common in most projects as you move through this guide.

Project coordinator

Usually project coordinators are found in organizations that are either strong matrix- or project-based. The reasoning is that smaller projects or functional organizations don't have the bandwidth for a project manager **and** a coordinator to help the project work. And typically, in those cases, the functional managers are in charge anyway. Even though a coordinator may be helping a functional manager facilitate project work, in a functional, weak, or balanced matrix type of organization, this particular role is specific to helping a project manager with a variety of different tasks.

A coordinator would only be necessary in a longer-term project, or if the organization is designed to accommodate that particular role. There are really no set responsibilities that a coordinator would take on, because they are there to support the project manager and project work. Coordinators who support large projects provide administrative support by answering emails, scheduling meetings, distributing agendas, and so on. They may also be helping the project manager with updates to schedules and budgets and change requests.

The coordinator may also be the go-between of different key stakeholders and resources.

The **Project Management Institute (PMI®)** has a certification designed for project coordinators called the **Certified Associate in Project Management (CAPM®)**. If you have some people on your team that want to get their feet wet in project management and improve their own skill sets, it's a good direction for them to go in, plus they will learn the same best practices you are learning here. It's not unusual for people to gain that certification, work as a coordinator on projects, and then pursue their **Project Management Professional Certification (PMP®)** once they have the related experience needed. Just like you are taking your CompTIA Project + certification and then gaining more hours of experience so you can obtain additional certifications if you have the desire to do so.

Scheduler

The project scheduler, much like the project coordinator, is usually found in larger organizations and on long-term projects. But I can tell you: if I'm managing a project and a scheduler shows up, be prepared to see my happy dance! That is because the scheduler is doing exactly what it sounds like they're doing. They are developing and updating the project schedule, keeping track of schedule performance, and communicating schedule performance. In Chapter 6, *Creating a Project Schedule*, we will cover the process by which you define your tasks, sequence activities, estimate resources and durations, and then get a schedule approved as a baseline.

For myself personally, I find scheduling to be the most stressful aspect of project management. It's not that I can't do it, it's just that it stresses me out! Still others love scheduling and are very good at it, so I prefer to leave it to them, hence the happy dance.

Project team

The project team is anyone who will be executing project work. Though in a strong matrix organization, some of the team may also be helping you plan. I know that the people who do the work know the work and are the best resources for me to turn to when developing my project management plan, its subsidiary plans, and baselines.

The project team can provide the following information:

- Duration estimates for tasks that they will be performing.
- The sequence that work needs to be performed in. This in turn helps with scheduling.
- In some cases, your project team will be able to provide cost estimates or procurement needs for materials and equipment.

- The team will be also be updating you on current project performance and working to implement corrective and preventative actions after they've been approved through formal change-control.

In some cases, you will need to acquire additional team members to help execute project work and they may come from functional departments or outside the organization itself. If you do find yourself negotiating for resources with functional departments, it is a good idea to understand the scope of work they will be performing, whether they're working full- or part-time on the project, and how they will be acquired and released on the project. If your project team is lacking the necessary number of humans to perform project work, that would be where the **sponsor** could be very helpful in helping to assign more resources.

Project Management Office (PMO)

The PMO is a governing body that oversees projects. We'll review PMOs in depth later in this chapter. They are considered key stakeholders.

Change Control Board (CCB)

Unsurprisingly, the CCB controls project changes by approving or denying them. Typically, the CCB is made up of project or program managers who are overseeing multiple projects and programs.

If a change is necessary on your project, you and your team would do the following:

- Assess the impact of the change on other project variables and constraints
- Come up with solutions for implementation of the change
- Bring it to the attention of the change-control board who would need to analyze the change you are suggesting, review how it would impact other projects and programs going on, and then make the final decision

Don't worry, you will not be running to the change-control board for every little change. Typically, these are big changes that involve scope, time, cost, additional resources, or the escalation of a risk event. A lot of times either the sponsor can approve the change or you yourself can make the final decision. Typically, the CCB is internal to your organization but if you have an external customer, they may also have their own change control board that may need to approve any changes to the scope of work that impact the customer and deliverables.

Functional managers

Functional managers may be considered stakeholders at some point in the project, specifically if you will be borrowing resources from those departments. Functional managers are key stakeholders in functional or weak/balanced matrix organizations because they are in charge.

In a strong matrix or project-based organization, the functional managers may not have any input in day-to-day project work, but they will be the deciding factor as to who you can acquire from their team, how long you can have them on your team, and whether they will be working full- or part-time on the project.

This is why it is important to create and maintain good relationships with functional managers, because you may be negotiating with them for additional resources. It's never a bad idea to know exactly what skill sets you are looking for before you negotiate for resources.

There have been times where I've acquired resources from functional departments and walked away thinking, *Well, that was easy*, and later found out the resources I acquired were given easily because the functional manager wanted to unload their worst resource on me. Since I learned the hard way, I'm passing this knowledge on to you. Go to the discussion prepared!

Some items to consider during the negotiation may be the following:

- Specific skills that are necessary to perform project work
- Whether the team member can be co-located or virtual
- What type of work-authorization system you will be using to let the resource know it's go-time
- How long you believe you will need the resource and whether you can utilize them part-time, so they can still perform their functional work

 It's a good idea to make sure that the actual resources you're considering are interested in working on the project. The reason I mention that is we want motivated team members, not people who are resistant to project work.

- Whether you will be tracking and documenting their project performance and submitting the documentation to their functional manager for their performance reviews

- Whether training is necessary for the potential resource and, if so, how to go about setting it up and figure out how much time you *think* is needed for the skill transfer
- And make sure everyone understands how they will be acquired and how they will be released from the project work

Remember, the sponsor is a key stakeholder and they are there in a support role to help you navigate functional managers and acquisition of functional resources. There is also the PMO who might be actually assigning resources to your projects without any negotiation necessary with functional managers. It just depends on your organization and how projects are run.

Sellers, vendors, suppliers, and procurement managers

Even though you will cover procurement more in depth in `Chapter 9`, *Monitoring and Controlling Project Work,* it's important to address the variables here because anything procurement-related will have stakeholders involved. Some may become part of your project team and some may be looking over your shoulder to protect the organization from arbitration, mediation, or litigation.

Sellers, vendors, and suppliers

Essentially sellers, vendors, and suppliers can all be considered one and the same. Mostly it's just semantics and what your organization uses as terms for anybody outside the organization that will contribute to project work. This could be human resources, materials, or equipment. In some cases, there will be a simple **service-level agreement (SLA)** or even a **master service-level agreement (MSLA)** that clearly defines the role of the seller and their role in the project.

Other times, you and your team may be performing a make-or-buy analysis to determine the procurement needs of the project.

In some cases, sellers may become part of your project team and therefore become key stakeholders. Your job would be to manage the relationship with your sellers but not necessarily to do contract negotiations.

If procurement activities are necessary on your project, you may be determining what the criteria will be for selecting your sellers, vendors, or suppliers. You may also be asked to create a **procurement statement of work (PSOW)** for each type of provider of people, equipment, and materials necessary for your project.

Your level of involvement in procurement activities is completely dependent upon your organizational dynamics, the level of influence from your PMO, and your experience with procurement processes. Either way, it is your responsibility to meet contractual obligations and protect your organization from future costs or litigation.

Procurement managers

Depending on your procurement experience and how your organization works with sellers, you may also be working with a procurement department. In general, it is assumed that project managers cannot legally or contractually bind their organization to another. It's also assumed (unless otherwise stated on the exam), that we are the buyer. That may not be the case in your real world, and in some cases on multiple projects you may be performing the activities of both the buyer and seller. First, you are the buyer to acquire equipment necessary for an install, and second, you are the seller for the customer whose install you are doing.

No matter what, there is probably a procurement department and a procurement manager overseeing contracts in your organization. Many times, the project managers do the pre-work for procurement needs.

Here are some items the procurement manager or administrator is in charge of:

- Performing the negotiations
- Determining which contract types are needed
- Procurement change-control
- Officially closing out the contracts throughout the life cycle of the project as needed

Because of the high level of interaction on some projects between procured resources and the project manager, it is important to understand terms and conditions, incentives, and different contract types. Mostly, we can leave the depth of contractual knowledge to the procurement managers. We will cover what you need to know about your role in procurement in Chapter 9, *Monitoring and Controlling Project Work*.

The Project Management Office (PMO)

More often than not, organizations see the value in setting up a PMO, especially if the organization offers a variety of products or services. The PMO's role is to specifically manage all projects and programs from a top-tier level with concern for the organization in mind. The value of a PMO to the project manager and the project team depends on how it is structured.

There are **three categories** of PMOs and each category provides progressively more support and more influence on your projects:

- Supportive
- Controlling
- Directive

 You will not be asked to define the types of PMOs on the Project + exam, but it is good information for the real world.

Supportive

Supportive PMOs are there to offer **guidance** and help to project managers and project teams. Even though they are considered similar to a functional department but designed for projects, their main goal is to help streamline project work by providing templates, support, and some standardized processes. I like to think of supportive PMOs as guidance counselors in a high school—there to help you decide your next steps.

Controlling

A **controlling PMO** would provide the same items as a supportive PMO, but they would take it several steps further. They may be responsible for working with a variety of different projects or programs and would make sure that the benefits to the organization are managed through project work. Just as the title suggests, a controlling PMO may even be setting deliverables and key performance indicators. I like to think of a controlling PMO like the vice principal in a high school who has some power but not all of it. They can still suspend you, however, for running in the hall.

Directive

Even though the phrase **directive** sounds less influential than controlling, it isn't—it is **more** influential as a PMO. A directive PMO has the **most** influence on organizational project work. Along with everything that the supportive and controlling PMOs provide, the directive PMO will set standards and processes, provide tools and templates, coordinate resources among a variety of projects and programs, may be responsible for signing off on baselines, and will make sure that projects are prioritized based on business value.

Just like being in the principal's office when you do something wrong, the directive PMO will be the ones to delegate the consequences for lack of project performance.

You might be thinking that if there is a PMO in place that you, as a project manager, have little to no power over your project. That is simply not the case. The PMO is overseeing all projects and programs at the organizational level and may influence your projects in some ways, such as dictating the rules and enforcing standardized best practices. They are not running your projects for you.

PMOs are considered key stakeholders, but in your everyday project work, you probably won't interact with the PMO too much unless you need help, or they need to provide you templates, tools, guidance, or other necessary items to better coordinate your project.

Creating a stakeholder matrix

Now that you have reviewed the different categories of stakeholders, you have to keep them all straight and create a way to keep track of who they are, how they want to be communicated with, what their expectations are, and so on. If only there were a specific document that you could use to do so. Good news, there is! It's called a **stakeholder matrix**, and while there isn't one way over another to create and use this document, it will go a long way to helping keep everyone straight. Especially if this is a brand-new project and you have never worked with them before.

Keep in mind during the exam that the assumption is you are managing a brand-new project, creating something you have never done before, and that the project is a large one. You will also get a variety of questions representing different industries managing IT-related projects and may need different best practices. All projects need excellent stakeholder-management.

The first step after identifying your stakeholders is to determine what their level of power/influence and interests are on the project. Be aware that things can change and sometimes change quickly. One stakeholder may be humming along minding their own business and be perfectly happy with weekly updates until something goes sideways on the project that affects them. Now, they are breathing down your neck and demanding daily updates. Trust me, it happens more often than you think.

The right way to engage your stakeholders is to do the best you can to determine their expectations (this week) and then work to meet those expectations. That is akin to having a bunch of preschoolers on the playground and trying to get them to come inside after recess. It's not the easiest task in the world. The stakeholder matrix can help.

In order to put together an effective stakeholder matrix, it's best to actually talk to the individual and ask probing questions, for example, the following:

- How do you prefer to be communicated with: by email, telephone, or meetings?
- How often would you like updates and status reports?
- Would you prefer to pick and choose which meetings to attend? If so, I won't put "required" on the invite.
- What are your needs or concerns about this project?
- What is the planned level of involvement you are expecting?
- What are your expectations of the deliverable, schedule, budget, and so on?

I realize that not everyone is going to be located in your office and some may not even be on the same continent. Understanding their time zones can help enable you to schedule these conversations fairly is important as well. Nobody wants to have a meeting at two in the morning. That makes for very cranky stakeholders, which is the opposite of what we are trying to do.

I find using checklists or interview questions to be the best way to gather information from a variety of people. This keeps the conversation on track and to the point without jumping down any rabbit holes that can sabotage information-gathering. There are a lot of ways to gather information about your stakeholders and no way is really the wrong way, as long as you feel that you have enough information to make the best decisions regarding stakeholder engagement and requirements-collection. The only wrong way is to **not** do it at all. Therefore, having a comprehensive stakeholder matrix is an excellent tool for stakeholder-management.

Typically (and I say typically because it may be different in your organization), my stakeholder matrix is a collection of information that then allows me the ability to update as needed when individual stakeholder needs on the project change. Trust me, they will change!

Best practice suggests the following headers, but be as creative as needed to engage your own stakeholders:

- Name
- Department
- Contact information
- Time zone (as needed)
- Preferred method of communication
- Communication strategy
- Role or title on the project
- Needs, concerns, and interest regarding the project
- Level of involvement in the project
- Level of influence over the project

For some project managers, this is a mental exercise because they work with the same people all of the time. The only new player may be the customer, and even then, it is a good best practice to document the information, if only as a tangible reminder to engage and communicate in the manner they are expecting. In Chapter 7, *Resource Management Planning and Communication Considerations*, you will review the creation of a communication plan and different ways to effectively engage your stakeholders.

There is a lot of overlap between stakeholder and communications management on the exam. Sometimes it's difficult to tell which knowledge area the questions are referring to. A good rule of thumb is to view communication as planning to distribute information, distributing information, and controlling communications. Stakeholder management pertains to creating and maintaining good relationships and meeting stakeholder expectations. Do we do that with good communication? Certainly, we do. This is why I recommend you read these types of questions carefully and refer to the exam tip to help you navigate to the correct answers.

Summary

In this chapter, we covered an overview of stakeholder roles and responsibilities and why it is important to be able to identify your project stakeholders. Then, you reviewed common stakeholder requirements and interests, which is one of the iterative responsibilities you will have as a project manager since those interests and requirements will change during the project life cycle.

You then reviewed different roles and responsibilities of potential project stakeholders by title or category, which included the project management office or PMO.

Lastly, you reviewed the importance of a stakeholder matrix and what headers could be used to collect information either at the beginning of the project or throughout. In `Chapter 4`, *Developing a Project Charter*, you will review the development of a project charter and why it is an important kick-off document.

Questions

1. Which of the following stakeholders could be considered the person (or persons) who oversees the project's finances?
    *   Business analysts
    *   Project sponsor
    *   Project manager
    *   PMO

2. Which of the following role can be found on large projects and whose main focus is to help support the project manager with administrative tasks?
    *   Scheduler
    *   Sponsor
    *   Coordinator
    *   PMO

3. A _____ is considered a project role that oversees projects and programs in the organization for the good of the organization.
    *   Program manager
    *   Project sponsor
    *   Coordinator
    *   PMO

4. You are working with your team to determine whether equipment from outside the organization is needed. Which of the following stakeholders would be a part of the process to obtain outside goods or services?
    *   Procurement manager
    *   Customer
    *   Project sponsor
    *   Project manager

5. Which of the following best describes a project-management plan?
   - Gives formal authorization to begin project work
   - The plan, once approved, can only be changed through formal change control. This includes the management plans and baselines
   - Includes the deliverables and can be changed when needed without authorization
   - Management plans and baselines are created to make sure everyone knows how the project will run

6. Of all the project documents, which one best describes who your stakeholders are and how they prefer to be communicated with?
   - Communication-management plan
   - Stakeholder-engagement plan
   - Project-management plan
   - Stakeholder matrix

7. You are a project manager working on a long-term project installing servers in multiple customer locations. Your customer asks you whether they can add something to the scope of work to make the install better for their organization. You determine that the impact is minimal to the schedule and the costs. What stakeholder do you need to review the change with before it is implemented?
   - Sponsor
   - Change-control board (CCB)
   - PMO
   - Customer

8. Which answer best describes a stakeholder?
   - A person or group that has a vested interest in the result once it's on the market
   - A person who buys the product or service after it's been marketed
   - A person or group who has requirements that must be met for the project to be considered successful
   - A person or group who helps create the project-management plan

9. Bill is a key stakeholder on your project and is discussing with you his high interest in getting regular reports on the project. This has changed since the beginning of the project when Bill didn't need updates on a regular basis. What would you update to make sure you are meeting Bill's new requirements?
   - Project-management plan
   - Business case

- Stakeholder matrix
- Stakeholder-management plan

10. Which of the following best describes the information you will need when negotiating with functional managers to acquire needed resources? Choose all that apply.
    - Whether you will be tracking and documenting their project performance and submitting the documentation to their functional manager for their performance reviews
    - Determining whether training is necessary for the potential resource
    - How the resources will be acquired and how they will be released from project work
    - If the team member will be loyal to the project manager
    - If the coordinator needs to get involved in acquisition

11. Which of the following plans can you expect to see in your project management? Choose all that apply.
    - Stakeholder management plan
    - List of all stakeholders
    - Schedule management plan and schedule baseline
    - Cost management plan and cost baseline
    - Stakeholder matrix

12. Your project sponsor has come to you to ask which stakeholders they should invite to the next all-hands meeting on your large project. Which of the following would not need to be invited?
    - Scheduler
    - Coordinator
    - Change-control board (CCB)
    - End user

13. Kelly, a member of your core team, reminds you as you are creating your stakeholder matrix that the project will need outside resources that will have to be processed through the procurement department in your organization. In this situation, what could your organization be considered?
    - Seller
    - Buyer
    - Customer
    - Procurement acquisitions

14. Which of the following certifications was designed specifically with project coordinators in mind?
    - CompTIA Project+
    - CompTIA A+
    - PMP®
    - CAPM®

15. All of the following are project stakeholders, except which one?
    - Functional manager at the customer's organization
    - Functional manager in your organization
    - PMO
    - Sponsor

4

Developing a Project Charter

In this chapter, you will review the different process groups found on projects and the different phase configurations that can be used. Then you will learn about how key deliverables and high-level requirements are determined based on a business case and stakeholder engagement, all of which will result in a formal project charter.

Once all project goals and objectives are determined, a kick-off meeting can be held and the planning of the project can begin.

In this chapter, we will cover the following topics:

- Life cycle of a project or phase
- Goals and objectives of a project charter
- Documenting high-level requirements
- Criteria of a project charter
- Holding a kick-off meeting

Life cycle of a project or phase

All projects are temporary and therefore have a life cycle with a beginning, a middle, and an end. Because you are working on projects, or will be very soon, you know that nothing about project management is very linear. Even though we are looking at a waterfall-type predictive project, meaning we can predict the result, that doesn't mean that it is a true step-by-step process from beginning to end. Project management is, for lack of a better word, messy. There are all sorts of things going on at once. Hence, a **life cycle**.

In a guide such as this, it would be difficult for myself or anyone else to say, *This is exactly how you run a project, and in this order.* You might be thinking, *Wait... what? I thought that is exactly what you were going to do.* In this case, you would be overestimating my project-management powers because all projects are unique, and not every single best practice, document, tool, and technique will be used every single time, *the perfect world versus the real world.* In the real world, my projects consist of some set best practices and documentation but not always and not necessarily in this order. I also have numerous templates I use to make this process a bit easier, for example:

- Project charter or a **statement of work (SOW)**
- Project schedule and budgetary baseline
- Risk-management plan and risk register
- Issue log
- Stakeholder matrix
- Glossary of uncommon terms

A glossary of uncommon terms is an important part of effective communication. If I start babbling about empirical process-control and daily Scrums, as a customer, you might not know what those are and be afraid to ask about them. Therefore, having a glossary of **three-letter acronyms (TLAs)**, and industry jargon definitions goes a long way toward effective communication and understanding. By the way, in case you didn't know those terms either, it's okay! It wouldn't be particularly good of me to give you a lecture on glossary of uncommon terms and not define the examples I used. The examples of empirical process control and daily Scrum are industry lingo found in the Scrum framework and is found in agile project management:

- **Empirical process-control**: Using expert judgment and experimentation to find the right answer or approach. It is the crux of the Scrum framework.
- **Daily Scrum**: The daily stand-up meeting on a Scrum team where the team discusses what they worked on yesterday, what they will work on today, and what speed bumps are in their way.

Many times, the project life cycle is driven by a unique product that needs a **specific phase-oriented** way of meeting requirements, and another is being driven by organizational processes and the order designated by your PMO. All I can provide are categories of life cycles that are different phase-oriented configurations that are *typical* in project management and found on your CompTIA Project+ exam.

In *Figure 4.1*, you can see that it is a cycle from project initiation all the way to the project or phase closure. There are multiple processes to plan, re-plan, execute and monitor, and control in project work before the project or phase is closed:

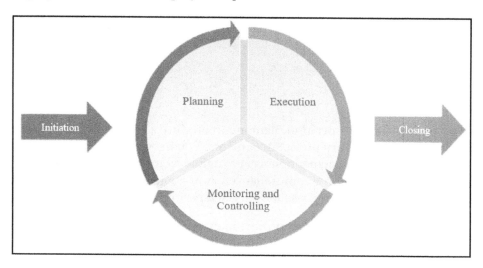

Figure 4.1

Because each process has its own role to play, we'll go through a high-level overview of each process group.

Initiation

Project initiation contains two important processes that are necessary to begin project work and determine initial requirements.

Initiation best practices will have been totally covered in Chapter 2, *Project Initiation,* and Chapter 3, *Project Roles and Responsibilities*; in this chapter, we will focus on the steps for the development of a project charter.

The key activities in initiation often include the following:

- The development of the business case
- Determining a high-level scope description
- Creation and approval of the project charter
- Stakeholder identification

Planning

There are many processes that occur in planning to produce a comprehensive project-management plan and necessary project documents. You have reviewed many of the baselines and subsidiary management plans at a high level in Chapter 3, *Project Roles and Responsibilities*. You reviewed how comprehensive how-to guides may be necessary for each knowledge area as well as specific baselines to track performance.

It takes work to produce an **integrated project-management plan**, but there are also a variety of living, breathing project documents that you will create and update on a regular basis. These do *not* need formal approval for changes. If you had to get formal authorization every time you added a new issue to the issue log, that would be all you ever did: *Hello, change-control board, I'm back again for the 85th time today!* That would be an outrageous waste of time. We'll visit the CCB when requirements for scope, time, cost, or quality need to change rather than for day-to-day updates that help us keep track of performance.

The list of project documents is not exhaustive because your needs will depend on the project.

You will review the following documents in later chapters:

- Risk register
- Issue log
- Activity lists
- Schedule (*not* the **schedule baseline**)
- Budget (*not* the **cost baseline**)
- Resource calendars
- Resource assignments
- Stakeholder matrix

Execution

This is where all the project work happens and when we find out how well we'd planned. Execution is where the deliverables are produced. It's where we acquire additional team members, as needed, and develop and manage our team of individuals. This is also the process group where we are auditing or *assuring* the quality of our process to produce the product, service, or result. This is also the point where we are collecting work-performance data from our resources, which lets us know what's really going on, in real time. We can compare that to the baselines and see whether there is a discrepancy between planned and actual. If there is a variance outside of our tolerance levels that needs to be corrected, this is where we process a change request and visit the CCB.

Monitoring and controlling

Remember I said project management is messy and there is a lot going on all at once? That is why monitoring and controlling is an important aspect of project management. It's important to keep an eye on project execution and determine whether the following are true:

- A visit to the CCB is needed
- Requirements have changed
- Risk responses are working
- The product is of a high quality
- The customer is validating the scope of work with signatures

All performance measurements and reporting occur here. Even though we spent a ton of time putting together our how-to guides and baselines, we also know that the best-laid plans don't always turn out the way we want. This is where corrective and preventative actions take place. Remember this is a cycle, so if you are executing work, and monitoring and controlling the execution of work, you may discover that something needs to change. How you manage that change has several steps:

1. Assess the impact on potentially affected knowledge areas with your team.
2. Re-plan and come up with a solution for implementation.
3. Visit the CCB and hope for approval. (I usually have two choices, one I want and one I can live with.)
4. You may also have to get approval from the customer, even if they are the ones who requested the change.
5. Once you have approval, you will need to update your plans and communicate the changes.

6. If you don't get approval, you still communicate the result of the decision.

There are many ways to keep an eye on the project, and it's important to be vigilant with documentation updates, tracking risks and issues, and making sure you are producing the right result based on requirements.

Closing the project or phase

We'll review different phase-oriented project configurations next, but let's assume all project work has been completed, the customer has signed off and formally validated that you produced the deliverable(s) correctly, they have accepted the result as completed, and all procurements have been closed. There is still some work left to do to formally close a project or phase.

It is quite common to have a final meeting to discuss lessons learned and create a final report. Administrative closure may include archiving project documents, and making sure all procurement items have been closed and waivers have been signed. At this point, the **product life cycle** is about to begin and may require a physical or technical transfer of the result to the customer/end users, and potentially you will release your team.

In some cases, there will be training for those that will support the product, or maybe the customer's help desk needs to take over, so they will be trained or updated prior to close.

Even if a project is canceled in the middle, you would go through a formal closure and would still need a signature accepting whatever deliverables have been produced before you could close the project formally.

The process groups, or life cycle, of a project are designed to have **time to plan** and build out comprehensive plans; while executing those plans, keep an eye on things and make changes as needed. If you just went back to re-read *time to plan* and snorted a bit, I understand. I'm snorting too.

The perfect world gives us time to be as comprehensive in our planning as is needed to be successful. If you go head first into execution and project work, I feel your pain. Maybe you can blame all these new best practices on me or CompTIA and ask for time to create templates and implement new skills to save the company money. Remember to include the money bit in your conversations and hopefully you'll have the time you need. My conversations usually start with *I have an idea on how to improve the organization with new best practices for project management.* The responses range from, *We've always done it this way* to *Yeah... no.* Those conversations usually end with me responding with, *Yeah, but that isn't working.* Organizational-process assets strike again!

If that is your world right now, choose your documents and best practices wisely to help plan (yet streamline) your project work. I always tell my project managers that the slow-moving wheels of progress need some help from time to time, and typically without proof, progress stops completely.

Keep note of any documents and best practices as you read through this guide that resonate with you or sound like something you need. Jot them down and try them out. These best practices, once implemented, can provide the documentation and actual cost and time savings to show to your organization to get those wheels moving again. Game on!

Common documents and process groups

There are some common documents that can be created and used as templates in other projects. This isn't an exhaustive list, but they are typical documents in most projects as best practices. Each document has the process group where it is *typically* created or used:

Document name	Process group
Project charter	Initiating
Project management plan	Planning
Issue log	Executing
Organizational chart	Planning
Scope statement	Planning
Communication plan	Planning
Project schedule	Planning
Project budget	Planning
Status report	Executing
Dashboard information	Executing
Action items	Executing
Meeting agenda	Executing
Meeting minutes	Executing

Overlapping phases

In some projects, it makes sense to have phases that are overlapping, especially if you have a tight timeline and the resources to perform work in parallel. It basically means one phase doesn't have to totally end before another begins. For example, if you are installing servers at 10 locations and you have 10 people on your team, it stands to reason that they could all be at various locations installing servers at the same time. Obviously, it doesn't always work like that. It may be that a test install happens first and, once the thumbs up happens, everyone else can begin their installs and work in overlapping phases. Any time you can execute multiple deliverables at the same time, you will finish faster than if you produced them one at a time.

In *Figure 4.2*, you can see a generic example of overlapping phases:

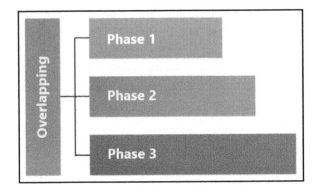

Figure 4.2 Overlapping phases

Sequential phases

If it makes sense logically that work cannot begin until other work is completed, running the project in sequential phases may be the best choice. Phase one would have to be initiated, planned, executed, monitored and controlled, and closed before the next phase could begin. Often there is a **phase-gate review** or a **quality-gate review** at the end of each phase. This would be a formal review of work completed in the phase and a determination of whether things can proceed to the next phase. Usually there is a go/no-go decision before the next phase can be initiated.

In *Figure 4.3*, you can see the progression of how each phase would begin after the prior phase has ended:

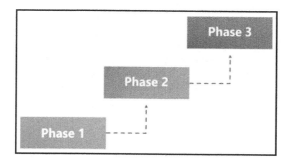

Figure 4.3 Phase progression

Adaptive or agile phases

The agile life cycles are vastly different from the waterfall life cycles. Just like waterfall is an umbrella term over the various life cycles we just covered, agile is an umbrella term for different frameworks.

Common agile frameworks include the following:

- Scrum
- **eXtreme Programming (XP)**
- **Adaptive software development (ASD)**
- Aspects of Lean and Kanban
- **Feature-driven development (FDD)**
- Crystal methods

While each framework is a bit different, the end goal is typically software development. Even though aspects of each are not just for software anymore and there are many hybrid frameworks, the core reason the frameworks were created was to create better software faster.

To do that, it was important that the scope of work was flexible, and that changes were acceptable. There are no comprehensive front-loaded plans, and if there are, work is only planned out for two weeks to a month to allow for progressive elaboration on the design. You will review agile frameworks and philosophies in depth in Chapter 10, *Formal Project or Phase Closure and Agile Project Management*, but for now the life cycles of agile frameworks are performed in iterations or sprints that are no more than 30 days each. Every 30 days, a new iteration begins and builds on the lessons learned from earlier iterations. For now, the differences between waterfall and agile may help explain why the dynamic is so different between the two.

In *Figure 4.4*, you can see a high-level comparative approach of the two most popular project-management approaches:

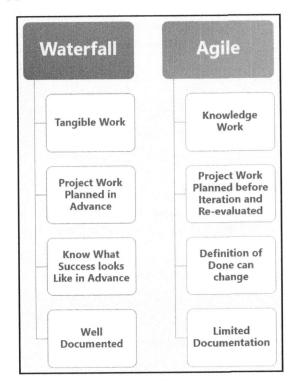

Figure 4.4 Waterfall versus agile framework

What is agile?

If you think of the word **agility** or **adaptable,** those are good definitions for agile approaches. The life cycles include the following:

- Iterative (over and over) cycles of work until the work can be called done or completed
- Incremental development of the result, usually software
- Frequent reviews of the results for customer approval and discussions of new features
- Adaptation is encouraged to include new features without formal change-control
- Uncertainty and risks during the iteration since not everything is known and can be planned for in advance

- No predictive front-loaded plan
- The result isn't predicted, it's adaptable

If all of that piqued your interest, don't worry, we'll cover all of it and more in Chapter 10, *Formal Project or Phase Closure and Agile Project Management*. For now, just know that agile is vastly different from waterfall, and even though we are covering much more of the waterfall types of best practices, the new skill to have in project management is to be able to *tailor* your best practices and approaches to meet the unique project needs. A dash of agile and a little bit extra of waterfall, plus your organizational processes can help attain better project-management best practices and better deliverables.

Goals and objectives of a project charter

There are many different paths to take to get to the same result in project management. In Chapter 2, *Project Initiation*, you reviewed a variety of project-selection techniques that organizations use to develop a business case. While that still occurs internally, some projects begin differently, perhaps via a contract or a request from a customer.

Once it is determined that a project will occur, it is time to decide the most effective way to accomplish it. A SOW could be created, stating intent to start a project on either the customer side or from your organization. Usually a SOW contains high-level requirements that will be better defined during the creation of a project charter. Typically, senior management or the PMO will also compare ways to execute a project by using different methods to determine cost effectiveness and feasibility, as you saw during the business case development. The best practice is to always have a project charter. You'll see why in just a moment, but in the real world, some projects begin with a SOW and a charter is never created.

If we go with the assumption that the decision has been made to charter a project, the actual charter will be developed once everyone making the decisions agree on a few things. There is most likely a selection committee who *could* be composed of the PMO, the project sponsor, business analysts, the customer, and additional key stakeholders. Included in the charter creation will be known problems, opportunities, risk events, time frames, and possibly a total amount of money the internal or external client wants to spend. This could be considered a **top-down estimate**. This means that until the true scope of work is defined, and the project is planned, it can be difficult to be as accurate as perhaps the organization needs the business case to be.

While money is important, and the business case can somewhat prove costs versus benefits, there are many reasons why a project may be undertaken, including projects for the good of society and the environment. Money isn't always the underlying factor for projects to be chartered. It's important, but it isn't everything.

There are many ways the selection committee may make the final decisions about the scope of work, potential costs and benefits, as well as schedule milestones or constraints. It isn't as simple as market projections.

It may be that you are already involved in the project now and are part of the decision-making process. After all, as a project manager, you will be accountable for the work and may have to be the one to reel in the pie-in-the-sky approach to the project itself. Expert judgment is imperative to make sure everyone is making the best decisions, either on whether to charter the project internally or to respond to a customer request. Even if you aren't involved at this point, part of your job responsibilities are to validate the project charter before project work begins and do your own benefit analysis.

My benefit analysis usually ends with a conversation involving the selection committee and starts with the question, *Where did you come up with those numbers?* They love it when you ask that question! All kidding aside, there are a variety of decisions and conclusions that need to be made before the project is chartered and actual project work can begin.

There are other considerations that are necessary before a project can be formally chartered. Some of them influence your day to day activities more than the others:

- **Project management methodology** basically means what approach you will take, what life cycle is appropriate, and whether a hybrid approach is necessary. The methodology or framework will influence the content of your charter as part of developing the project charter process.
- **Project Management Information System (PMIS)** is basically all the software you will use on your project or any computer-related help your project will have. How will you store your documents, create reports, and communicate? There are many software programs we all use to help do our daily work, and a PMIS is the system or software we will use for this.
- **Expert judgment** is a comparative approach to selecting a project or a process. It is a group of experts who confer and give opinions on your project or how to manage it. Expert judgment is considered the number-one tool and technique used in project management.

The Delphi technique

The Delphi technique is a form of **Expert Judgment** or **Analysis** and was created at the Rand Corporation in 1950 to forecast or make decisions. The entire crux of the analysis works from the assumption that group judgment is better than the judgment of individuals. Organically based on the Greek story of the **Oracle of Delphi**, this process is a way of determining consensus in a group environment. A bit of a small history lesson may help explain the process. The Oracle of Delphi lived in a cave at the top of a mountain and the cave entrance was protected by a priest. Villagers would climb the mountain to ask questions about their fate of the Oracle through the priest. The priest would take the questions to the Oracle who would provide the answers. The villagers never knew who actually answered their questions, so they remained anonymous. For all we know, the Oracle had a meeting of the minds and consensus was reached about that question and they all determined *Yes, we believe your crops will be fruitful this year, pass it on.*

The **Delphi Technique** is used to reach **anonymous consensus** among a group of chosen experts who review initial project information and give advice on the best ways to proceed. The answers most alike will be considered the *best* way to move forward. The experts usually aren't aware of the others (keeping it anonymous), or their results are analyzed by a facilitator and they aren't aware of the chosen way to proceed.

There are many ways to execute this process, and it is mostly used to prevent **groupthink**.

Groupthink happens whenever a group of people get together and the stronger personalities push their decisions and everyone else just goes along with it. *What do you guys want for lunch? I was thinking pizza.* Everyone says, *Okay pizza is fine,* and thinks to themselves, *I would have preferred a sandwich, but I'm not going to be the one that rocks the boat.*

The Delphi technique is used often in **risk identification**, but is considered expert judgment in project selection and initial risk documentation during project initiation. Gaining the advice of experts who aren't close to the project can be immensely helpful.

Documenting high-level requirements

At the beginning of a project, not much is truly known about the ins and outs of the scope of work, what things will cost, and how long the project will be. Yes, it is predictive, but it's tough to predict everything at this point. That is why high-level requirements are made and agreed upon, and why all projects are progressively elaborated on. **Progressive elaboration** is a fancy term for *go with what you know today and expand on that knowledge once you have it.* Elaborate progressively on scope, time, and cost as well as risk, quality, and resources.

For example, we are planning to build a bridge over the Delaware River between Pennsylvania and New Jersey. Predictive means we know we are building a bridge, we know where it will be built, and we know how long the last bridge took and what it cost (maybe). When we are finished, we will have a bridge. So, the statement of work is created; the business analysts crunch the numbers and determine it will cost $3.5 million to build and should take about a year to complete, barring risk events such as weather impacting the timeline. You will review that information, and offer your opinions, and the project will be chartered. That doesn't mean we know much of anything more today than we did when the statement of work was created. But because we can predict the result, we can outline the expectations.

At the end of the project, it may end up taking two years to complete and $6.5 billion, but we won't know that until we are in it. It's not unusual for the high-level requirements to be overly optimistic either; you can probably bet that they will be. That is where your analysis, communication, and validation are important, because you are the one being held accountable for the result.

High-level requirements

High-level requirements often include a broad stroke of the scope of work – enough to make the decision to charter without many of the specifics. Much like diet soda is all the taste without the calories, high-level requirements are specifics without context:

- **The predicted result for scope of work**: A bridge between Pennsylvania and New Jersey with some basic design specs
- **The results of the business case analysis**: $3.5 billion
- **High-level schedule expectations**: One year
- **Mandatory milestones**: Key date considerations to meet the high-level schedule
- **Constraints**: Scope, time, cost, quality, risk, resources
- **Pre-approved sellers or vendors**: Not even sure they are available or can work on this project yet
- **The selection committee**: Those who make these decisions

Once everyone agrees on the project scope and the high-level requirements, a contract may be negotiated between the customer (states of PA and NJ) and your organization. Most organizations have a procurement or legal department that handles all of this, so we can leave those details to them and it may just be an SOW at this point until the scope of work is clearer and the project has been officially chartered.

Criteria of a project charter

The first thing to note is that a project cannot begin without a charter. I know you are thinking, *We do it all the time!* and I'm not surprised at all. Not every organization uses a project charter to kick off their projects, but we must return to the perfect world for a moment and assume you need a charter to begin project work.

You may see questions about the project manager being asked to start work without a project charter – in that situation, what do you do? You are expected to explain the risks of not having a charter and turn down the project until the charter is created. I'll pause for virtual laughter… but that is the correct answer! In my world, turning down a project without a charter is called an RPE. A **resume-producing event**! As we move further through this chapter, I'll cover why that is the correct answer, but for now let's assume we are still chuckling a bit and move on.

Typically, a project charter will be developed once everyone making the decisions agrees on all the items thus far: scope of work, the business case, and the like. Included in the charter creation will be known problems, opportunities, risk events, time frames, and possibly the total amount of money an internal or external customer wants to spend.

The project charter is the first documentation of a project after a statement of work. Typically written and signed by the project sponsor, the charter gives formal authorization to begin a project. Your organization may call this something different, but the premise is the same. Usually the project manager is named or chosen for the project and the sponsor will document what is currently known about the project's schedule, budget, risk events, and milestones.

Why a charter is important

Project charters go a long way to beginning a project the right way, a formal project kick-off. I refer to the project charter as the ticket to ride the roller coaster of project management, because it gives us project managers the ability to begin project work formally.

Typical aspects of a charter include the following:

- Describes the agreed-upon scope of work
- Names the project manager and gives you formal authority to begin project work and use company resources
- Identifies key stakeholders
- Is a written agreement to take on the project

There are many elements of a project charter to consider – even though there may only be high-level information, getting all that information in one place is important. Chances are that the project charter will go through some revisions until the powers that be approve, but once that occurs, it is rare that the charter will be updated or used as anything other than a reference point going forward. Then why is it so important and how can I tell the difference between a project charter and other documents I've seen already? Great questions! The project charter is the culmination of business-case development, a SOW, an agreement between your organization and that of another, and a decision by your organization to take on the predicted scope of work.

Once that work is better elaborated on, it will lead to the creation of other documents such as a scope statement, a work breakdown structure, a schedule, and a budget. All cannot be created without the formal authorization to begin the project via the charter and all will be reviewed once we get to those chapters. Much like in project management, the charter must come first.

Project charters, much like projects, come in all shapes and sizes. There are some standardized headers that can be used as a template if your organization does not currently use project charters.

You will not be asked on the exam to define specific headers. You may need to know how to identify the project charter based on the information found in it though, so we will go through the most common headers and I'll show you which items to be aware of in situational questions.

Example of a project charter

The headers of a project charter are fairly consistent in most projects. Of course, you can adapt and adjust as needed on your own projects but you will find the following headers very standard:

- **Executive summary**: Not all project charters have an executive summary, and if they do, it is usually the last thing written, much like what you see in the business case. It is sometimes good to have an executive summary to show support on the organizational level for the project and to help create buy-in with other stakeholders.
- **Project name**: Usually the project name is something generic such as the "bridge project," this is mostly just to identify it as unique and differentiate it from other projects that are being chartered.

- **Authorities**: The authorities are usually key stakeholders, and may include the customer, the PMO, the business analysts that created the business case, and a variety of other decision-makers. This is a good section for the project manager to review because it can enable them to identify key stakeholders who may have extremely specific requirements for the project.
- **Initiating authority**: The initiating authority is typically the project sponsor. Remember the project sponsor is the one that writes checks for the project and is in a supportive role to help the project manager navigate the project. It's typical that the project sponsor is internal to your organization, but in some cases it could be an external customer.
- **Project manager**: This is an important section for us, because this paragraph gives us project managers formal authorization to begin project work and utilize organizational resources to produce the deliverable. Remember I mentioned in an exam tip earlier that project managers are supposed to turn down the project and explain the risks of not having a project charter? This is the reason why, because once the project manager's name is added to the project charter, they are formally assigned to the project and are responsible for managing it. Without that documentation, it is risky for a project manager to begin project work.

It is also important to note that this section will identify the authority level of the project manager, meaning they are responsible for things such as budgets and schedules, or they are working in a different organizational dynamic and sharing some of the responsibilities with the functional manager.

Naming the project manager is an important piece of this process:

_____ is authorized as Project Manager for this project and will be the primary point of contact. _____ is responsible for meeting all key milestones within the time, cost, and performance constraints of this project. Furthermore, _____ has the authority to apply organizational resources to accomplish the goals of this project.

- **Business need the project addresses**: In this section, it's important to describe why the project is being undertaken, and the business need that is being met by chartering this project. This may also include sections of or the entire business case. Even though ROI isn't always about money, chances are that money will be addressed in this section.
- **Project description**: At this point, there are only high-level scope descriptions, high-level milestones, and a budget based on a business case. But it is important for contributors to the project charter to describe to the best of their ability the true scope of work.

- **Product/service characteristics**: This may be key features and expected results and be generated from high-level scope descriptions, the business case, or a contract.
- **Project relationship to business need**: This section addresses why the business is chartering the project. Was it due to a change in the market? A customer request? A regulatory compliance update? This will help with buy-in and to tie business needs to project results.
- **Assumptions**: These are aspects of the project we assume to be true without any specific proof. Assumptions are usually made based on past experiences on other projects, taken from historical information or lessons learned.

If I walk by a bench that has a *wet paint* sign on it, I won't sit on the bench because I assume the paint is still wet. The sign could have been there a month, but I won't take any chances. It is an assumption that may or may not be true. Until it can be proven one way or the other, I will proceed as if the paint is wet. In projects, though, we should test assumptions regularly to see whether they can be eliminated.

Project assumptions will change and be proven or disproven as the project progresses.

For that reason, *all* assumptions should be documented before project kick-off and then questioned throughout the life of the project and updated. Projects that have never been executed before or a brand-new product rollout will have more assumptions than facts in the beginning, and those assumptions will need to be monitored, documented, and controlled. An assumptions analysis is also a large part of risk identification.

- **Constraints**: Anything that limits the project in any way. The competing constraints of time, cost, scope, quality, risk, and resources are definite constraints to document currently. Other constraints may include having to use one specific seller because the organization has a single source agreement with them. Constraints can hinder the project manager's ability to truly plan effectively because they may have to work around constraints that aren't flexible. The more constraints a project has, the higher risk the project may become, because if you change something in one constraint, the rest could be affected. Constraints aren't inherently bad, or risky. If all of the constraints are reasonable, with acceptable buffers, risk will be low. Unreasonable or restrictive constraints, of course, will definitely introduce risk. If you lengthen your schedule, that could affect your cost, the scope of the project/product, and potentially the quality. Not all changes are necessarily negative, however, it's important to assess the impact to other constraints before making changes on the project.

- **Risk Events**: Typically, there are categories of risk that come with every project. Some are industry-specific categories such as cyber security, or diverse categories such as technical risks, weather risks, and external risks. Even though risk identification has not yet formally occurred, knowing what categories might influence the project is important. Risk isn't always a terrible thing, although that is what we are used to considering first. Risk can be a threat or an opportunity. It may be that the organization is trying to be first to market with a brand-new product and the risk of being first is worth the money. It's an opportunity but it still carries a probability of not occurring. It isn't guaranteed. This is referred to as a known/unknown. You will review risk in depth in Chapter 8, *Budget and Contingency Plans for Risk*. For now, knowing some of the threats and opportunities categories can go a long way to helping you and your team identify, analyze, and create responses for risk.
- **Approval**: Signatures are important because it makes the project charter formal and means buy-in has occurred with a variety of key stakeholders. If the sponsor signs off on the charter, it means everyone agrees that the project is necessary and is ready to be kicked off.

Agile project charter

You will review agile in depth in Chapter 10, *Formal Project or Phase Closure and Agile Project Management*, but it's important to note that even though agile isn't considered predictive, and is instead adaptive, a charter is still used to kick off a project.

Traditional project charters are not as flexible as an agile charter because a traditional charter documents a lot of set information; high-level requirements are included but it's clear that the organization knows what it is trying to achieve. Agile projects are more open to changes and need a bit more flexibility in the chartering process.

A large part of agile project management is transparent communication; determining what kind of project to charter will be determined by engaging stakeholders in the process prior to chartering. Many topics will revolve around features and functions, rather than a set deliverable. Another difference is that the project charter can change and be updated prior to the project and possibly throughout to keep on top of the changes to the scope of work, therefore it is not a static document like a traditional charter.

It is important to have a charter on an agile project, but it's also important to make sure that it allows for flexibility and responding to changing needs and technologies.

The structure of an agile charter could depend on your organizational processes. If the project benefits from a hybrid approach between predictive and adaptive best practices, you may find the charter is more like a waterfall charter than an agile charter.

These are the typical headings on an agile charter:

- **Who** are the key stakeholders involved in the project, including participants and team members.
- **What** is the high-level description of the project goals and vision today? This is documented but is also expected to change or adapt.
- **Where** are the work sites, client sites, and where is most of the work going to be done? Most agile teams are colocated, but they may be off-site at a client site to run the project or the client can be internal to the organization.
- **When** does the team anticipate the project will start and end? Scheduling is done in sprints or iterations in agile environments, typically lasting a month or less. It would be exceedingly difficult to pinpoint total duration or how many iterations in the beginning, unless it is designated by the organization or the customer.
- **Why** is the project being done? What is the value to the organization and the customer?
- **How** will the project be run? Full agile or a tailored approach to the framework?
- **Signatures** allow an initial buy-in to the charter and makes the project formal and approved. It isn't uncommon for agile projects to have a business case created in advance of the project charter and that tends to be adaptable too.

Holding a kick-off meeting

A kick-off meeting not only signals the beginning of the project, it also gives everyone a chance to communicate their vision of the project. Some teams hold their kick-off meetings prior to planning, to give everyone a chance to discuss the scope of work and other constraints. Some do all the planning and then hold a kick-off meeting to signal the beginning of execution of the project. Still others have two kick-off meetings, one after the charter and one after planning. There isn't a wrong way to do a kick-off meeting except not to do it.

There are certain best practices or key aspects of a kick-off meeting, but I'll keep this generic since it tends to adapt based on the project type or the organization's way of doing things:

- Confirm everyone understands the goals and objectives of the project
- Project description
- High-level milestones
- General project approach
- Should include the project sponsor, key project team members, and key stakeholders
- Address and discuss the project charter

One way to make sure that the key aspects are covered is to have an agenda. I prefer to send out the agenda a couple of days in advance of the meeting to those who will attend. I do this so everyone has a chance to review, and if anything needs to be added or removed, there is time to adapt the agenda. I am also not the only one who should be talking. People who do the work know the work. Therefore, my agenda may include attachments of the charter or other project documents and who is presenting what information, in what order, and for how long. It isn't unusual for a kick-off meeting to run an hour or longer and is certainly dependent on the estimated project length.

Keep in mind that not every kick-off meeting will have everyone in the same room. There are numerous virtual teams around the world that participate in a virtual kick-off. It's important to account for some of the challenges that are found in virtual meetings, such as the following:

- Time zones
- Language differences
- Slang/jargon
- Lack of body language
- Technology
- Lack of buy-in

Most of the exam questions are written from the perspective of a colocated team, but you may get questions about the challenges of virtual teams and the importance of a comprehensive communication plan. You'll cover communication and team dynamics in Chapter 7, *Resource Management Planning and Communication Considerations*.

Summary

In this chapter, you reviewed the distinct types of common life cycles of a project or phase in both waterfall and agile project management. Then you reviewed the goals and objectives of a project charter, and learned why documenting high-level requirements and understanding the criteria of a project charter are important. Lastly, you reviewed common best practices and the topics of a kick-off meeting. In `Chapter 5`, *Creating a Work Breakdown Structure (WBS)*, you will review the **work breakdown structure** (**WBS**) and why it is considered the *most important* planning document.

Questions

1. The definition of a project is:
   - Progressively elaborated on and unique
   - Temporary and chartered
   - Temporary and unique
   - Unique and has a life cycle

2. Which of the following is the correct order for the process groups of project management?
   - Initiation, executing, monitoring and controlling, and close project or phase
   - Planning, execution, monitoring and controlling, and closing
   - Initiation, execution, and project or phase closure
   - Initiation, planning, executing, monitoring and controlling, and close project or phase

3. Which of the following are key activities in the initiation process group? Check all that apply.
   - Creation of the risk register
   - Development of the business case
   - Schedule baseline
   - Project charter creation
   - Identification of stakeholders

4. Which of the following is the main goal for planning?
   - To create a comprehensive project-management plan
   - To create a schedule baseline
   - To create a budget that meets the business plan
   - To understand the scope of work

5. Which of the following process groups is where the deliverables are produced?
   - Initiation
   - Planning
   - Monitoring and controlling
   - Execution

6. To process a change request, which of the following departments would you most likely need to get approval from?
   - The PMO
   - The CCB
   - The sponsor
   - The customer

7. You are working on a long-term project with 25 stakeholders. In the middle of the project, the customer asks for a change in scope that will impact the entire project and consequently will not align with the project charter. Which of the following is the best way to handle this?
   - Process a change request with the CCB
   - Discuss everything with your sponsor
   - After approvals, go through formal project closure for this project
   - Explain to the customer that the change is too different from the original scope of work and can't be done

8. You have received a project charter to work on a project that involves installing data centers at multiple client sites with a very tight timeline. Based on your current team and understanding of the scope of work, the team has decided that, after the planning and delivery of equipment, each team member could work in pairs at a variety of locations at approximately the same time. What type of project phase configuration would be the best?
   - Adaptive
   - Sequential
   - Overlapping
   - Predictive

9. What are the major differences between predictive project management and adaptive project management? Select all that apply.
   - Predictive projects know the full scope of work in advance
   - Adaptive projects typically correlate with knowledge work
   - Predictive projects don't really know the scope of work in the beginning
   - Adaptive projects are only for software development

10. What is the main goal or objective of the project charter from the project manager's perspective?
    - Explains the scope of work to stakeholders
    - Defines the business case
    - Formally authorizes the project manager to begin project work
    - Signed by the sponsor

11. Which of the following represents a PMIS?
    - The project charter
    - The stakeholders involved in the project
    - The project-management system or framework
    - The software and hardware used to manage communications, reporting, and performance

12. Which of the following would be considered an assumption in the project charter?
    - Who the project manager will be
    - Who the sponsor is
    - Who the customer is
    - Schedule milestones

13. An agile charter differs from a project charter for which of the following reasons?
    - Offers less flexibility for the scope of work
    - Offers more flexibility for the scope of work
    - Offers more information about the software design
    - Doesn't document how the project will be run

14. You are about to hold a kick-off meeting for a large group of stakeholders to announce a new project and get buy-in. What is the best document to present to everyone prior to the meeting?
    - A schedule
    - A budget
    - The name of the team members
    - An agenda

15. What is the main goal of any kick-off meeting?
    - Confirm everyone understands the goals and objectives of the project
    - Get everyone's thoughts on the project
    - Assign your team to work in the charter
    - Begin planning

5
Creating a Work Breakdown Structure (WBS)

In this chapter, you will review the knowledge area of scope management in the planning process group. You will begin with the scope management plan, which describes how scope will be managed, and then review why a comprehensive scope statement is so important to define the scope of work and the requirements for the deliverable.

Once the requirements have been collected and approved, the **work-breakdown structure (WBS)** can be created.

Here are the topics we will cover in this chapter:

- Developing a scope management plan
- Requirement documentation
- Creating a scope statement
- The work breakdown structure
- The WBS dictionary

Developing a scope management plan

In Chapter 3, *Project Roles and Responsibilities*, you reviewed what an integrated, comprehensive project management plan does and why it is so important. You also learned that other than baselines for tracking performance, there are subsidiary management plans that are the how-to guides for the knowledge areas they represent. The scope management plan is one of those subsidiary plans, and honestly scope of work really drives the project management train when it comes to planning other areas such as schedule, costs, resources, procurement, and the like. That is always why it is the first plan we talk about.

Remember that the scope management plan is like the YouTube video for scope of work and may contain several helpful best practices to not only plan the scope of work but to execute on requirements and learn how formal acceptance of the result is accomplished.

This is an important how-to guide because without it your stakeholders may not be aware of your strategy to meet all their requirements.

Remember, a lot of how you run your projects is based on you being at the mercy of your organizational processes and enterprise environment. I've mentioned this a couple of times and how those influencing factors may render it unnecessary to create certain management plans. This is because the plan could contain well-known or innate best practices, rendering it excessive documentation. That is true in a sense. But what if your customer isn't aware of how you manage your scope of work? What if they aren't privy to your change control processes or that they need to formally approve the result? Now, that documentation may become necessary.

Permit me a sidebar about organizational influences while I'm thinking about it! It may seem as if organizational processes and the enterprise environment are working successfully together to help you manage your projects. Uh…nope! Think about them this way: the day you first started your current job, the organization may have given you a tour and a handbook, and possibly even some training about how they *do things around here*. This is how we manage projects, here are the rules, and here is what is expected. Those are organizational process assets. This seems perfectly OK so far. Then, you go to lunch with someone and they tell you *how it really is*, nudge, nudge; wink, wink. That is your enterprise environment. Of course, I'm being a bit snarky when I put it that way, but if you have ever experienced politics in your organization or how things *really* work, then you know that what I speak of is true. So, why does this matter? Because as a project manager it is up to you to determine how best to manage your project. If you feel like you can effectively manage the scope of work without a how-to guide, then carry on! Nobody is running around calling you a bad project manager if you don't follow every *single* best practice out there. I know I don't. I do what works for me and what is best for the project.

OK, sidebar concluded.

The importance of scope management plans

There are a variety of reasons why having a scope management and/or a requirements management plan could be helpful. It's most helpful when the scope of work is totally unique, and you have never worked on this type of project before. It may be relevant to describe the specifics. After all, the scope of the work and the requirements are the driving force for everything else on the project. Get this right and you're well on your way to mastering project management!

The specifics of the plan may include the following:

- How the scope of work will be clearly defined
- How the scope of work will be broken down to a level that can best and most effectively estimate time, money, and resources
- Documentation on how the customer will accept the deliverable(s) or results
- How changes will be managed
- How you will communicate scope updates, completions, and changes throughout the project

 Much of the how-to information that needs to be included here will be covered in detail throughout this chapter or in other chapters, pertaining to change control and formal acceptance of the result.

Remember, I'm using the word customer loosely here as a blanket statement of whoever the project is for and however the influencing party will need to accept the finished product, service, or result. With that said, it is important for you and your other stakeholders to know and agree upon how scope of work and requirements will be managed on your project.

Once you have a scope management plan in place and everyone agrees, then you can move forward with collecting requirements and defining the scope of work.

Requirement documentation

Collecting requirements is easier said than done. It's important to make sure that you speak to the right stakeholders, ask for clarification as needed, and document the requirements in such a way that you can trace and manage them throughout the project. It's also an iterative process that could involve project scope or product scope requirements, which are two vastly different things. **Project scope** is what you are learning about in this guide. It's the best practices, tools and techniques, documentation, and diverse ways of managing your projects effectively – all of which are dependent on the **product scope** requirements.

This spot is as good as any to stop and remind you that reading carefully is the most important exam tip I can give you. Project management exams are notoriously vague in the situational questions they present, and many of the questions you answer in this guide may not even be close to what you get on your exams. I say this because practice exams are designed to make sure you understand the information and can put yourselves in the shoes of a project manager in multiple situations and decide the best way to handle that situation. If you don't read carefully, you may miss the nuance of the question and answer incorrectly! That is the last thing I want, so while you are answering practice questions, remind yourself that this is about understanding the content and solidifying information, rather than mirroring the exam. Reading the situational questions carefully on your actual exams can help navigate to the correct answers.

Collecting accurate requirements is the key to project success. Not only is it important to collect requirements from the right stakeholders, but to be able to understand those requirements well enough to analyze, document, and execute the work to specification. This is the key to project success. There are multiple ways to collect requirements, and no one way is better than any other. You may be brainstorming with your team and other key stakeholders and you may even have pre-built questionnaires and surveys so that the right questions are asked of the right people in a comprehensive manner. You may also be looking at documentation that is currently available to you. This could include any procurement agreements, the business case, the project charter, and stakeholder documentation.

Keep in mind that you will be collecting requirements iteratively throughout the project, so even though in the beginning, there isn't much documentation to refer to, you will have multiple documents to refer to once you begin executing project work. This could include the integrated project management plan, the change log, lessons learned, your assumptions log, as well as any updated project documents as you are executing and monitoring and controlling project work.

I find compartmentalizing requirements into categories makes it easier to determine how to execute them and how they all fit together on the project. It also allows you and the team to specifically focus on individual categories to determine if anything is missing or needs to be adjusted. There are several diverse ways to document requirements. Many of you are used to opening your **Project Management Information System (PMIS)** and entering them into an outline and/or structure that will inevitably become your schedule. Even though there's nothing wrong with that, because, believe me, I'm guilty of it as well, it is important as a best practice to focus first on requirements, and then decompose those requirements in the form of a work breakdown structure, and then, and only then, begin your scheduling.

I realize project management is not a linear thing and much of this is all going on at the exact same time, but for the purposes of your exams, it is important to compartmentalize these processes as separate entities to understand the role that each plays. We start first with requirement documentation and categories that might be useful, and then we will move into the scope statement and the work breakdown structure a bit further into this chapter, and you will see how each plays its role of importance in defining the scope of work.

One thing to consider is not everyone is going to know what they want and what requirements are necessary right out of the gate. There may be many meetings, discussions, and brainstorming with the team and key stakeholders to get everything in order and to classify requirements as well as the priority of identified requirements.

Typical categories to describe how requirements meet business needs

There are numerous categories that could be used and many of them are based on your industries or specific project focus. The categories are not exhaustive, but they are typical:

- Overall project requirements including set constraints
- Requirements to meet the business need, as seen in the business case and project charter

- Individual stakeholder requirements for both project and product scope
- Requirements based on the solution that you're trying to provide to the organization
- Phase or quality gate review requirements or transitional requirements between phases
- Requirements involving quality to make sure that the results are fit for use
- Documentation of how requirements will process through change control, and be updated and communicated

I often find it helpful to present requirements in a visual manner, not just for communication with stakeholders but to provide traceability from the requirement's origin to the deliverable that will come from those requirements. This is sometimes known as a **requirements traceability matrix**, which ensures that all the requirements are in one place. It's also a good thing to have if a change were to occur in one requirement; you would be able to see the domino effect of that change on other requirements. It's also useful as a checklist of sorts to make sure the requirements are being executed on, traced, and tracked through the life cycle.

In *Figure 5.1*, you can see very generic way to trace requirements through the life cycle. This isn't necessarily in your exam, but it is a good practice to utilize when you are collecting requirements from a variety of stakeholders:

Requirements						
Project Name:	Anti-Phishing campaign for employees					
Description of the result:	Resigned process including software and corporate training					
Requirement number	Requirement description	Business value	Objectives	Requester	Deliverables impacted	Change control
1						
2						
3						
4						
5						
6						
7						
8						
9						
10						

Figure 5.1 Tracing requirements

The importance of understanding all the requirements throughout the life cycle and making sure the changes don't impact requirements that are necessary is exponential. Understanding what your requirements are will allow you to comprehensively create a document called the **scope statement**, which will build on your requirements and allow buy-in to happen from stakeholders on your projects.

Requirements in agile project management

Collecting requirements is the same in any project. Make sure we understand what the customer wants, get it documented, and get it accomplished. In an agile environment, requirements are less known in the beginning, and typically requirements change from iteration to iteration. Planning for something that can't be easily planned for means the team will have to work with what they know from iteration to iteration and update the requirements as they come in. Priority can change in requirements as well.

When you review Chapter 10, *Formal Project or Phase Closure and Agile Project Management,* I'll explain the project backlog and some prioritization best practices. For now, assume that predictive project management requirements are planned upfront and we manage changes through formal change control. Agile teams plan requirements from iteration to iteration without a need for formal change control. Otherwise, requirements are requirements, and they need to be documented and produced to specification.

Scope statement

Before we get into what makes up the scope statement, this is a good point to circle back and see how far we've come. Even though much of this is easier said than done, we have covered a lot of the information that you would need to create a detailed scope statement. We may have been contributors to the business case, we were probably utilized as expert judgment on the creation of the project charter, we have identified stakeholders and what their levels of interest and impact are on our project, and we have collected requirements.

There is a reason that the **project scope statement** is considered the most important scope document, because you will be using the scope statement to very specifically detail major deliverables and confirm scope understanding with stakeholders.

Scope categories

In the IT world, you may spend a lot of time translating high-level deliverables to distinct deliverables based on certain categories.

Those categories could include the following:

- Functional specifications
- Systems analysis
- Systems engineering
- Value analysis
- Value engineering

The collection of requirements is an iterative process, but the goal in creating a scope statement, at this point in the project, is to define specific project requirements for scope of work and what the acceptance criteria may be. Certainly, the scope statement will be progressively elaborated on and may be built on assumptions and constraints as well as a specific scope of work. Therefore, there may be several versions of the scope statement as the scope of work becomes clearer throughout the project's life cycle.

Keep in mind that the scope statement is considered a formal document and once approved by key stakeholders will become part of the scope baseline. That baseline will be integrated into your project management plan, which as we already know we must go through formal change control to update. Because we are working with a predictive deliverable, it is sometimes easier to see the big picture at this point in the project. That does not however mean that the scope of work won't change.

You might be thinking to yourself that the scope statement sounds an awful lot like the project charter, and in a lot of ways you would be correct. But remember the project charter is the formal authorization to begin project work and is documented at a high level of what success looks like in the realm of scope of work.

Here's a little tip for identifying the scope statement from other documents, specifically the project charter: the key to the project scope statement is that it not only defines what scope of work *will* be completed, it also defines what scope of work *will not* be completed. Now, you might be thinking to yourself what won't be completed is everything else in the world other than what we will be doing, and that sounds like excessive documentation. Here's the key to why the scope statement is the **number one most important scope document** for confirming or developing scope understanding across the project: it describes what we will produce and what we *won't* produce for the customer.

Let's say you are working with the customer who wants a 12-speed cherry-red bicycle. They have set the scope of work and defined some of the key characteristics of what they want on the bicycle. Perhaps they are looking for a specific kind of street tire, shifting mechanism, seat type, and so on. You would document that in your project scope statement as part of what you will do to accomplish the customer's needs. You will also document that you *will not include a bell on the bicycle*. Why is the bell stated as something that will not be included? Because a bell is often added to bicycles. On the other hand, orange tires and fuzzy handle bars will not be included, but also will not be listed, because they are not commonly included with any bike. This is a key step, because what if the customer assumes that every single bicycle has a bell on it? They may figure that they didn't need to tell you that, because everybody knows there's a bell on every bicycle! Except for the fact that there isn't a bell on every single bicycle.

What we will not do is a crucial aspect of making sure that all requirements are well-documented, and everybody understands what success looks like. Documenting what will not be part of the scope of work keeps any assumptions to a minimum, prevents risk to the scope of work, excess costs, and time, but still gives the customer time to decide that in fact they do want a bell on the bicycle. That would lead to an update in requirements and an update to the project scope statement and would help plot out the schedule and budget in advance of execution where changes aren't as easily made. It's best to find all of this out as soon as possible in the project, but that does not mean that your customer won't decide they want to bell later in the life cycle. The chances are they will if the price is right. If that is the case, it would involve formal change control at that point.

The scope statement will also include the acceptance criteria by which the customer will formally accept the scope of work throughout the project and final acceptance at the end of the project. This is very typically a formal process with which we would collect signatures from the customer to **validate** that we have met scope of work. That allows us to not only get paid, but hopefully to formally close out the project successfully.

In *Figure 5.2*, you can see a comparative approach between the project charter and the project scope statement. I look at the scope statement to go to stakeholders and say, is *this what you meant by your scope requirements in the project charter? If so, then we will move forward with all of this until further notice*:

Project Charter	Project Scope Statement
Project purpose or justification	Project scope description (progressively elaborated)
Measurable project objectives and related success criteria	Acceptance criteria
High-level requirements	Project deliverables
High-level project description	Project exclusions
High level risks	Project constraints
Summary milestone schedule	Project assumptions
Summary budget	
Stakeholder list	
Project approval requirements (what constitutes success, who decides it, who signs off)	
Assigned project manager, responsibility and authority level	
Name and authority of the sponsor or other person(s) authorizing the project charter	

Figure 5.2 Project charter versus project scope statement

The scope statement is also important because it sets the stage for you and your team to begin to see the trees through the forest and break down large deliverables into groupings of smaller level deliverables. Once you do that, you can begin to address scheduling, budgeting, resourcing, and pretty much everything else you will need to do to accomplish the work in the scope statement. In the next section, you will review the work breakdown structure, which is the output that breaks everything down to a level you can most appropriately plan and execute scope of work. Until then, be aware that the scope statement is the number one most important scope document, and now you will cover the most important *planning* document: the WBS.

Understanding the work breakdown structure

I have already alluded to the fact that the work breakdown structure is the number one most important planning document, but why? Because the WBS is utilized to organize 100 percent of the scope of work represented in the currently approved project scope statement. If the scope statement changes, then the work breakdown structure will be updated. Understanding how they both work together can help you understand why they are the most important scope and planning documents.

Imagine if somebody came to you and said, *I want you to set up helpdesks in all 87 of our corporate locations in 15 countries, train everyone, and do it in a timely fashion.* That is a massive amount of work! It would be impossible for you to even comprehend that much information, let alone create a schedule and budget to meet the requirements right away.

It is true that much of the scope of work can be duplicated in each location – at least the processes that you use can possibly be similar – but you have multiple stakeholders, speaking multiple languages, needing multiple specifications, and perhaps even diverse ways of being trained in different languages. It would be impossible at this point to even define what a timely manner means, much less what an actual schedule might look like, how many resources you would need, and how much everything would cost at this point.

That's why the project scope statement alone isn't good enough.

The scope statement does describe the scope of work specifically and what success looks like, but it is not broken down enough to plan efficiently. We then have to take things a step further and organize and define the scope in a deliverable oriented, hierarchical way. Therefore, the WBS is so important, that it forces us to plan out all the scope of work in a methodical manner based on deliverables that can be broken down to smaller packages of work to most effectively estimate time, money, resources as well as determine risk and procurement needs.

One thing to keep in mind is that the WBS is not a schedule. In the real world, we may define scope of work and create a work breakdown structure while at the same time, trying to determine what tasks would need to be done to help to determine the timing. For exam purposes, though, the work breakdown structure represents the scope of work only, *not the schedule*. However, the WBS is a fundamental planning tool, and therefore will be the basis for breaking down scope of work to the task level, and eventually sequencing those tasks and producing a schedule. For now, though, we want to make sure that we don't miss anything as far as the scope of work is concerned, so were going to hold off putting things in logical order or trying to create a schedule at this point.

If you've ever gotten half-way through your project and realize you missed something, it is possible that you jumped right from scope into schedule. To avoid that from happening, we will break down the scope of work in a methodical manner. There isn't really a wrong way to do this, except not to do this – especially with all the software we have available to us these days.

Old school, using no real software so to speak, work breakdown structures look like an organizational chart, and in some ways, that's an effective way to think about it. Organizational charts take top-level positions (CEO, CFO, president) and break the organization down to the team or functional level. For the scope of work, we will take large deliverables or features and break them down to a group of work that can be accurately estimated.

These days, we're utilizing software programs to help us create our schedules, our Gantt charts, our budgets, and resource scheduling. The creation of the WBS is also being done in software programs, so your real-world WBS may look more like an outline than an organizational chart.

I think of the WBS and the project scope statement working together to produce something to specification. An analogy that I use in my classes to describe both especially important scope documents is in the form of a jigsaw puzzle.

When you go to the store to buy a jigsaw puzzle, the chances are the one you choose is based on the picture on the puzzle box. Maybe today it's the Eiffel tower, or a basket of puppies (aww!); whichever one you choose, the picture on the puzzle box shows you what success looks like. There is nothing extra. The box tells you how many pieces are in the puzzle, how much the puzzle costs, and what age groups it is appropriate for. So, you go home all excited to build your jigsaw puzzle, and you open the box. There is no way that that jumble of pieces is easily sequenced, or even managed in its current state. What is the first thing that you will do? You will start taking the pieces out of the puzzle box and organize them. Corners with corners, reds with reds, blues with blues, and so on. Once you have your piles organized, you will then refer to the picture on the puzzle box, to help you execute putting the puzzle together. In this case, the project scope statement is the picture on the puzzle box. It is exactly what success looks like at any given moment. The work breakdown structure is the piles of puzzle pieces that are organized, like with like. This is a necessary step to be truly ready to begin putting a puzzle together and creating the result.

The one thing to be aware of with the WBS is that it utilizes a tool or technique called **decomposition**. Decomposition isn't the friendliest of terms I agree, but it is an apt description of what we are doing. We are taking large deliverables and scope of work and decomposing or breaking it down to a level that is easier to manage.

With the puzzle analogy in place, let's look at that massive help desk project again and work through a basic and small piece of what work breakdown structure might look like.

In *Figure 5.3*, your WBS will be represented in an old-school organizational chart-looking thing, then in *Figure 5.4*, the same information will be represented as an outline, which is more realistic to your day-to-day work:

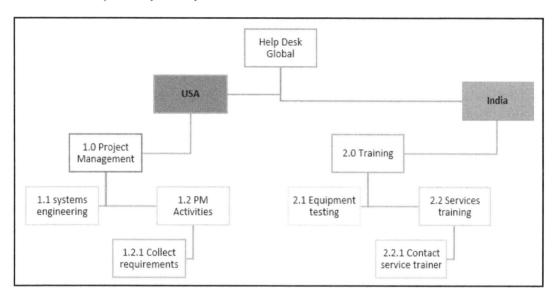

Figure 5.3 WBS represented as an organizational chart

And the same information represented as an outline:

Figure 5.4 WBS represented as an outline

You can see from both figures that there's really no wrong way to create your work breakdown structure, and you can even think of it as an outline or a visual flowchart. This allows you and your team to determine the best way to accomplish scope of work by organizing it in such a way that you and your team can focus on one deliverable at a time in the hope that nothing gets missed. The people who do the work know the work and will be the best resources to help you create your work breakdown structure. You are not in this alone! The other thing to note is that just because we're specifically documenting scope of work, it does not mean that we are not thinking about the order in which the work needs to be done in, how long it's going to take, how much is going to cost, and which resources are doing what.

Now is probably an appropriate time to give you some of the terminology that you can see regarding the WBS. You might've noticed the outlining system or numbering codes on the WBS examples. These are called the **code of accounts**. This outlining number system is an excellent way to keep track of top level deliverables, all the way down to lower level deliverables. Many times, the code of accounts is used in budgeting, in change control, or if you need to export your WBS into a spreadsheet program, to help keep track of the hierarchy.

Don't confuse the code of accounts on the exam for the chart of accounts. Chart of accounts is an accounting term and could be used as a distractor in an exam question, but will never be the correct answer.

The lowest level on the WBS is called a **work package**. It's important to understand that we are not breaking the WBS down to the task level because that would be jumping head first into scheduling, and we're not there yet. What we want to do is avoid the temptation to **excessively** decompose the scope of work at this point. We are not creating a schedule yet. The WBS is not a schedule, is not a schedule, is not a schedule. Just in case you missed it the first time, I want to make sure that you don't answer question incorrectly, because I forgot to mention that it's not a schedule. We will get there in the scheduling chapter, and you'll see the pieces fit together, but, for now, we are utilizing a function of scope best practices. Yes, it will help us create a schedule at some point, but not yet. Say it with me now: *The WBS is not a schedule!*.

A simple rule of thumb to keep in mind is that work packages should not be any smaller than eight hours' worth of work or any larger than 80 hours' worth of work. This isn't a hard-and-fast rule, but just another way to show the piles of puzzle pieces. Some piles will be bigger than others. It also depends on the types of projects you're working on. If it's a three-week project, then the chances are you are going to jump directly to scheduling after defining the scope of work. But, remember, the assumption of the exam will be that we are working on longer-term projects, where it might be necessary to work through the WBS first.

Another thing to consider with the WBS is that it's always going to follow the 100-percent rule, meaning 100 percent of the scope of the work will be represented in the WBS as it is known today. If we create a WBS correctly and roll-up the work packages from the bottom up to first-level deliverables, all scopes of work will be accommodated. That is tough to do if we don't have all the information at the beginning of a project.

We may have to engage in something called **rolling-wave planning**, which is essentially waiting for the next wave of information to come crashing into your project. Rolling-wave planning is the act of updating your scope statement and your WBS as additional information is determined and a new scope of work has been added to the project. Rolling-wave planning is a type of progressive elaboration. Trust me when I say you're going to feel as if the waves are crashing down on you any time your customer changes the scope of work! It's to always be expected though, and we do want to make sure we have everything updated through formal change control.

Hi, change control board, the customer wants something else added.... again! The goal is to avoid another scope term called **scope creep**.

Scope creep is unauthorized or uncontrollable changes to the scope of work without any regard to scheduling or budgeting. It's the project management equivalent of having too many cooks in the kitchen trying to make soup. Everybody decides to walk by the pot and add salt to the soup. It isn't going to take awfully long before the soup is ruined.

Even though scope creep happens on every single project in some way shape or form, the goal is to have formal change control to prevent as much scope creep as humanly possible. Let's think back to that bicycle project, and let's assume that somebody on your team added a bell without any regard to the true scope of work documented in the scope statement. They just decided one day that this bicycle needed a bell.

One of two things is going to happen: either the customer is going to say, *Wow! I didn't want to have to pay for a bell, but I really wanted one, and now I've got it for free. I'm going to call my friends to order bicycles from you!* Pretty soon, your organization is losing massive amounts of money providing free bells for all its new customers' bikes.

Conversely, the customer may look at that bell and say, *I never asked you for that; everybody knows not every bicycle has a bell on it, so remove it right now!* Now you and your team must spend time and organizational money and resources to remove the bell from the bicycle. Whether it's too much salt in the soup, too many bells on the bicycles, or a very slight scope edition done without regard to formal change control or the true scope of work, scope creep should be avoided at all costs, or it will cost you and the company you work for.

I'm hoping that it is extremely easy to see why the WBS is the number one most important planning tool because it truly defines scope and project success in a hierarchical manner by representing 100 percent of the scope of work. It will then be an input to just about everything else that needs to be planned for, including scheduling, budgeting, resources, procurement, and other aspects of the project that will support scope-of-work success.

Now that we have two particularly important documents, the completed the project scope statement (the picture on the puzzle box), and the WBS (the pile of organized puzzle pieces), there is just one more document that we need to create to be the most successful with scope of work, and that is called the **WBS dictionary**.

When I was younger, and I didn't know the meaning of a word, my parents would tell me to look up the definition in the dictionary. Once I found the word in the dictionary, I would read a very specific definition of the word and a variety of uses for the word, as well as whether the word was a noun, a verb, an adjective, and so on. The same can be said for the WBS dictionary.

There is no way that you and your team can break down 100 percent of the scope of the work, compartmentalize, and get it organized, without throwing a ton of additional information into the mix. You may be asking them what the work package is for a certain piece of scope of work, and instead of just giving you the work package information, they start giving you information about how many resources they're going to need, how long it took them to do something similar in the past, that they need to confer with the procurement department about parts and equipment. You will not say *no, no, this isn't a schedule, and we can't discuss this now, because my study guide said so.* Quite the contrary! All of that information is important to successful scope completion, and nobody is suggesting that that information isn't being discussed or thought about during the process of creating your WBS. It is also safe to say that some work packages may not be well-understood by your customer or other key stakeholders. You can then refer them to the WBS dictionary, where definitions can be found for the work packages and deliverables as well as a multitude of other planning information that can be useful for understanding.

For many of us, the WBS dictionary can simply be a text column next to our outline where we jot down the information that we were gathering as we plan. For others, the WBS dictionary can be a formal document that is in addition to the WBS itself. No matter what, it's never a good idea to make assumptions about what your customers and other key stakeholders know. We very much want them to understand the scope of work, because inevitably they will be the ones that sign off on the baselines of scope, time, and cost. We know we need approval for a scope baseline, and we also need everyone to be on the same page about the result, so this is as good a time as any to tell your stakeholders to *look it up in the dictionary.*

WBS dictionary information

Here is some information that could be found in the WBS dictionary. Not every single work package and deliverable will have all of this information, but it is valuable information to document if needed:

Code of account descriptions	Resource Requirements
Description of work	Cost estimates
Assumptions/Constraints	Quality requirements
Responsible organization	Acceptance criteria
Milestones and schedule activities	Tech references and agreement information

Having documents all stakeholders can refer to is a major step to building good relationships, communicating effectively, and getting everyone on board. Even more important is getting all three documents signed off on as a **scope baseline** because at this point you have created all three documents that could be considered everything needed to execute on the scope of work.

A good example of a WBS dictionary working as a companion document to the WBS would be the following:

- **WBS Work Package**:
    - 1.1.3 install servers
- **WBS Dictionary: 1.1.3**:
    - Contact procurement about our vendors for hardware
    - Determine if outside resources are needed to help with the install
    - Be sure they can speak the language of the country we will send them to

What is the scope baseline?

The scope baseline is comprised of the three scope documents you have covered in this chapter:

- The currently approved version of the project scope statement
- The WBS of 100 percent of the scope of the work to date
- The WBS dictionary that defines the work packages and deliverables in such a way that all stakeholders can understand and put their signatures right on the bottom line

Let's discuss baselines at this point and their importance to the project. Baselines are basically your game plan. Imagine yourself as the coach of your favorite sport's team. Mine happens to be an American football team. I know that once kick-off happens it may be necessary for the quarterback (team member) to call an audible (a last-minute adjustment to the play call or for our purposes the baseline) because things aren't exactly going the way everyone expected. It happens. But when the coach is in the locker room pre-game, they are confident in their plays and their team players. It's not until you get on the field that you realize that you may have to make some adjustments as soon as possible. Baselines work the same way. It's the plan we put in place with every confidence everything will work out. And a healthy skepticism that if it doesn't, we can adapt and adjust in the moment. You are the coach; your team believes in the plays and it all looks good. So good in fact, your stakeholders agree and sign off on the plan. If your scope baseline says no bell on the bicycle, that is the expectation, and without change control or scope creep, that is how it should work out.

Change control is good and scope creep is bad.

Well, I hate to say this, but scope creep will probably happen. The best we can do is to clearly define the scope of work and if changes are necessary we assess the impact of those changes, create solutions for implementation, get approvals, update our baselines as needed, and implement the change. Don't forget to validate that the solution worked as well. Scope of work is the driving force of every other baseline you will review. Any changes to the scope of work will inevitably drive changes to your schedules and budgetary baselines as well as other plans to support scope of work.

 It's important to memorize what makes up the scope baseline. Remember, when I promised to tell you whether memorization can help you in certain questions? This is one of those times. The scope statement, the WBS, and the WBS dictionary.

You've reached a crucial step in the planning process, and, even though you will plan in an iterative, rolling wave, fashion throughout the project, for now, you have locked down scope of work and gotten your strategy approved by key stakeholders. It's at this point you are ready to start looking much more specifically at the other important aspects of the project, including scheduling, budgeting, risk, resources, and so on. Once your scope of work is set as a baseline, everything else can fall into place.

Summary

In this chapter, you reviewed the importance of a scope management plan and how it sets the stage for all of scope planning. Then, you reviewed some aspects of collecting requirements, so they can be well-documented and organized in a requirements traceability matrix.

Then, you reviewed the importance and the contents of the scope statement which gives everyone a detailed review of the expected scope of work.

Finally, you reviewed the work breakdown structure (WBS) and the WBS dictionary. All three of the documents from the scope statement to the WBS and dictionary create the scope baseline. Now, you have a formal baseline to track scope performance while executing project work as well as the information needed to begin scheduling and budgeting.

In Chapter 6, *Developing a Project Schedule,* you will take the WBS and decompose it down to the task or activity level, which will allow you to begin sequencing work and estimating duration to create a schedule and get a schedule baseline approved.

Questions

1. You are the project manager for a large installation project. Your key stakeholders are discussing what is needed to be accomplished to set up their new data center and have some specific ideas about what they want. What is the best document to collect all their requirements?
   - Requirements list
   - WBS
   - Requirements traceability matrix
   - Scope statement

2. Which of the following is the best description of a WBS?
    - Hierarchical decomposition of 100% scope of work
    - Organizational chart for scope of work
    - What will and will not be included in the scope of work
    - An outline

3. Bill is your sponsor, and he has come to you and asked for an overview of the work package you and your team have decomposed. He is concerned because your customer doesn't really understand your WBS, and before they sign off on the baseline, they would like a clearer understanding of the scope of work. What is the best document the customer can review to gain a better understanding of the requirements?
    - Scope statement
    - WBS dictionary
    - WBS
    - Requirements traceability matrix

4. Which of the following would your key stakeholders sign off on as the baseline for scope of work? Choose all that apply:
    - WBS
    - Requirements traceability matrix
    - Scope statement
    - Project charter
    - WBS dictionary

5. You and your team are doing some brainstorming and breaking down large deliverables into more manageable planning packages? What technique are you using to do that?
    - Scope planning
    - Requirement planning
    - Decomposition
    - WBS creation

6. You are working with your team to decompose scope of work and your coordinator Jim suggests that you organize the WBS using a numbering system. What is the numbering system called?
    - The chart of accounts
    - Outline numbers
    - WBS dictionary
    - The code of accounts

7. You have taken over in the middle of a large IT project after the previous project manager was pulled to work on something else. You are reviewing what they have accomplished so far and have determined that the requirements have been collected. What do you do next?
    - Double check everything is properly documented
    - Discuss with your team your plans to document scope of work
    - Create the scope statement
    - Explain to the team that you need to review the charter first before you can do anything

8. You are working on documentation for a project that involves installing data centers at multiple client sites with a very tight timeline. You have described the scope of work in a formal way, but have also mentioned that your team would not be involved in the testing of the equipment. That would be left for operations. Which document would be best for this information?
    - WBS
    - Charter
    - WBS dictionary
    - Scope statement

9. What are the major differences between the scope statement and the WBS? Select all that apply:
    - Scope statement describes what will and will not be done, and the WBS formalizes that
    - Scope statement describes what will and will not be done, and the WBS decomposes to a level you can estimate effectively
    - Scope statement is very descriptive, and the WBS is more of an outline
    - The scope statement is very high-level, and the WBS is very descriptive

10. What is the main goal or objective of the WBS from the project manager's perspective?
    - Helps create a schedule
    - Decomposes work to the activity level
    - Formally authorizes the project manager to begin project work
    - Decomposes the scope of work to the work package level

11. Kalil is a key stakeholder on your current project and is also new to project management best practices. He has asked you to explain the difference between the project charter he signed and the scope statement he is about to sign as they look like him. How would you answer Kalil's question?
    - The project charter gives formal authorization to begin project work, and the scope statement breaks down scope of work for scheduling
    - The project charter gives formal authorization to begin project work, and the scope statement clearly describes what features will and will not be produced during the project
    - The project charter is just an overview to begin project work, and the scope statement is hierarchical
    - The scope statement is just an updated project charter

12. You are working with your team to determine the structure of the WBS, and you have collected all requirements and have a good handle on the scope of work. Even though you know that the scope could change, what is important to include in the WBS at this point?
    - High-level scope
    - Major deliverables and work packages
    - 100% scope of work as it is known today
    - The business case

13. An agile charter differs from a project charter for which of the following reasons?
    - Offers less flexibility for scope of work
    - Offers more flexibility for scope of work
    - Offers more information about the software design
    - Doesn't document how the project will be run

14. Your project has been decomposed, and the WBS has been constructed. Your final WBS contains five levels. All the following are true regarding the WBS, except which of the following?
    - This project's work package level is level one
    - The code of accounts will show the outline structure
    - The WBS is a deliverable-oriented grouping of project deliverables and elements
    - Level five for this project will facilitate resource assignments and cost and time estimates

15. Which of the following best describes what a WBS dictionary is?
    - A document that describes technical terms used for scope management
    - A document that describes the details for each component in the WBS
    - A document that translates essential WBS terms for global project teams
    - A document that helps translate functional into technical requirements

Developing a Project Schedule
6

In this chapter, we will review schedule management in the planning process group. We will begin with the schedule management plan, which describes how to manage your schedule, from creation to monitoring and controlling. Then, we will review how to define and sequence tasks in a logical order, to best estimate durations, as well as the creation of the project schedule and the schedule's baseline.

The following topics will be covered in this chapter:

- Developing a schedule management plan
- Defining tasks
- Sequencing tasks
- Estimating task durations
- Creating the project schedule

Developing a schedule management plan

As with any other management plan, a schedule management plan is a how-to guide. While this plan helps you get your schedule priorities in gear, it may be a plan that you wouldn't use in the real world, because those who schedule, schedule. They already understand how to put together a schedule baseline and the rules of the organization. But what if you are new to scheduling? What if your customer needs more clarity on how the schedules will be created and updated? What if you don't have a schedule coordinator? Oh, the horror! I mean, you can do this! Now, it may be realistic to at least get everyone on the same page about the rules and how changes will be managed.

 You probably will not be tested on the value of the schedule management plan, but it is considered part of the integrated project management plan.

The high-level overview of what may be included in the schedule management plan allows for several schedule management best practices to be addressed in one place.

Schedule management plan considerations

Being able to answer the following questions will help guide you as to whether you need a schedule management plan. Remember to ask yourself the questions from the perspective of your team and other key stakeholders as well. Just because you know the answers doesn't mean they know the answers. Remember, schedule changes can impact everything else, so knowing how to manage changes is a big consideration.

The questions that can be answered with a schedule management plan are as follows:

- How will you monitor and control the overall schedule?
- What are the approved schedule development tools and techniques?
- How will changes to the schedule baseline be managed?
- Who is responsible for developing and maintaining the project schedules? (Please say a schedule coordinator!)
- How and when will schedule performance be reported?

You will see as you move through this guide that we spend less and less time on management plans. There are a few exceptions though, and they are communication management and risk management, which we will go into in more depth in Chapter 7, *Resource Management Planning and Communication Considerations* and Chapter 8, *Budget and Contingency Plans for Risk,* but until then it's time to move on to the *what* of schedule management.

The completed schedule will be a major constraint, so it's important to have a management plan that can address some of the challenges of scheduling. All constraints, not just the schedule, are **competing constraints.** This is because they not only affect one another, but some constraints are more important than others to customers and stakeholders. Does your organization care more about time, scope of work, or money? You may have heard the saying, *you can have it fast, good, or cheap, but you can't have all three.* This is because they are competing. How long will this take, and how much will it cost? Did we build the right thing, and did we build the thing right? These are questions that will be asked and need to be answered as you progress through the project. By planning effectively, you will be able to answer those questions.

Defining tasks

Remember when we discussed the **work breakdown structure (WBS)** and you reviewed how to decompose large deliverables down to the work package level? Now, we will take those work packages and decompose them to the task level. This is where the WBS begins to influence the schedule but is still *not* a schedule. We will use the WBS to get to the task level, and once that occurs we will have a **task list** and **milestones** that will guide the creation of the actual schedule and the baseline. I realize that for the most part I'm writing philosophy here. We are involved in the realm of *easier said than done* right now. This piece can be very time consuming especially if you have never done a project before or you are working on something totally new. For the sake of the exam, the defining of tasks process is self-explanatory, meaning you don't need to know a whole lot about the process to answer questions because it just is what it is. This is generally because CompTIA and PMI® could never say specifically, *this is how you define activities on your projects*. Every project is unique, and every project will have differing levels of task decomposition.

Suffice it to say that every project is different, and you will have to decide how far down you want to take your tasks. It's probably not a great idea to take them down to the nth degree. Nobody, and I mean nobody, wants an eight-thousand-line item schedule when all is said and done, except for maybe NASA, because it's necessary. For the rest of us, the more concise we can be, the better we will manage things. This comes with a caveat though: **make sure you have enough information** so that nothing is missed. Even though the scope of the work may not be 100 percent clear right now, it will be progressively elaborated on throughout the project. This would lead to updates to the scope statement and the WBS through formal change control, and that could/will drive changes to your task list and milestones. That is why the WBS and the currently approved scope statement are the biggest influencing factors right now. Couple that with the process of breaking deliverables down to the task level, and it's probably best to call in reinforcements. Remember, even though project management is a big job, you are not working in a vacuum by yourself. It is assumed that you are in a strong matrix organization on the exam, unless otherwise stated in the question. That would mean you have a core team of people to help you plan. The best advice on the work breakdown to the task level is from the people who do the work, because they know the work and can help with this process.

 Expert judgment is the number one tool or technique in project management.

Now, you have large deliverables and work packages that need to become tasks. The best practice is to break them down to the level where everyone understands the work to be done and assumptions are clearly documented and discussed. It's always a bit of a guessing game to determine how far the work packages should be broken down. Some project managers like to stick to the heuristic or rule of thumb that each work package be no larger than 80 hours' worth of work and at least eight hours. This can vary from project to project, but it is easier to plan one day or two weeks' worth tasks than a month or greater. The difference could very well be a concise task list versus an 8,000-line-item project plan. I know from experience that that type of task list leads my software to fight back and become an unmanageable list of work. I realize when you are first starting out, you don't want to miss anything, and I totally get that, but try to balance both sides as much as possible. It will help you in the end. Plus, if you have resources who understand the work they are going to do, it becomes unnecessary to break it down any further than their understanding.

Install software for HR doesn't need to be documented as follows go to HR, turn on computers, wait for them to boot up, put software in the computer, and so on. That is too much information for your task list, and your resources already know how to do the work and what the work entails. Unless you have contracts that force you to document every single item for the purposes of compliance, try to keep it simple and executable.

Once you have completed the process, you will have a task list. This process is iterative as well because it is dependent on the currently approved scope baseline. If scope changes, so will the tasks to complete the work. **Progressive elaboration** and **rolling wave planning** are very typical when defining the tasks and putting together a schedule you can probably meet.

The other main output of the defining tasks process will be **milestones**. The origin of the word *milestone* takes us back to the third century, when Romans were building their network of 53 thousand miles of roads. Every one-thousand paces or so a stone marker would be placed so travelers knew how far they had traveled. Granted, most of the milestones had names of Roman emperors on them, and you won't see that in your schedules, although it would be interesting in a meeting: *We have reached the Marcus Aurelius milestone and plan to catch up to Commodus by next week.* It stands to reason that using milestones lets you know how far you need to go and how far you have traveled through your project.

Typically, there are two types of milestones: **mandatory** and **discretionary**. Mandatory are the ones we are used to. Those dictated by the project charter, the customer, the sponsor, and those that may act like Roman emperors. Discretionary milestones are typically used by project managers to set goals for their team. This allows for checkpoints of successes without all the pressure.

Once you have your task list and any additional information or **attributes** you can use to help you plan as well as milestones documented, you now have a skeleton of your project. Now, it is time to put the sequence together. The knee bone is connected to the shin bone.

In *Figure 6.1*, you can see the WBS and how it influences the task definition process:

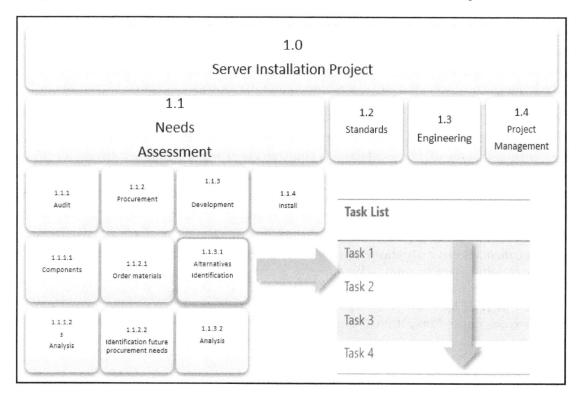

Figure 6.1 WBS

This is also why the WBS isn't a schedule, because you will need to break it down from the work package level to the task level in a progressive way as new scope is determined. Then, you'll need to sequence those tasks and estimate durations and resources, before you can even think about what your schedule will be.

Sequencing tasks

I find sequencing tasks to be the most stressful piece of project management, because if you get the order incorrect, the entire project goes sideways. That's a lot of pressure! Still, others love this piece and are exceptionally good at putting the puzzle together. If you have never done this before, it can be a bit daunting, especially if you are using scheduling software for the first, or even the one hundredth time. It isn't unusual to see (me) project managers gesticulating wildly at their computer screens and asking why the finish date just jumped out four thousand days into the future. This is because of several reasons. First, the order in which things occur will affect the dates, and then the resources you assign to the tasks will affect the level of effort, and finally the durations that are added to the tasks which will affect the rest. That is the process of schedule creation, but it starts with sequencing tasks. It's also important to attempt to do these scheduling processes in the order we cover them, in sequence, if you will. The good news is you won't be using scheduling software for the exam; you will be answering questions old-school, without software. You may find, after reviewing this chapter, your software stops controlling you, and you start to control it a bit more. Are you ready? Let's begin.

The goal of sequencing is to determine the **relationships** between the tasks and determine the dependencies that drive the sequence. There are many reasons why certain tasks are done in certain orders. It could be because there isn't any other way to perform the tasks, or because you don't have enough resources to do the work in the order it is presented (*because that never happens*, I say sarcastically). Dependency determination is typically the first step when sequencing and may drive the order or relationship between activities.

Dependencies

There are four dependencies that may drive the order in which you perform work:

- Mandatory
- Discretionary
- Internal
- External

Let's discuss **mandatory** first, because in IT this may be the most influential dependency, since it is based on logic. You must turn the computer on before you can use it. You can try it the other way, but you won't get too far. The good news with this dependency is you probably are already aware of the sequence of many of your tasks on an IT project. It won't be something you can debate or that is flexible; it just is what it is. This is known as **hard logic**.

Discretionary dependencies are the opposite. It is up to our discretion the order in which we perform tasks. This could be because a resource isn't available now but will be soon, or you have received parts and equipment for one task but not the other. You can perform these tasks in any order. A first, then B, or B first and then A. Either way will work. This is what is known as **soft logic**. It isn't unusual to have fewer tasks up to your discretion, especially on technical projects, but it is good to look for areas of flexibility, in case they are needed during the execution of project work. It may be the difference between being behind schedule or getting creative, so you don't slip your baselines.

Internal dependencies are typical on any project. These are based on organizational processes. Your organization states that you will do this first and then that. That is usually followed up by a project manager saying, *Yeah, but...there is a better way*. This is quickly followed by *Yeah, but...no*. In some cases, the internal drivers of task sequence are based on perfected ways of doing things in an organization. More than likely, the opposite is usually truer; it's just always how the organization does things, and that is always how it will do things. Make sure you understand organizational protocols and best practices well enough to accommodate internal dependencies.

I always tell my classes that you can't change the internal cogs in the wheels of your organization without proof. Therefore, it is important to document and make note of where any organizational influences are outdated or negatively affect your projects. The first thing that popped into my head is too many meetings about meetings and planning for next week's meeting to finish the meeting from last week. I know you understand! Meetings are internal processes that can affect your project duration, your sanity, and your baseline. Without proof that meetings take up more schedule time than necessary, nothing will change. I add meetings to my schedule to keep track of the time spent, and in `Chapter 10`, *Formal Project or Phase Closure and Agile Project Management*, I'll show you some ways to have meetings that don't take up too much time at all.

External dependencies are typical of any project. These are the outside forces that push us to do things in a certain way. That could be the customer who requests something be done a certain way, or you have regulatory requirements that must be met. Could you break ground for your new data center without a permit? Logically, sure you could. Would you want to? Nope. Anything that forces your sequence to conform and comes from outside your organization is considered an external dependency.

I would imagine both mandatory and external dependencies drive many of your projects. Sprinkle in some internal and a couple discretionary influences and you can see why sequencing can potentially lead to hair loss and wanting to chuck your computer out a window. No? Just me? OK, we will carry on.

Relationships

Relationships can be difficult. These will be the true driving factors for the order in which tasks are executed. You may have heard this referred to as **linking** tasks together. Linking will provide you with a map through your project. And just like any road maps there are multiple directions you can go to reach your destination. If you have ever taken a long road trip, you may decide to find the most direct route which will get you there the fastest. The same can be true for sequencing your tasks together. The shortest distance between multiple points. Many highways diverge from and converge with each other, as will project tasks. Some will abruptly end, and some will carry on to the destination.

The goal is to create the main output of a **precedence network diagram.** The precedence diagram is a visual map (Gantt chart for those using software) of all your activities connected by dependency and relationship. The precedence diagram isn't a Gantt chart, so don't tell CompTIA or PMI® I said this, but it really is the best way to describe what it is we are trying to accomplish without software. The network diagram will show visually how the tasks are connected and their flow from the beginning of the project to the end. That network will also drive how the project is resourced, budgeted, and duration estimated.

There are four relationships that can be used in any precedence network diagram:

- Finish to start
- Start to start
- Finish to finish
- Start to finish

There is also an arrow diagram (activity on arrow AOA) that can only accommodate **Finish to Start** relationships and is typically used on exceedingly small projects. The activities sit on the arrow connecting them together. The *PMBOK® Guide* has already phased out the arrow diagram because it isn't typically found in scheduling software programs anymore, but it may be a question or possible answer on the Project+ exam.

Finish-to-start relationships

We'll start with perhaps the easiest and most popular relationship, which is **finish to start**. The reason it is the easiest is because like many things you must finish one thing completely before you start another. This could be due to hard logic or lack of resources or because it makes a pretty Gantt chart. A first, then B. This relationship will also give you the longest total duration a project could take if you use it on every single linked activity. *A's duration + B's duration + C's duration*. Even though we haven't covered duration estimating yet it would make sense that you are thinking about how long things may take. The relationships you choose will also drive the total duration of the project along with the resources you assign to it. More on that later in the chapter. For now, it's important to both recognize the relationship visually and be able to identify the relationship in a situational question. I'll give you examples of both.

In *Figure 6.2*, you will see a finish to start relationship. Be sure to look at where the arrow is because that will help you identify relationships visually:

Figure 6.2

Notice the circles on the left and right of each task. The left side of the task is the start and the right side of the task is the finish. Where the arrow connects shows you the relationship. In this case the arrow is at the *finish* of **Task A** and at the *start* of **Task B**. If I were looking at durations as well, I could easily see that if I took A's duration and added it to B's I would have the total duration for both tasks. I must finish setting up my brand-new computer before I can *start* loading software.

Start-to-start relationships

In *Figure 6.3*, you will see a **start-to-start** relationship. Again, notice the arrows. Keep in mind that these are examples. You may have a larger gap between activities due to lag time, or a different configuration due to resources being able to start sooner or later, and so on:

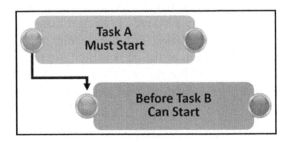

Figure 6.3

The **start to start** is also a common relationship, especially when you are trying to condense the total duration of two or more activities. This can be referred to as **fast-tracking** or making the boss happy. This is because the activities are running in parallel.

A good example is the writing of this study guide. I need to start writing the first chapter, so my very patient editor can start editing. We carry on this way throughout the writing process until we complete everything. If my editor had to wait until I finished writing this guide and then started editing, then this study guide wouldn't be in your hands or on your computer screens right now. It would have taken twice as long to complete the entire project.

This relationship is useful in a lot of ways, but most especially if you have the resource availability to run things this way and only if it is logical to do so. In this case, if you were thinking of duration estimates, it makes more sense. It takes me about six months to author a book. It takes about four months to edit and get it ready for publication (I'm guessing here). In this case, four months is fewer than six, so the entire process should take about six months. Conversely, if this were run in a finish to start manner, it would take ten months. Therein lies the value of this relationship.

Finish-to-finish relationships

In *Figure 6.4*, you will see a **finish-to-finish** relationship. Look at the arrows to see them both connected to the right side of the activities or the finish of both. We are also running in a parallel format, only this time activity A needs to finish so activity B can finish. The relationship driving these activities doesn't necessarily mean they will both finish at the exact same time. In fact, **A** may finish before **B**, but **B** is dependent on **A**, so it can be completed:

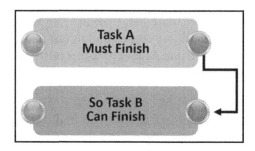

Figure 6.4

The finish-to-finish relationship may be necessary in an IT project but isn't usually as common as the finish to start and start to start. It stands to reason though that somewhere on your projects you will have a dependency that forces this relationship. I need to finish installing the software, so I can finish testing it. Now, you might be thinking, *Hold on a second; I can also finish installing the software and start testing it,* and you would be correct. Remember, I said this sequencing thing can be a bit trying. It's up to you to determine what works best for your project and then sequence accordingly. Each relationship will affect the total duration of the activities and like a row of dominoes, once the first is knocked over the rest will follow.

Here's the true indicator of the relationships and how they affect your total duration. If A takes five days to finish and B takes six days to finish, then both activities should take about six days to be finished if there aren't any other types of influence, such as **lag time** or necessary gaps between the activities. If you revert to the finish to start relationship, then it would take eleven days to be totally completed.

As I said, finish to start is the most common relationship and if you are just starting out you may feel more comfortable keeping everything finish to start. Trust me when I say you would not be the only one who does it. Yes, it makes for a pretty Gantt chart when everything waterfalls to the end of the project, but the **FS** relationship also allows project managers to build in contingency time. What if you scheduled a finish to finish relationship with a total duration of six days and a risk event occurs that forces the total duration to eleven days? Then, you are behind schedule. If you have it set as a finish to start, then you are right on schedule and may even finish a bit early. Then, you are the hero of scheduling! It is just this philosophy that keeps most project managers from venturing out to other relationships too much and they keep themselves in the range of finish to start. It gives you buffer time, contingency time, and allows you to breath out a little during the project. It isn't padding your schedule because padding is bad, but buffer time and contingency? Well, that's OK! (It's kind of the same thing.)

My best advice is to use some of the relationships sparingly until you understand them. Because we are using software, I recommend that you play around with these a bit in a demo schedule. Add resources, add durations, add dates, and then change the relationships that seem logical and see what it does to your finish date and your resource allocation. Then, you can start to see the power of logic and how it affects time. You may still decide to leave it as finish to start and that is okay too, if you can squeak that by your customers and key stakeholders. After all, they will have to approve the schedule and you will be held accountable to it. More than likely, they will kick it back and ask you to cut about a month off your month and half-long project, but I digress. Let's move on to the last of the logical precedence relationships: the **start to finish**.

Start-to-finish relationships

In *Figure 6.5*, you will see the start-to-finish relationship. You can tell it's a bit different from the ones you have just reviewed. There is a reason this is the least used relationship, although I see this more on IT projects than anywhere else. There was a time when I saw these relationships in large projects and thought to myself that they were just showing off by using it. *Look, we can use the least-used relationship. Top that regular project managers!* Now, with the technological age in full swing, this relationship may be something useful on your project schedules:

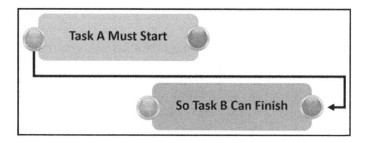

Figure 6.5

A start-to-finish relationship sounds the most logical doesn't it? You start the race, you finish the race. What is so weird about that? In the case of a start-to-finish relationship, you must *start* something to *finish* something else. Let that sink in a bit. Let's say you decide that you are going to a sporting event and will buy tickets at the ticket window before the event starts at 8 pm. You also know ticket sales will stop once the event begins, so you had better be on your way. This means you want to get there before 8 pm because once the sporting event *starts*, ticket sales will *finish*.

Here is the best example in an IT environment I can give you. Your customer has asked that you install a brand-new server system in their office building, and they want you to do it during business hours. They have expressly stated that you are not to halt organizational productivity during the install. So, you wheel in the new server, get it turned on, and set it up before you unplug the other server system and wheel that out of the building. You must start the new server before you finish the old server.

Other than that, you probably won't see much of this relationship on the exam or use it much in the real world. It is a good one to know though, if you find yourself in a situation like the one I just mentioned. Then, it is the most realistic for that type of project.

Lead and lag time

During the sequencing of tasks and determining relationships, you may identify a need for either lead or lag time to be included in the relationship. Lead time condenses the overall duration and lag time adds to it. There are some extremely specific nuances to that statement though. Lead and lag time do not add to costs or to resource schedules. If I am laying concrete and that needs to finish before the frame goes up, I have a finish to start relationship. However, the concrete will need to cure and harden before any frame can go up. So, I will need to add some lag time between laying the concrete and putting up the frame. I'm not sure how your organization works but I don't take kindly to paying people to stand around and watch concrete cure when they could be doing other things. Logically though that time needs to be there. *Laying concrete = 4 hours, concrete curing = 4 hours* and *putting up the frame = 14 hours*. I only need resources for the first and the last task. I will use a finish to start relationship with 4 hours of lag. In this case the entire duration will equal 22 hours, but I'd only be resourcing and paying for 18 hours of work.

In *Figure 6.6*, you will see what lag time looks like on a network diagram:

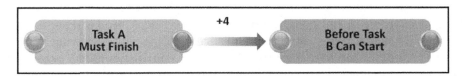

Figure 6.6

As we move further through this chapter, and most specifically when we go through duration estimations, you will see that dates, duration, and effort are all distinct types of schedule drivers. If I look at budgeting, I'm paying for activity A and then B, but I'm not paying resources for the lag time. Plus, there is the other side of the duration estimates in which lag time is accommodated in the duration total. This probably wouldn't happen on your team, but it has for sure happened on mine in a galaxy far, far away. If I put in my schedule that the laying of concrete takes 8 hours total. Not only do I have to pay for the curing of the concrete, but chances are my team may believe I have added some buffer time to the task and wait until the last minute to lay the concrete. Then, the framing people show up and the concrete hasn't cured. Lag time is an asset when used correctly and when necessary.

In the case of *lead time*, the total duration of both activities will shorten because lead subtracts from the total. Much like running activities in parallel, the total duration on a calendar is shortened.

In *Figure 6.7*, you can see an example of lead time. Also notice that both lead and lag sit on the arrow between activities. This is a visual cue to show that it isn't the actual duration of activities but a necessary addition or subtraction of time:

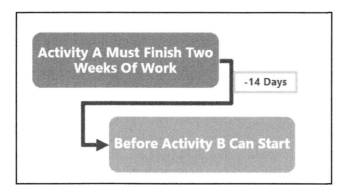

Figure 6.7

In this example, we still need to finish a certain amount of work before task B can start, but we do not need to wait for them to finish the first task, we just must wait for two weeks' worth of work to be completed. Even though a finish-to-start relationship is used, the total duration will compress and run a bit in parallel, thus shortening the overall duration. Otherwise, had it been a true finish to start without the lead, it would have taken the total duration of both activities added together. Now, we have compressed the duration and shortened the total. Remember, these are just quick examples and reference points for exam purposes, but I also believe understanding these relationships and sequencing can help you put together a more comprehensive and realistic schedule.

When you have sequenced your tasks appropriately and plotted out everything you know today, you will have a precedence network diagram or an **activity on node** (**AON**), *since the activities sit inside the node or box*. In *Figure 6.8*, you can see a quite simple version:

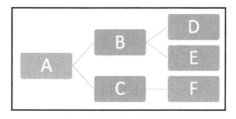

Figure 6.8

What do you notice about the diagram and the activities? Hopefully, you noticed they are all finish-to-start relationships, that, and the fact that it is the smallest project ever! Here's the bad news: you do not have a ton of time to answer questions on the project as well as the exam. It's less than a minute per question. Some will be faster, and some will take longer. Here is the good news: there would be no way you could analyze a network diagram that is too involved for a massive project on the exam, so they will tend to be small examples such as this one—a bit more in depth but not by much, and most of the relationships will be a finish-to-start relationship. That makes it easier to analyze.

 Hammock activity is something you may see on your exam. The topic probably is not going to be prevalent, but just in case it shows up, I want you to imagine a hammock. Two trees with a comfortable hammock, a summer resting place in a field of flowers next to a stream. Ahh! Brain break. That is my idea of a hammock activity or lack of activity, as it were. For the exam, a hammock activity is a group of subtasks that hang between two end dates. You won't see them in your software, and you probably won't see them on the exam either, plus they are not as exciting as my original example.

When we get to the schedule creation and discuss critical paths further in this chapter, I'll show you what you could see on the exam and how to navigate it. Until then, let's move on to the next step in the schedule creation, the estimation of durations.

Estimating durations

Duration estimating is more of an art form than a science. Some people are good at it and others, well, not so much. You know that one friend you have that is always early or the other friend who is always late? Both are annoying, but you love them anyway. Which one do you love more? The first one probably. Most estimates are either too much or not enough, and that is because time is a concept. If we turn to the story of the three bears to explain this, we are looking for *exactly right*. Exactly right is tough to attain though, so we must use a multitude of different techniques to get a duration estimate that is realistic for each activity. **Dates**, **duration**, and **effort** are three totally different things that affect your project schedule equally. These concepts and sequencing activities can drive a project manager into hurling the computer out of the window. Let's start with dates.

Dates

We all use calendars; it's how we maintain ours day to day. A calendar shows the dates and the days and anything that is scheduled for us to do. Most organizations run on a Monday-through-Friday schedule. I say *most*, because that isn't always the case. I'll use this to make a point in a moment. Let's assume your work week is Monday through Friday and you work 40 hours a week (I'll pause for virtual laughter), this is also what your scheduling software is betting on, unless you tell it differently. The very first thing I teach when I teach scheduling software is how important calendars are. Typically, there are three main calendars that all scheduling software works with: a project calendar, a resource calendar, and a task calendar.

The project calendar

A **project calendar** is what your scheduling software refers to always, unless it's told differently. It runs the 9-5, Monday through Friday. What it doesn't do is address non-working days such as holidays. It will be up to you to enter those company holidays into your project calendar. If you have multiple global locations, it's best to build the calendar out where the project originated. I'll talk more about global calendars in just a moment because it is important to accommodate *all* non-working days. The reason this is important is we want our schedules to be realistic. If the company is closed for a holiday and you have work scheduled or deliveries expected, you will find yourself behind schedule, and your team may become disgruntled if forced to be behind schedule due to a scheduling snafu. I typically go to our HR website and find out what holidays the company is closed, and enter them all in at once into my software and share that calendar with all my projects. That way, I'm not duplicating effort or focusing too much on when my next paid day off from work is. Once you have your calendar for the project sorted, you can start to look at other influencing factors. This is where resource calendars come into play.

Resource calendars

Since the project calendar is driving the project based on the corporate calendar, it is also important to address when your resources are on vacation or have a different holiday calendar all together. This is where global calendars are *so* important. If you are working in the United States as the project manager and have team members in another country, they will for sure have different dates that their holidays fall on. I experienced this on a global project where the UK was expecting deliveries from China in February, and they were late. The UK wasn't happy, but then we discussed the dates, and I said, *That was during Chinese new year.* We can't expect those team members to work on their new year when we just took our new year break in January. When we get further into the people side of project management, we'll touch on how important it is to be globally conscious. Resource calendars can help you schedule around a variety of holidays that are applicable to the resource and their countries. I typically go out to a website that lists all the dates of holidays in every country we represent or work with for that year (because they change) and add them to specific resources as well as any scheduled vacations I'm aware of. If everyone is running on the same holiday schedule, then I would just add individual vacation time to the resource calendar.

There is another reason why resource calendars are important and that is when a resource doesn't work full time on your project. They may be working on a variety of projects and can only focus on your project on Monday and Thursday from 12 pm to 5 pm. If that isn't correct in their calendar, you will have a schedule that looks good on paper but is impossible to meet.

Task calendars

In every project, there is always a task that doesn't conform to the regular schedule. In IT, that could be the testing of a system that is automated but necessary to track. Nobody is going to be sitting there watching all the flashing lights all night long, but it is a task that is necessary to add to your schedule. In that case, a task calendar may be appropriate. Different durations or timeframes from the norm that need to be tracked will also need a different calendar. Let's say it's a 12-hour task for automated testing. If you followed the normal project calendar, then it would schedule eight hours for one day and four hours the next day. That would make it look like the entire task took one and a half days spanning over 24 hours, and that simply isn't the case. Task calendars may not be used as heavily as the other two, but may be necessary once or twice a project. We are going to look at hours, dates, duration, and effort, and you will see that they are vastly different, and you may find that task calendars can help get the schedule corrected as needed.

Effort

I touched on effort a bit in the calendar section while looking at resource calendars. Effort is assumed at 100 percent in most scheduling software, unless you adjust it. That means that every human resource you assign to a task is assumed to be working full time on that task. That is almost never the case. In fact, even if your resources are working full time, it's probably safe to say they aren't at 100 percent all the time. Let's say you have a part-time resource who works on multiple projects, that would make their level of effort 50 percent maximum, and it may even be 25 percent. It will take them twice as long to get the work done across a calendar at 50 percent and four times as long at 25 percent. It's important to effect effort appropriately when creating your schedule because otherwise you will find yourself with over allocated resources and inevitably behind schedule. That doesn't include holidays and vacations either, all of which can affect your finish date. That brings us to duration.

Duration

Duration, dates, and effort are three totally different things, but all three impact your schedules and your ability to effectively set a baseline for tracking performance. Durations are typically documented in your schedule as hours, days, and weeks in normal schedules. Anything that is larger than that on the task level probably needs to be decomposed further down to effectively resource it, unless you are progressively elaborating and do not have enough information to decompose effectively at this point. Here is how dates, effort, and duration all work together.

Task A is scheduled at a 10-day duration. That roughly translates to 80 hours of work or two work weeks that you would pay for out of your budget for your resource. It is the amount of assumed time it will take that resource to complete the work.

The calendar would put the total of that work at 12 days because there is a weekend in between. Not in effort or task duration, but because of the project calendar and non-working days.

If the resource is working at 100 percent effort than we can assume for now they will complete the work in the ten-day duration across two work weeks, barring a risk event or issue that impacts that total during the execution of the work.

Now, let's imagine that same resource is part time. The duration is the same. They will do 80 hours or ten days' worth of work except on the calendar it will be four weeks instead of two. This is enough to drive the best scheduler a bit crazy. That is why it is important to have an idea of who and what your resources will be and their levels of effort. Otherwise, your estimates may be off completely.

Another consideration with resources and durations is how many resources will be working on the tasks. There are certain tasks that if you add another person the duration is cut in half. For example, you have one person painting four walls of a room. The duration is four days. If you add another person to help them the duration is cut in half. That's awesome if you have the right amount of resources and they are skilled in painting rooms.

There are, however, certain tasks that it doesn't really matter how many resources are assigned the activity will take the same amount of time as if one person were doing the work. The first example that pops into my mind is road work. Every day I drive by road work, it's like they are constantly fixing roads around my home. As I sit there with tons of other irritated drivers moving at a snail's pace, I have to opportunity to marvel (yet again) at the fact that there is one person doing the work and fifteen people standing around drinking coffee watching them do the work. Inevitably another truckload of people arrive on the scene before traffic starts moving and wouldn't you know it one person is still working and now 30 people are drinking coffee. It's going to take until the end of the universe to fix our roads around here! Whoops! I'm sorry about that little rant, but it is an excellent example of how some tasks could have multiple people assigned and still take the same duration to complete. Mostly, the example would be two people riding in a delivery truck. That doesn't cut the total duration in half. The duration is fixed.

As you can see, there is a lot more involved in estimating time and creating schedules. Here's the good news for you: the exam will only use durations and estimating durations in questions (yay!). In the real world, well, you know, it's different. I'll give you some techniques you can use to help estimate as effectively as possible and still consider risks to your schedule that can cause a less than frenetic pace while work is being executed.

The techniques you could see on your exams and could use in the real world are the following:

- Analogous estimates
- Parametric estimates
- Three-point estimates
- Reserve analysis

Analogous estimates

I like to think of **analogous** estimating technique as an analogy for your duration estimates. You will be looking at the recent past to predict how long a task or tasks will take in the future. If you know that your team upgraded everyone's software in the finance department six months ago and now you will be doing the same in another comparable department in size and scope, it's a safe bet you will probably take the same amount of time. Even though this could be the one time that it takes twice as long due to a risk event it's a safe bet estimate. A lot of the time, the business cases are developed using analogous information, which is why I like to ask business analysts where they came up with *that number*. They love it when I ask that. It's also probably the way you will estimate many tasks that are repetitive on multiple projects. It isn't the most accurate way of estimating because it is based on history and assumptions, but it is a good jumping-off point.

Parametric estimates

Parametric, metric, math. These estimates are based on the resources, level of effort and their estimate on how long the task will take based on the task duration and the number of tasks that need to be done. If my painters can paint one wall in three hours and they have four walls in total to finish, then I can use that to forecast the total duration of 12 hours in total. This type of estimate is more accurate and is typically what your software is doing in the background when you determine the task, the duration, the resources, and the effort. Boom, it's got a number for you because the software used math and your inputs to calculate. This is a much more accurate estimate because it based on the actual work on the current project and the actual resources assigned and their assumed levels of effort.

It's doubtful you will need to calculate using a parametric estimate on the exam, but you may be asked about its level of accuracy. By the way, all these techniques can be used for **cost estimating** as well. Time and money are very tightly integrated.

Three-point estimates

I'm not kidding when I say I use this technique with my customers. It all stems from the psychological factor of calculators and math. For some reason, when you explain something with a calculator or jot down the equation on paper, people are like, *Whoa! It must be right, it's math!* It's true; try it sometime. This estimating technique is my favorite because I am risk averse, and any time I can take potential risk into consideration I will. I'll expand on being risk averse in Chapter 8, *Budget and Contingency Plans for Risk*, but it is never too early in a project to think about risk. In fact, the first place we see risk is in the Project Charter, and we try to stay in front of it as much as possible. I'm sure when you think risk you immediately think it's something bad or damaging to your project and you would be correct, I do it too. There is the other side of the coin though and that is opportunity. A risk is anything that carries a probability or an impact, good or bad. We know it could happen, but we just aren't sure it will or what the true impact is going to be, so we plan for it.

Three-point estimates help us plan for schedule risk and cost risk. I'm a bit of a history buff and always want to know where these practices came from. The three-point estimate is also fondly known as **PERT**. No, not the shampoo. **The Program Evaluation and Review Technique**. PERT was created in 1957 by the US Navy Special Projects Office. It was designed and used to support the US navy's Polaris nuclear submarine project. PERT has also popped up in numerous projects in aerospace throughout the years and even showed up in the planning of parts of the 1968 Winter Olympics in Grenoble, France. It will also make an appearance on your exams. The concept is to take into consideration the optimistic, pessimistic, and most likely estimates of tasks and provide a duration estimate that is more accurate. These durations can then be used to determine the total duration or cost or used in correlation with overall project duration or cost estimates with risk included.

Since PERT was created by scientists and engineers, I typically imagine three rocket scientists sitting around arguing about how long things will take to accomplish. I would imagine it isn't just rocket scientists having that conversation, but it makes me laugh so I use it. The first rocket scientist is risk averse (me too) and sees threats to the project everywhere and inflates the duration estimate to protect it just in case. The eternal optimist also has an opinion and sees progress everywhere, thereby estimating that things will move much faster. The most likely or expert says, *hey listen I've done this a gazillion times and it always takes this long to do.* Who's right? They all are! Here is the formula that will make you a big hit at parties when people ask you what you do for a living. This formula is also considered a **beta distribution or weighted average** formula. You might be wondering why we divide by six. That is because we have six variables: 4: most likely, 1: pessimistic, and 1: optimistic. Hence, the **weighted average** distinction:

Time estimate or TE = (O+4ML+P)/6

Basically, you trust the expert judgment four times more than your catastrophic thinker or your eternal optimist. That is because experts have the experience, and we can trust it. This is what is known as a **weighted estimate.** The most likely estimate carries more weight. We trust it four times more than the other two estimates. Let's assume we have three estimates from our rocket scientists:

- **Optimistic scientist**: It will take five days to complete, because we are all awesome
- **Pessimistic scientist**: No, no, it will take 15 days to complete, with a variety of risk events that will occur
- **Most-likely scientist**: Uh, nope. I've done this tons of times before, and it usually takes about nine days

If you are like me, a bit mathematically challenged, make sure you follow the normal order of operations in math. Because if you run it like the formula is presented, you will get the wrong answer. Please Excuse My Dear Aunt Sally, or Parentheses, Exponents, Multiplication/Division, Addition/Subtraction.

You will have a calculator and something to write with and on during the exam, so you don't have to do math in your head—phew!

Here is how to run the math for the PERT expected duration formula, using our rocket scientists:

$$[O + (4*ML) + P]/6 \text{ or } [5+(4*9)+15]/6 = 9.33$$

The answer works out to be about 9.33. You might be thinking *That seems like a big waste of time, seeing as the answer is pretty darn close to the original estimate—what gives?* I typically use the example of being late for a flight. If I'm even 25 seconds late after they shut the door, they don't open it for me. What if we were calculating in weeks? Now, our schedule is a bit behind because of poor estimates. It also gives the expert time to *I told you so* the others involved. This formula is typically used for tasks that have been done before. We trust the expert judgment four times more. That is why there is another formula for those things we have never done before. This formula is called **triangular distribution**. Instead of a weighted average distribution, we need to consider all points equally. There isn't any true historical knowledge to guide us therefore we must take risk into consideration equally with our estimate. Much like a triangle has three sides, this formula is a true average, and we divide by three. In this case, our scientist's estimates would look more like this:

$$TE = (O+ML+P)/3 \text{ or } (5+9+15)/3 = 9.66 \text{ or rounded up to } 10$$

Many times, this exercise helps explain why we have added some buffer time to our schedules to accommodate risk because frankly if something goes sideways it could take 15 days to accomplish or certainly more than the nine we have scheduled. Therefore, we also need to consider another aspect of risk in our estimates in the form of reserve estimates or standard deviation.

Reserve analysis

No matter what, all projects have risk. It may not be enough to run PERT analysis to determine the impacts of risk on our schedules; we may also need to determine how much time or money we should to set aside in reserves to manage identified risk events. Threats cost time and money; opportunities save or gain time or money. It's the threats we are really concerned about. Most of the estimates will be +/- a certain amount of time or money. This is because risk carries a probability less than 100 percent, and it would be impossible to honestly say the impact to the schedule or budget will be XYZ. The goal is to have some contingency in our schedule for **known/unknown** risk events that can be fixed or managed with time or money. Known, because we have identified a probability a risk event will occur, and we have estimated the impact but it's unknown whether the risk will happen or if we were correct in our assessment of it.

Here's a quick lesson in statistics but don't worry too much if the following gives you a bit of a headache, you will not have to calculate this more than once, if at all. I give you permission to forget this entire section on standard deviation. Proceed with caution.

Standard deviation is a statistical concept that gives a measure of the range of the values of a random variable around the mean of a distribution. It shows how much variation there is from the average or the mean value. The more the variation, the more the uncertainty or risk in the process. If you have normal distribution, and you try to calculate those values which are plus or minus 1 sigma or standard deviation from the average (or the mean), you will learn that 68 percent of the values fall within that range. The standard deviation formula takes the most likely out of the equation and instead focuses on the pessimistic and optimistic variables. The formula is as follows:

$$SD = (P-O) / 6$$

Our job is to determine how many days, hours and so on +/- the original duration estimate. This will all be factored based on our confidence level in the original estimate. If you are familiar with sigma variables for quality management, then this may look familiar:

- Confidence level in estimated value +/- 1 x SD is approximately 68%
- Confidence level in estimated value +/- 2 x SD is approximately 95%
- Confidence level in estimated value +/- 3 x SD is approximately 99.7%

What if your customer asked you what the duration variables are for a certain activity? You would need to be able to answer that.

Let's go back to our rocket scientists:

- **Optimist**: 5
- **Most likely**: 9
- **Pessimist**: 15

If we take the expert judgment out of the picture and run the math, the standard deviation would equal:

$$(15-5) / 6 = 1.7 \text{ rounded up}$$

Now we must determine how confident we are in the original weighted duration estimate of 9.33. We will use N to represent the sigma levels.

If $N = 1$ *Sigma*, then we would consider the original estimate $+/- 1 \times SD$ is approximately 68 percent or the sigma level we estimate is correct. For example, if:

$$9.33 +/- 1 \text{ sigma*} 1.7$$

Then:

$$9.33 + 1.7 = 11.03$$

$$9.33 - 1.7 = 7.63$$

If $N = 2$ *sigma*, then our confidence level in an estimated value $+/- 2 \times SD$ is approximately 95 percent:

$$9.33 +/- 2 \text{ sigma*} 1.7 \text{ (or two times } 1.7 +/- 9.33)$$

Then:

$$9.33 + 3.4 = 12.73 \text{ or } 13 \text{ rounded}$$

$$9.33 - 3.4 = 5.93 \text{ or } 6 \text{ rounded}$$

All this information provides us with a range of estimates, so you can build in contingency or adjust your estimates. In this case, it's more than likely we will go with one standard deviation or sigma if we are doing something we have never done before. This builds out more accurate estimates. Now, you can tell the customer and your team that activity A *should* take about nine and half days but could be finished early at 7.63 days or late at 11 days, depending on the risk impact to the work.

There are several items to consider with risk. First, not every single risk event can be solved with time or money. These estimates would be reserved for tasks that can be adjusted with additional time or money. Typically, finish-to-start relationships are so common, because they present the longest total duration a task or string of tasks can take, thus building in contingency. The other consideration is that contingency reserves are typically money and will be ours to distribute as needed throughout the project and is considered part of our cost baseline. In Chapter 8, *Budget and Contingency Plans for Risk*, we will review risk, contingency, and budgetary considerations. For now, our focus is on schedule risk and creating a schedule that we will probably meet. The goal is to get your schedule approved as a baseline and to be able to answer the question of *How long will this project take?* That question can be answered by putting all the pieces together and creating the project schedule and determining your critical path.

Developing the project schedule

Let's look at the road so far. First, you created a task list and milestones by decomposing the work packages in your WBS. Then, you sequenced activities based on dependencies and relationships. After which, you estimated your resources and durations, taking into consideration dates, and effort, lead, and lag time, along with those estimates for the duration of the tasks. Now, we have a schedule. What we don't have is a finish date, a total duration, and the answer to the question of how long it will take. That brings us to schedule creation. There are several techniques we will go through and I'm sure you have noticed that time management takes a lot of time to review!

The techniques we will cover are these:

- Critical path
- Critical chain
- Monte Carlo technique
- Schedule compression
- Resource optimization

Before we dive into the critical path method, let me make a few comments regarding this for your exam. First, it takes me longer to explain the concept than you will ever get questions on your exam. Most people fall on one side or the other with this technique. Either they have used it and it makes sense or they haven't, and it looks and sounds confusing. If the latter is the case, do not fear! You may get about three to five questions on critical path that ask you to navigate a network diagram or determine float or slack time (interchangeable terms). Unfortunately, people spend too much time studying these confusing concepts instead of taking a well-rounded approach to the content and find they don't have the amount of questions on the exam to have warranted late nights studying critical path and the inevitable caffeine jitters that come with it. I am going to make this as easy as humanly possible to understand the concepts and how to read a network diagram for exam purposes. In the real world, we have software that does all the heavy lifting for us.

Critical path

In the simplest of terms, the **critical path** is the *string of linked activities* that takes the longest to complete in duration. Therefore, the critical path determines your **finish date**. That finish date is your baseline, it is the date you are being held accountable for once you begin to execute. Remember we have a map of sequences in our project, different relationships, durations, and resources. It is critical that we finish by that date or we are behind schedule.

Here's a quite straightforward way to understand critical path, we will use the example of making dinner. Even if you don't cook, you'll get the reference. My husband doesn't cook, but he does want to know what is for dinner and the all-important answer to the question of *How long until dinner?* Here is what is on the menu tonight:

- Steak
- Baked potato
- Salad

Now let's put some things into order and the context of duration:

- Baked potato takes one hour and 20 mins to cook in the oven.
- Steak must rest for 30 minutes and will grill 12 minutes total and rest again for six minutes. The total duration is 48 minutes.
- For the salad, I'll open the bag, put dressing on it and voila! Salad! (I know, I know…judging is fine, I'm busy.) Let's say with my lazy salad making it takes 5 minutes total and trust me it isn't even that long, but, for the purposes of learning, we'll call it a solid five minutes.

Which of the dinner items will take the longest? The baked potato. What is the answer to the question of how long until dinner? One hour and 20 minutes. That is my critical path. Everything else can happen in the timespan it takes to cook the potato. Now, if I want everyone to come to the table where the hot food is hot and cold food is cold, I have some decisions to make regarding the steak and the salad. If my steak takes 48 minutes and the potato takes 80 minutes, I could literally wait to start the steak until minute 32 of the entire potato process and the salad (as easy as it is), I still don't want it to be soggy by starting too early. Instead I'll wait until the baked potato has 5 minutes left to cook before I start shaking the bag and putting dressing on it. That means for the steak I have 32 minutes of float time. I could start it when I start the potato but that wouldn't work for the hotness factor and I have 75 minutes of float for the salad because, you know, the soggy factor. When my senior *steakholder* asks how long until dinner, the critical path is 80 minutes or one hour and 20 minutes.

In *Figure 6.9*, the same scenario is presented in a simple network diagram. The critical path is the longest total duration the project can take and the absolute fastest the project can go:

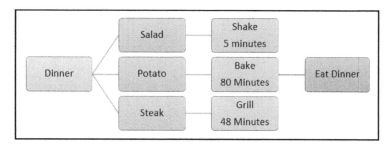

Figure 6.9

Here's where things start to get interesting. On a network diagram that you will have to analyze for the exam questions, you could be looking for several different variables. For example, you may get questions that ask, *What is the early start (ES) and early finish (EF) of each task and the late start (LS) and late finish (LF) of each task?* The problem with this is it sounds like you are starting something super early, which would put you way ahead of schedule or super late which would put you behind schedule. That isn't the case at all. The ES is asking what the earliest possible time is that the task can begin based on its relationship with other tasks and on its duration. Then, based on that duration when will it be finished is the EF. This is called a **forward pass** and allows us to determine the durations of all paths and find the longest or the critical path.

The LS is asking if there is any conceivable way that a task can be pushed out a bit, and if so, when can it start and based on its duration what with the LF be. This is called a backward pass and it will provide the information on float/slack time for non-critical tasks. The critical path doesn't have any float/slack time. If my husband asks when dinner is going to be ready and I say 80 minutes and then two hours later, I finally serve dinner that *steakholder* will not be happy at all!

The good news is you have already figured this out with the dinner example, but I want to show you on a network diagram how that works. In *Figure 6.10*, you will see the same network diagram, except now the finish to start relationships and the durations are represented in the task box:

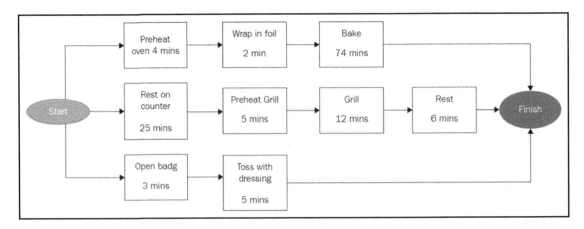

Figure 6.10

All projects start on day or minute one and finish after the longest path has been completed. The easiest way to calculate critical path is to jot down each path and add up the durations. The biggest number is the critical path. Then, take the critical path and subtract each additional path from it and that will tell you the float/slack.

Let's look at a typical network diagram and work through it. In *Figure 6.11*, you will see a network diagram with the early starts. Critical path is used without regard to weekends or other non-working times. A forward pass is calculating all the path durations moving from the start of the project to the finish.

For the exam, you will most likely be using finish to start relationships and calculating durations only. You won't have to worry about dates.

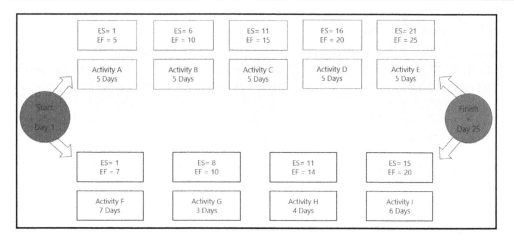

Figure 6.11

In this case, 25 days is longer than 20 days, so path **A-B-C-D-E** is the critical path.

In *Figure 6.12*, you can see that critical path can be calculated beginning with zero. This was the way it used to be done in earlier iterations of the exam. While it will still provide you with the critical path total, it will not provide you with the correct answers regarding the ES and EF or the LS LF for the exam. I get this question a lot when people begin taking practice exams. They have seen it somewhere online, but for the newest version of the exam PK0-004 and beyond, it will use a start of day one of the project. Besides, who the heck starts their project on day zero anyway?

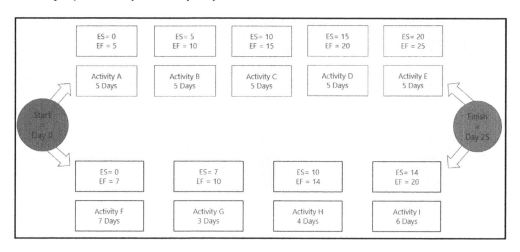

Figure 6.12

Float/slack time

Float time is the longest we can possibly push out non-critical tasks, without slipping our schedule. That allows us to have some breathing room to move resources around as needed to critical tasks without falling behind schedule. If you are late on your critical path you are behind schedule. Float is calculated by subtracting durations from the critical path to determine the difference. This is done by using a backward pass or working from the finish of the critical path and working back to the start.

In *Figure 6.13*, you will see the late starts and finish for the non-critical path. The critical path has zero float/slack:

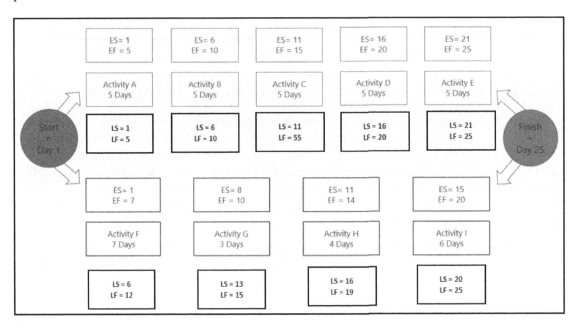

Figure 6.13

There are several distinct types of float or slack to consider. Even though these are interchangeable terms it is typical that float is used on the project and the exam:

- **Positive float**: This is the opposite of negative float and is basically the unicorn of project management. The date constraint is further out than your assumed baseline—woo-hoo!

- **Negative float**: This is when you have float/slack on your critical path. You can read negative float as being behind schedule. Typically, this comes from a date constraint that defies reason. You already know you are going into the project sideways. The customer says get it done in three months and you know it will take six. That is negative float.
- **Free float**: This is the amount of time a task can be delayed without delaying the early start date of any following activity. You are free to use your float however you like! It's typically best to use it at the end of a non-critical path because Murphy's law is a very real thing in project management. Having buffer time at the end, if possible, is the best course of action. Otherwise, you can use it as needed, two days here, three days there.
- **Total float**: This is the amount of time a task can be delayed from its early start without delaying the project finish date.

There are distinct types of float, depending on what you need for your projects but for the exam you should be working with total float the most. Many times, in exam questions and precedence relationships, you will see task relationships represented as the **predecessor and successor**. That is just a fancy way of saying the task that comes first and the one that comes after it.

Both will give you the exact same answer. Look at activity on the bottom right of the diagram in *Figure 6.13*. If I subtracted *LS 20 - ES 15 or LF 25 - LS 20*, I get five. If I took the total of the first path of 25 and subtracted the total of the second path 20, I get five. There are five days of float.

Another way to calculate float/slack is to use these formulas:

$$LS-ES = Float \ or \ LF-EF = Float$$

If you found all of that confusing, just remember the critical path is the longest string of connected tasks in duration. To determine float, you take the critical path total duration and subtract each individual non-critical path from it. The difference is the float time. You could have 85 tasks that take four days and three tasks that take 40 days. It's all about the duration. In your software, you will see dates, and that is why we have software. For the exam, they are just testing your knowledge of the concept as a tool or technique and will only use durations and quite possibly all finish to start relationships as well. This makes it much easier and faster to answer questions, *A+B+C*.

You may also see the term near-critical path. This would be the second longest path of tasks in duration and would need to be watched closely as well. If a risk event lengthens the near critical path it could create a new critical path total and you would be behind schedule. It isn't unusual on complex projects to have multiple critical and near critical paths.

Critical chain

Critical chain in its simplest of forms adds buffer time to the critical path to accommodate limited resources. That may be the only way you see it on the exam. This is what we are doing by using all finish to start relationships when sequencing. FS relationships give us the longest total duration the project could take and provides some buffer time on the critical and non-critical paths to allow for a limitation in scheduled resources.

Monte Carlo technique

The Monte Carlo technique uses probability and impact along with specialized software to determine the *odds* of meeting your schedule in its current form. I'm not sure who has time to sit around running different computer-generated schedule models on regular projects but clearly people do. **Random number generation**, **computer generated**, and **iterative** is how this technique is described. Let me give you an easier explanation and use a casino to do so. After all Monte Carlo was the first and oldest casino as it was built in 1856 after permission from Charles III of Monaco to help with some pesky financial problems he was having. The house had to win for those problems to disappear. Let's say you are a new casino owner, and you are setting up a blackjack table on the floor. Charlie knew, and we know the house always wins, not because you are psychic but because you are going to run the odds first and choose the best configuration for your house to win. Let's say you set up your table to begin with and use five decks of cards, five players and five US dollars a hand. You would enter that into the software system. Then, you would take away a deck of cards. Four decks of cards, five players and five US dollars a hand. Then, you would put the deck back and take away a chair. Five decks of cards, four chairs and five US dollars a hand and so on until you find the best configuration based on the odds. It could be six decks of cards, ten players and five US dollars a hand. Winner, winner, chicken dinner!

For your exam, Monte Carlo analysis won't be heavily tested on, but if you do get a question, it may relate to *what if* analysis and random number, computer-generated and iterative, which means repeatedly.

Schedule compression

There will be multiple times when your schedule will need to be shortened or compressed throughout your project management career. Typically, the first time will be when you have worked so hard to put all of it together and turn it in to be approved as a baseline and are told to remove at least a month from the total...meh! The other times may be during the execution of the project and finding your project behind schedule. To get back on track you will need to take some corrective action and compress what is left to do to finish on time. There are only two ways to compress your schedules before execution or during and those are fast tracking and crashing.

Fast tracking

This is where understanding different relationships and lead time comes in handy. Fast tracking is running tasks on the critical path in parallel rather than sequentially or finish to start. That isn't going to work for everything because remember we have dependencies that may not allow for compression due to logic. We will have to look for areas we can adjust tasks. This is typically the best way to compress because it doesn't cost additional money or need additional resources. You may have to move some resources around, but you don't need more resources. Fast tracking is considered the *best*, **first choice** because of that very reason. There is always a downside though and in this case the downside is that doing things faster than you are supposed to can create risk events. I know this to be the case because when I was twelve years old I had a steep driveway and a skateboard and the two together were shortly followed by a broken ankle.

We will have to keep a pirate eye on the scope and quality if we are fast tracking because you are rushing it but again, what does your organization value most? Good, fast, or cheap? It's far easier to plan to fast track before execution than it is to use it as corrective action. The current project trajectory may not handle it well.

Crashing

Crashing sounds as if it would fit my skateboard story more appropriately, but in fact, crashing is throwing money or additional resources at the critical tasks. We would have to look for areas where if we added more people the tasks would move faster. Extra people cost extra money. The trick to crashing is to look for tasks that will move the fastest for the least amount of money or the **least incremental costs**. We need to move it along, but we don't want to break the bank either!

Watch out for exam questions asking about least incremental costs. Some equate that to fast tracking because it is free but crashing is spending money to move faster.

Many times, as a preemptive strike during planning, we can get support and approval for more people or equipment if we can prove our case. This is great because we are in the process of getting baselines approved and haven't done any of the work yet. After the fact, it may be like pulling teeth to get approval, fast, cheap, or good?

Optimizing resources

Often when we are scheduling, we are also assigning our resources, updating their calendars and effort and everything looks good until you realize that you over allocated Karen and have her working 16 hours in one day on multiple activities. Trust me when I say Karen isn't happy so it's up to you to fix it. When resources are over allocated it not only impacts their state of happiness, but it also affects the budget due to overtime costs. There are only two ways to fix over allocation and those techniques are leveling and smoothing.

Leveling

Leveling happens on the critical path and will extend your total project duration. This is because Karen needs to have two eight-hour days instead of one 16-hour day. This could lead to rescheduling work and pushing out the dates. Much like dominoes falling, if one falls the rest do as well. As soon as you push out her schedule, it impacts the other activities and resources. It can't be helped though unless you have other people willing to step in and help Karen, and it's the type of task that can be compressed with more than one person.

 Just a quick note about leveling in software: find the button, and forget you saw it. Any time you allow a computer to make decisions for you, it can be an unwise decision. If you tempt fate and try it anyway you may see that your project will be completed in the year 2670. This is because the software will look for Karen's next available day to do the work and that always ends badly. Locate the *undo* button; undo is your friend.

Smoothing

Smoothing is the easier of the two if you are lucky, because smoothing is on non-critical paths and will not extend your finish date. You can use your float time because you are free to use your total float however you like. In this case, if Karen is over allocated, then you simply apologize profusely and move the rest of the work to the next day if possible or the next available day that is realistic. That will utilize float but that is what float is there for. Sometimes you'll use your float time to crash your critical path if you are lucky enough to have additional resources you can pull away from non-critical tasks in the moment you need them.

The schedule baseline

After all this effort and work to put together a comprehensive schedule, it is now time to get a formal version of your schedule approved as a baseline.

There will be three major baselines. The schedule baseline, the cost baseline, and the scope baseline. All baselines are used to track performance and would have to be updated through formal change control.

You will need to present your schedule to your sponsor, customer, and other key stakeholders to gain approval and acceptance on the dates/duration of the project. Once you get that approval (after multiple revisions and some tears) you will have your schedule baseline. The schedule baseline is a formal, approved version of your schedule and will be used to manage schedule performance during execution and to determine if you need to make corrections.

All baselines are static documents, meaning they don't change unless there is a reason to change them. If so, the change would have to be processed through formal change control. You can't just update your baseline whenever you want, as tempting as it may be. The baseline will reside in the formal integrated project management plan and be used to compare planned versus actual. The schedule itself is a living breathing document you will update as you progress through the project.

During execution, you will ask your team how long the tasks *took* to update your schedule. You will then compare actual to planned, baseline to schedule. If there is a variance or difference between planned and actual, you will determine whether it is bad enough that you need to take corrective action such as fast tracking or crashing, or both. Usually, part of this process is asking your team just how in the world it took them twice as long to do the work as scheduled and reminding them about the long walk to the sponsor's office you now need to take to get approval for baseline updates.

Most of the time, schedules are presented as Gantt charts, bar charts, or milestone charts to senior management. The best is a milestone chart for senior management; give them an easy-to-follow, easy-to-read chart. This is so they know that you are on track without all the noise of a Gantt chart. Next week, Commodus!

Scheduling is a lot of information to take in and it takes practice to become proficient in your day to day. So, don't worry too much. As for the project and the exam, there is so much information we just covered; it is rare to get questions on everything. If you do well on the practice exam, then you are halfway there. If you don't do well the first time, do not despair; answer the questions open-book, and look up what you don't know, not what you do. You'll get there! This is one knowledge area out of ten, and perfect practice makes perfect. Ready to move on to something else? Oh, yeah…me too!

Summary

In this chapter, you reviewed schedule management concepts such as creating a schedule management plan, and defining and sequencing tasks, as well as some best practices for duration estimating. You wrapped up with critical path and float determination and diverse ways to compress your schedule and reduce over-allocation of your resources, as well as having an approved schedule baseline to track performance with.

In Chapter 7, *Resource Management Planning and Communication Considerations*, you will be covering resource management planning and communication considerations. This is basically the human side of project management and is typically easy on the exam. It will be valuable information, but it won't create a brain cramp, as this chapter did.

The topics we will cover include resource management concepts, conflict management, monitoring team performance, and techniques for developing a performing team.

Questions

1. You are the project manager for a large installation project. Your key stakeholders are discussing the best ways to manage changes to the schedule. Which is the best document to refer them to?
   - The schedule baseline
   - WBS
   - The schedule management plan
   - The schedule

2. You are working with your team to decompose the work packages of your WBS down to the task list. What other document will you be preparing?
   - Milestone list
   - Sequenced tasks
   - The schedule
   - An outline

3. You have just completed the development of the task list and your milestones for the project. What step do you take next?
   - Create the schedule
   - Sequence tasks
   - Estimate resources
   - Estimate durations

4. Bill is on your core team for your new server installation project. As you are working together on the beginning of the schedule creation, Bill mentions that you will need complete all the tests on the new equipment and then you can schedule the install, if everything passes. What kind of relationship is Bill referring to?
   - Mandatory
   - Start to finish
   - Discretionary
   - Finish to start

5. Your sponsor is discussing the project schedule with you and has alerted you to the fact that the customer would like a process flow diagram of your proposed install process. Once they review it, the customer wants you to adjust your process to accommodate the process in their organization. This is an example of what kind of dependency?
   - Mandatory
   - Discretionary

- Internal
- External

6. You have just been assigned to a project in the middle of planning due to the original project manager being pulled to work on something else. Before they leave the project, they let you know that they have defined all the tasks they are aware of for now, but scope could change. What best practice will you need to utilize to keep on top of scope changes that will affect your schedule?
    - Formal changes
    - Progressive scheduling
    - Rolling wave planning
    - Schedule updates

7. Which of the following is the most common precedence relationship?
    - Finish to start
    - Start to start
    - Finish to finish
    - Start to finish

8. You are working with your team and analyzing the current version of your precedence network diagram as well as the durations that have been added to it. You are trying to figure out the critical path. If the following options represent all path durations, which would be considered the near-critical path?
    - 20 days
    - 19 days
    - 10 days
    - 5 days

9. During the planning of a large install project, your key resource lets you know that the first roll out will include tests of the system before the rest of the installs happen. He estimates that the automated tests will take about five hours to do and it isn't necessary for him to be there when the testing happens. Which of the following could the testing time be considered?
    - Lead time
    - Total duration
    - Lag time
    - This isn't considered schedule time

10. Lisa is one of your main go-to resources when estimating time because she tends to be right on schedule. You have asked her to estimate the time it will take for phase one of the project. Lisa lets you know that, based on other projects she has done that are similar, phase one should take about two months. What kind of estimate did Lisa give you?

    - Analogous
    - Parametric
    - Three-point
    - Reserve analysis

11. Your customer tends to always have an optimistic view of your schedule and doesn't consider risk if they don't see it happen. You are trying to convince the customer that you have some concerns about the total time an activity will take due to identified threat events and your expert on the project has experienced the same on other projects. You have presented the customer with three different durations. What is the expected duration of the task using a three-point estimate?
    Optimistic: 10 days
    Pessimistic: 32 days
    Most likely: 17 days

    - 17 days
    - 16.6 days
    - 18.3 days
    - 32 days

12. Which of the following schedule compression techniques involves performing tasks in parallel to speed up critical tasks?

    - Fast tracking
    - Crashing
    - Resource optimization
    - Monte Carlo technique

13. Both Karush and Rebecca have come to you and pointed out that on the schedule they are over-allocated for several tasks and will not be able to meet the request. They have asked if you could possibly adjust the schedule. After reviewing the schedule, you have determined that Rebecca is working on critical tasks and Karush is not. What adjustment would you have to make for Rebecca?

    - You would need to fast track
    - You would need to crash
    - You would need to level
    - You would need to smooth

14. You are reviewing your precedence network diagram and are attempting to determine float time for one activity after your assigned resource asked for a vacation day. You have determined that the late start of the activity is 30 and the late finish is 38. How much float time does the activity have?
    - Eight
    - 10
    - Five
    - There is not enough information to answer this question

15. Your customer is working with you on your schedule creation and they have made it noticeably clear that they want this project completed by the January 5. By your calculations, it appears you will wrap up the project on December 15. This is an example of which of the following?
    - Float
    - Negative float
    - Positive float
    - Total float

Extra credit!

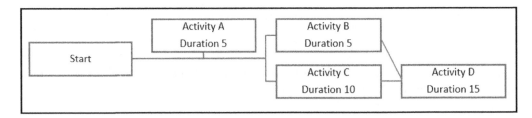

Figure 6.14

16. Based on the network diagram in *Figure 6.14*, what is the critical path?
    - ABD
    - ACD
    - ABCD
    - BD

7
Resource Management Planning and Communication Considerations

In this chapter, you will review the knowledge areas of human-resource management and communications management. You will begin with some common resource management concepts and how your organizational dynamic affects your resource usage and allocation. Then, you will review how to manage conflict on your project team as well as motivate and develop a team of individuals while monitoring their performance. A large part of doing all of this successfully, as well as engaging your stakeholders, is to practice effective communication.

In this chapter, we will cover the following topics:

- Resource management concepts
- Organizational charts and position descriptions
- Developing a performing team
- Conflict management
- Monitoring team performance
- Communication management

Resource management concepts

The first thing you probably think of when you hear the word resources is the human side of project management, and mostly you would be correct. However, resources are also equipment and materials. All three resource types would need to be estimated, scheduled, and paid for. In fact, estimating resources is very tightly integrated with costs and budgeting. You will cover costs in more depth in Chapter 8, *Budget and Contingency Plans for Risk*, but until then, just know that people, equipment, and materials cost money. Some of these would be considered **soft costs**, meaning your organization is probably already paying people their hourly wage or salary through the organization's payroll. Thus, those costs would not be considered part of your budget.

Materials and equipment may also unilaterally be a part of your organizational processes, through a procurement department, or everyday needs of the organization to run the business effectively. For your exams, it will be considered your budgetary costs for resource utilization as well as aspects of procurement that would need to be considered to acquire any resources from outside your organization.

Most of this chapter will be based on the human side of resources and how to acquire, develop, and manage your team of individuals.

I'm sure it's obvious that having your own team that you work with all the time is a perfect situation for project managers. You know your team, you know their skills, you know their work styles and personalities, and that makes it easier to schedule work correctly and interact with your team daily.

 The Project+ exam assumes a strong matrix organization (unless otherwise stated in the question). This assumption would provide a team of core resources for the project and the potential for acquisitions outside of the team for functional resource needs or through staffing and procurement. Therefore, it would be necessary to acquire your team. This would include acquiring the *rest* of your team when it's time to execute the work.

This is not always the case though, and since projects are temporary and unique, it would make sense that some of your resources are as well. The disadvantage of this type of team is that they may be part-time on your project, they have a *real job* in their own functional departments, and they may be more focused on their day job than what is going on during your project. Those team members may also be more focused on their performance reviews from their manager than their performance on your project.

I'm not sure why that is though, as most managers in my distant past only remembered the last two weeks of my work life and the one stupid thing I did all year and that was my yearly review! I always keep that in mind and after I shudder a bit in remembrance, I make it a habit to keep a file on my acquired team members to keep track of their wins and the challenges that they have overcome. I turn that in to their managers when the work is completed so they are aware of additional weeks of their team member's work life when it's time for reviews.

It's very typical on longer-term projects that your resources will be over-allocated because they are working on multiple projects at once. In Chapter 6, *Developing a Project Schedule,* you reviewed **leveling** and **smoothing** as techniques to reduce over-allocations. The techniques that were not mentioned are begging, pleading, negotiating, and possibly crying to gain the resources you need to avoid over-allocations of the resources you currently have scheduled. Since there is no crying in project management (yes, there is), you may need to brush up on your negotiating skills to acquire the right resources for your project team.

How good are you at negotiating? I thought I was great at it until I raised my daughter. I tried the normal phrases parents use when their children are about to do something stupid. I chose, *If all of your friends jumped off a bridge, would you do it too?* Her response at nine years old was, *where is this fictional bridge? I'd like to see it before I answer that question.* Now our negotiations result in me paying her credit card bills and student loans on time while she is in college; I lose all and any money negotiations. Of course, I'm kidding (not really), but negotiation is a key aspirational skill that project managers need to hone, especially when trying to acquire resources from functional managers. I've learned the hard way that negotiating with functional managers for their best resources often ends with acquiring the only resource they want to unload from their team. Their problem is now yours. Therefore, honing your negotiation skills is important.

I'll share a negotiating trick with you that I learned (by accident, actually): the person who talks first loses in most negotiations. Being an American, I am not used to the haggling that occurs in other countries when shopping. I ask, *How much?* they tell me, and I say, *Here you go,* and pay full price. I traveled to Thailand a couple years ago to do seminars for a client and while I was there I went to a street market where they sold a variety of items. At the time, I was looking to buy a piece of jade jewelry for myself (my daughter ended up with it), and when I found one I liked I asked, *How much?*

I should preface all of this with the fact that I'm a bit mathematically challenged and basically needed a currency exchange app to determine the American dollar to the Thai baht, but didn't have my phone with me. So, when the shop owner said the jade is 5,000 baht I stood there with a dumb look on my face trying to do the exchange in my head and was saying nothing. *Okay, okay, 4,000 baht.* D 'oh! I'd just figured out 5,000 and now I have to do the math again. Same dumb look. Still not speaking. *Okay, okay, 1,000 baht.* The only words I uttered were *Do you take dollars?* Because at that point, I knew it was much lower than my original math and even if I were totally wrong in my calculations, I was comfortable with the numbers. I learned a valuable negotiating skill that day. By saying nothing, it forced the other person to fill the space and all of a sudden I had new jewelry. I couldn't wait to try the tactic on my husband! Unfortunately, he knows that little trick already so sadly no new jewelry to report. Other than family members, it's a good trick when trying to acquire resources via negotiation.

It's also important to know several things about your projects before entering said negotiation. Preparation is key in any negotiation, but in this case it's for a cohesive team or additional resources to round out your current team, so it's important to know what you are looking for and prepare to do some haggling.

The information to have prepared is as follows:

- Dates of acquisition and release, to the best of your ability.
- What skills are needed from the resource?
- Whether that resource will be full- or part-time on your project.
- How you will track their performance and report on it.
- Whether that person is working on other projects at the program level.
- Virtual or colocated?

I also like to ask the potential resource (if possible) whether they want to work on the project. I find this to be important because if they don't want to work on the project, you may be dealing with a poor attitude during their tenure. I would much rather acquire a person with a great attitude with fewer skills than a rock star with a poor attitude.

Just like projects, borrowed resources are temporary and therefore you will need to develop your team so that they perform well and are successful. Therefore, it is important to plan for your human resources much like you would plan for scope of work or your schedules, budgets, and the like.

Human resource planning

Most of the human resource planning is determining roles and responsibilities, so they can be clearly expressed to your team, as well as how team communication will occur. It is also important to clearly understand the chain of command, as well as your expectations on performance reporting. Organizational charts and position descriptions can help with this. The organizational chart is a hierarchical, visual overview of department heads and their teams. This can be useful if you are new to an organization or if you are trying to figure out which functional departments you might need to engage with to suit your project team needs. I'm also a huge fan of creating a **project organizational chart**, especially if you have a large team, multiple stakeholders, and possibly remote or virtual team members. This is good for communication and excellent for those times when someone comes to your office with loads of questions when they need to be taking those questions to someone else. It helps keep things organized. If we go with the assumption that you have a core team of people to help you plan and that you may need to acquire others to help with execution, it's safe to say that you will need to determine who does what. You may know your team well and what their skillsets are so that may be the easy part, but if you acquire others, you need to know what gaps they are filling. In some cases, you may not even know people's names yet because they haven't been acquired or negotiated for, but you do know the role or skills needed for the project. Either way, a **responsibility-assignment matrix (RAM)** may be immensely helpful.

In *Figure 7.1*, you can see a very generic RAM that shows what activities need additional resources to execute the work and how many are needed. You can adapt the RAM as you get further into planning and add names and other necessary information, but for now we'll keep things simple:

WBS Code of Accounts	Team Role 1	Team Role 2	Team Role 3	Team Role 4	Team Role 5
1.3.5	2			3	8
1.3.6		1		1	
1.3.7	1		5		7
1.3.8				2	
1.3.9			3		1
1.3.10	5				
1.3.11			3		3

Figure 7.1 A generic RAM showing activities that need additional resources

Another way you can represent resources and roles is by using a **RACI chart**.

RACI stands for:

- **Responsible**: People who execute the work
- **Accountable**: People who will be held liable for the result of the task's execution
- **Consulted**: People who can provide expert judgment on the task at hand
- **Informed**: People that need to be updated about the task progress

RACI charts are a great and effortless way to show resource needs and allocation visually. Sometimes people wonder whether someone can be both responsible and accountable, and the answer to that is yes, they can. The goal is to keep the RACI chart as simple as possible and use it as a guide to fill gaps, review allocation, and help the team determine their experts and communication strategy for the tasks.

In *Figure 7.2*, you can see a simple RACI chart:

RACI Chart	Person				
Task	Ann	Ben	Carlos	Dina	Ed
Create charter	A	R	I	I	I
Collect requirements	I	A	R	C	C
Submit change request	I	A	R	R	C
Develop test plan	A	C	I	I	R
R = Responsible	A = Accountable		C = Consult		I = Inform

Figure 7.2 A simple RACI chart

Know what the acronyms RAM and RACI stand for in case you get a question on it and be aware that a type of RAM is a RACI chart.

Of course, these are not the only ways to plan for your human resources, and most of us will schedule out our resources across multiple tasks that need to be accomplished throughout the project without trying to over-allocate Karen in the process. Whatever works best for you and the team is the right way to plan for resources.

Whether you use org charts, negotiation with functional managers, submit resourcing needs through a procurement department, beg, borrow, or steal your resources, it's never a bad idea to have an idea as to how you will acquire, reward, recognize, motivate, release, and manage your team of individuals.

Developing a performing team

Even if you have worked with the same people for years, it's still a good idea to understand human behavior and how a team of individuals work their way up to the full performance level as a team. The other thing to consider is that you may be very new to project management. Maybe you were awesome at your job and got promoted to project manager and now you oversee people who you used to work with in the trenches. I call this being an accidental project manager. This can be difficult because many organizations rarely provide management training to their new managers and instead provide the trial-by-fire and school-of-hard-knocks version instead.

Even more important than executing the work, having pretty Gantt charts, and making sure your sponsor is happy, is being able to guide, manage, and motivate your team, because a motivated team will typically perform well. I say typically this because I've seen a high-performing team's epic fail due to scope creep and customer interference, and low-performing teams knock a project out of the park and get all sorts of accolades for their *impressive performance.* It's frustrating to see that happen, but it does.

All we can do is our best on the human side of project management. Some days you will be a rock star at it, some days you will feel like you are chasing squirrels around a yard, and still other days you will wonder whether project management is right for you. It is, or you wouldn't feel that way. Self-awareness is an important skill!

Don't worry, we are going to dive deep into the project team psyche, review some cool human motivational theories from the experts, and hopefully generate some ideas to help you manage, motivate, team-build, and understand your team.

One particularly important caveat before we begin this journey is there isn't any way that I, CompTIA, or PMI® could ever tell you the exact way to do all of this. The reason is because we don't know your team like you do. We don't know the personalities, the career goals, or the challenges of your team. Therefore, we are all going to pass it over to the experts and theorists of motivation and team-building with the hopes that you will answer questions correctly on your exam and glean some additional information to help you with the human side.

Our first theorist is psychologist Dr. Bruce Tuckman, who created the team-development model unsurprisingly called **Tuckman's ladder**. Tuckman theorized that all teams go through certain levels of development, and at each level there is a variety of input necessary from the manager. In *Figure 7.3*, you can see the ladder in its simplest form:

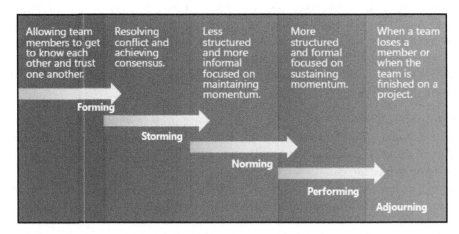

Figure 7.3 Tuckman's ladder

Tuckman believed that to reach the level of true performance, the team had to adapt, adjust, and grow, and part of that was through resolving conflict. Of course, there are people you may work with that love the drama! Someone's name just popped into your head, didn't it? Most conflict in team development is functional conflict, which is how teams deal with being behind schedule, reaching consensus, and making collective decisions.

There is also a varying level of necessary influence from you, the project manager. In forming, the team is very much looking to you to set expectations and explain the vision of the project. In this stage, the team is pretty much on their best behavior. You may have a mix of people who have worked together and some who have not, but at this stage, everyone is saying things like, *Great to work with you, Excited for this project to begin,* and other such niceties. Eventually, the storm clouds will roll in and people will start to show their true colors and begin to disagree on a variety of things. They will figure out people's work styles and whether it works for them and so on. We hope for functional conflict, but sometimes personality clashes occur as well, and it may be necessary for you to have a private meeting to help them work through it.

The team is still very much dependent on the project manager to *parent* until they can begin to normalize and agree to disagree as needed. In *norming*, you can begin to step away a bit and focus on other things. Even though they will still look to you, you may be doing less squirrel organization and more of your own work. When the team reaches the performing level, they can work on their own and are executing effectively. You will be in the role of updater, coach, facilitator, and communicator.

Adjourning was added to Tuckman's ladder later after testing his theory for a while. It was determined that when someone leaves the team, the team will have to adjust to the new normal again. If a new person joins the team, then they start forming, storming, norming, and then performing again. Much faster this time of course, but still the adjustment is necessary.

Virtual teams

This may be an appropriate time to discuss the differences between colocated teams and remote or virtual teams. Remote workers are becoming more and more the norm in many industries around the world, and having virtual employees is great for organizations who can downsize their building complexes and hire from all around the world. While there are many benefits to virtual teams, there are also some downsides, many of which rest squarely on team-building and communication. It's tough to do team-building with a virtual team, even with all the technology we have available to us. It's much more realistic to get everyone together at some point in the project to allow the team to get to know each other and work together. I'm a virtual team member and my headquarters is on the other side of the country. We stay in contact via conference calls, emails, and the like, but at least twice a year we all go out to have face-to-face meetings and engage in team-building efforts. It's a bit easier in our virtual environment since we are all instructors, and must engage with our live virtual classes on a regular basis. We are used to it. For others on a project team, it may be more difficult to build a performing team. Difficult but not impossible. The hardest part is informal communication and team-building. Because of this, it will be important to create a communication strategy that works for your team.

 Most of the Project+ exam is focused on colocated teams and how they work together, which makes the questions easier to answer. You may get a question or two about virtual teams and what the challenges are, but for the most part, the exam focuses on teams that are all working together in the same building, at the same time.

No matter whether you have a colocated or virtual team, it is important to lead by example and build trust among your team members. The way to do that is to practice transparent communication to make sure there are no misunderstandings about the project, the roles, expectations, and what the project vision is. Trust-building on a project team includes the same practices you would use to build trust with anyone. Practice honesty and empathy, respect others no matter what their situation, act on performance problems in a timely manner, and actively listen to your team.

Active listening is probably the hardest because our brains are going 8,00 miles a minute and we may think we are listening, but instead we may be thinking about why the project is behind schedule, what you need to do after work, and how badly you need caffeine right at that very moment. Active listening means quieting all that noise and focusing on the message another person is sending you. This is not only verbal, it is also tone and body language. In fact, according to the experts, 55% of all face-to-face communication is conveyed via body language. 38% is tone of voice, and only about 7% are the words coming out of the other person's mouth. Yikes! Guess what happens when you take away the face-to-face? You got it, tone takes over. Therefore, you read and re-read your emails because you are checking for tone (and spelling and grammar).

Unfortunately, perception is reality, and even if the tone sounds good in your mind, it may come off differently to the other person. I bring this up because on virtual teams, much of your communication will be via the written word with less opportunity to explain yourself. This is originally why emoji were created, to take the place of body language. That way, if your tone sounds sarcastic and you put a crying laughing face, the receiver knows you are just kidding. Emoji aren't necessarily business-appropriate in all industries. Can you imagine an attorney filing a brief with emoji? Insert crying laughing face here! But you will know in your industries what is appropriate and what isn't.

If you don't have the type of industry where emoji are used, it may be more important to make your message clear and check your tone while doing it. It's also important to understand how communication happens in other countries, especially if you have a customer or a team member who lives outside of your own country. Some communication is low-context and other communication is high-context. Low-context communication is extremely specific and clearly spelled out, weighing very heavily on the words that are used. In high-context communication, the way the message is said is more important than the words that are written or expressed. It's never a bad idea to do some research if you have a multicultural team. This is another way to build trust among your team.

Motivational theories

Your ability to manage your team effectively may come down to how you reward, recognize, and motivate. Remember the caveat though, we can't *tell* you how to do any of this – all we can do is provide information that is found on the exam, along with my hope that it will spark some interest and help you uncover some ways to motivate your team.

What are you motivated by? Is it money? Is it the work itself? Is it taking care of your family? What would you say is your greatest motivation?

Permit me a sidebar here with a theory that isn't the most well-received in the motivational guru world; the theory is that people can be inspired but they can't be motivated by someone else. My thought behind this is that people go to see motivational speakers for whatever they need to help themselves with in life. When they are there, they engage in a lot of adrenaline, high fives, and tools to begin to adapt their behaviors. Three days later, the euphoria wears off and many are back in old patterns, with nothing having changed. Instead, they must be inspired to change, and then be self-motivated to make the changes stick.

With that in mind, it is important to recognize human behavior in such a way that you are not responsible for the challenges of your team members, especially if you have done everything you can to help them, guide them, and coach them. It simply comes down to the fact that they either are not inspired, and if so, they are not self-motivated. That could be for a variety of reasons, but you can only do what you can do. I ran large teams and every day I would ask myself, *How can I help my team be successful today?* That was my inspiration to get to know everyone, their kids' names, their birthdays, their personalities, and work styles/habits. Then and only then could I help the individual reach for success. But they had to want it. Our job is to inspire and guide and help where we can. The motivational theorists we are about to cover understood human behavior and were collating theories that could help explain the behavior of humans and humans at work.

There are four theorists you will review and all four could be found in questions on your exam:

- Abraham Maslow's Hierarchy of Needs
- Douglas McGregor's Theory X and Theory Y
- Frederick Herzberg's Theory of Hygiene
- David McClelland's Theory of Needs

Maslow's hierarchy of needs

In 1943, Abraham Maslow posited his theory of needs after studying hundreds of individuals and found that all humans have basic needs that must be met before they can strive for or attain other things. In *Figure 7.4*, you will see a basic overview of the hierarchy of needs, and then I'll break each one down. Many of you may already be familiar with this theory as it typically shows up in psychology classes or in management training (both can feel like the same thing):

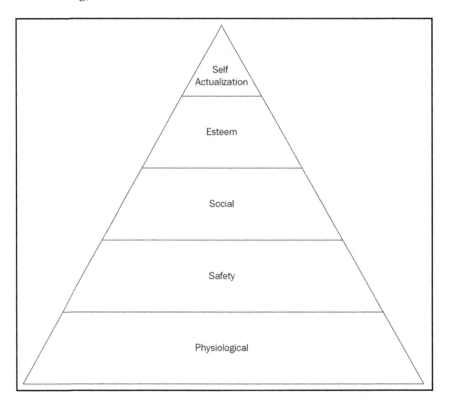

Figure 7.4 Hierarchy of needs

The theory starts at the bottom of the hierarchy with physiological needs, and goes up as a visual way of representing growth or moving up to the top of the hierarchy, which is self-actualization.

Physiological needs

All humans need air, food and water, shelter, and sleep. Without those basic needs, the human will not survive, and if they are in the process of lacking any of those variables, that will be all they can think about. If you are starving, you will think about food constantly, if you're thirsty or can't breathe, same thing. It would make sense that those needs would come first. Lack of sleep can affect every aspect of your lives, so thank goodness for caffeine!

Safety needs

Humans need to feel safe in their surroundings and their lives. Once the basic human needs of air, food, and water are met, safety needs become the dominant concern or need. Safety falls under numerous categories, including personal safety, psychological or emotional safety, financial security, and health and well-being. Safety is another core need and if you live in a war-torn or poverty-stricken country or are suffering personally or psychologically, those impacts will be at the center of your life. Safety is necessary for all humans.

Social needs

Humans need to feel a sense of belonging and have friendships and relationships. Sometimes the social need can far outweigh the other core needs of physiological and safety needs, especially in young children. The need to be loved and have relationships on the individual and group levels is extraordinarily strong in humans, and if someone feels like they are being shunned or avoided in groups of people, it will lead to depression. I think now about all the keyboard warriors on social media who shun and ostracize people who do not agree with their thought processes or opinions. Bullying and other types of removal of social acceptance are devastating at all ages.

Once the physiological, safety, and social core needs are met, the person can begin to seek esteem.

Esteem needs

Esteem involves our ego and the need for respect. Maslow believed that there are two core levels of the esteem need. First, the need of respect from others and self-respect. People who have low self-esteem, those who need recognition or accolades from others, will seek external validation over self-respect. Those who are respected by others can focus more on self-respect. One doesn't lead to the other though and it may be a constant struggle for some. You have seen cases of famous people who took their own lives due to low self-esteem or depression, even though the world loved and revered them. That is a sad example, but strikingly like Maslow's thoughts on the matter. With that, let's focus on the top of the hierarchy, with self-actualization.

Self-actualization

What is your full potential? Have you realized it? Then you have reached self-actualization. No? Don't feel bad about that, many people don't reach self-actualization, which is essentially saying all the other needs have been totally and fully met and you have a powerful desire to meet a difficult-to-obtain goal or something that you aspire to be great at. A great musician, a great football player, a great public speaker. Once one has achieved it, one has reached self-actualization. If you have the motivation to accomplish something and be the most you can be, you are experiencing the pinnacle of Maslow's theory.

Later in life, Maslow also added self-transcendence, which is a more spiritual way of being and doing things for the good of the universe and an understanding of it. I met five Buddhist monks in Thailand and they had reached self-transcendence. For the rest of us earthly folks, it may be a bit of a struggle to reach that with bills to pay, children to raise, friends, family, and the day-to-day in 2018. Therefore, you won't see self-transcendence on most models of Maslow's theory.

You may get a question on Maslow's hierarchy of needs in one of two ways. One is the simple question of what the highest level of Maslow's hierarchy of needs is. The correct answer would be self-actualization. You may also see a situational scenario that describes a team member and where they are in the hierarchy and you would need to match the scenario to the correct level. Most of the questions are not too difficult on this subject; it's more difficult to work through them in the real world.

Douglas McGregor's theory X and theory Y

Maslow really set the stage for an influx of human-behavior specialists who were trying to determine how people were managed and motivated in organizations. Doulas McGregor created Theory X and Y in the 1950s and later adapted it in the 1960s, and frankly not much has changed since then with this theory. McGregor studied workforce motivation by management and postulated that management styles fall into two categories: the X manager and the Y manager.

X managers

Managers that conform to the X style of management essentially go through their lives with the assumption that they must micromanage their employees because their team doesn't really want to work. They believe each person is there for a paycheck only and must be forced to do their jobs with the threat of punishment. They are **authoritarian managers**.

This could be based on the personality of the manager or it could be because of how they perceive their roles and the motivation and performance of their teams. I worked for a theory X manager once (notice the usage of the past tense) and never again. They were the type of person to wear t-shirts that said things such as, *Morale will improve, or the beatings will continue.* But let's face it, there are some jobs and some employees who are at work for their own self-interests; they want a paycheck because they need it, but they don't really want to work. You often find them in the break room for the 95th time in an hour. It's tough to be a manager when you have staff like that, and some may have to resort to threats and punishment to get everyone back on track.

Y managers

Y managers are much more my style as they are **participative** in nature and rarely find themselves needing to micromanage their team. Usually when you have a performing team, it is unnecessary to do so. If you don't, then this style would act as more of a coach and facilitator to guide performance and help the team member. There is a downside to being a participative manager, though. I found this out with my first large team, and that is you get totally run over by your team if you are too nice. There is an exceptionally fine line between being a manager and being a coach. Finding that balance is important and if the time comes when you must micromanage one or several team members, then that is what you need to do. For the most part, I'm more geared toward being a Y manager because it suits my personality and I enjoy developing people to be successful in their careers. That is the reason I teach and write. I want you to be successful on your exams and in your position, and I want to help where I can. Some see that as a weakness, so have an X in your back pocket as needed, but focus on building your relationships with your team and get them to that performing stage, if they aren't there already.

Frederick Herzberg's theory of hygiene

Frederick Herzberg began his research in the 1950s and developed what has been called the two-factor theory or the theory of hygiene. It's not what you think, although shower-fresh employees are always appreciated. Instead, hygiene in this case means health. How healthy is your organization? Herzberg basically separated **satisfiers** and **motivators** from each other to show that satisfiers must be in place so that the employee could be motivated, and if they weren't in place then demotivation would occur, and people would leave the organization. In *Figure 7.5*, you can see the differences between hygiene needs or satisfiers and true motivators:

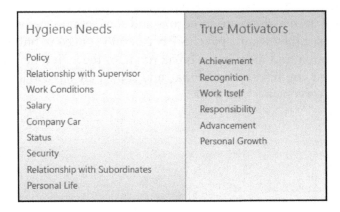

Hygiene Needs	True Motivators
Policy	Achievement
Relationship with Supervisor	Recognition
Work Conditions	Work Itself
Salary	Responsibility
Company Car	Advancement
Status	Personal Growth
Security	
Relationship with Subordinates	
Personal Life	

Figure 7.5 Hygiene needs versus true motivators

Even though this isn't an exhaustive list, Herzberg wanted companies to know that they had to have several perks in place and good working conditions, health care, time off, and the like, to recruit and retain good employees. Without those things, they would leave or be demotivated. Did you notice that salary is a satisfier? If I had asked you if you were money-motivated at the beginning of this, I'm sure the answer would have been a resounding YES! Let me ask the same question from Herzberg's perspective. Have you ever worked at a job that you totally loved but they didn't pay you enough money to survive and you eventually left? That is because that satisfier was missing. Everything else was great but that one thing led you to another position and maybe even one you don't like as much, but hey you've got bills to pay. Make sense?

The true motivators are when people have the satisfiers they need to stay at the position and then experience reward, recognition, achievement, and personal growth on top of that. Now, your team is happy and feels safe. Much like Maslow's safety level, many things must be in place organizationally to truly motivate your team.

David McClelland's theory of needs

In a survey published in 2002, McClelland was listed and ranked as the 15th most cited psychologist of the 20th century and there is a good reason for that. His theory of needs is applicable in many situations and he believed that all humans could be taught to change their behaviors once they understood what their driving factors or needs were. The theory states that all humans, regardless of where they grew up, whether they are male or female, and their cultural heritage were driven by three needs:

- The need for achievement
- The need for power
- The need for affiliation

McClelland felt that all humans have a mix of all three needs, but one stands out more than the rest in individuals. Once you determine what that core need is, you can drive their behavior to change or use it to motivate the employee because you understand what is driving them internally.

The need for achievement

People whose driving need is achievement tend to be risk-averse when it comes to taking on things they don't think they will be successful at. They also tend to want to work alone in a commission-based environment or work on their part of a project without a whole lot of collaboration. If you recognize this need in yourself or a team member, it's important to realize that training, guidance, checklists, cheat sheets, and feedback on a regular basis are necessary for achievement. To motivate these folks, as their manager, it's important to let them know the path to success in very specific terms, guide them when needed or asked, and let them know when they have achieved success and why they got there. Specific feedback and specific praise for their taken actions are key.

The need for power

The theory on power states that there are really two distinct driving power factors. One is **personal power** and one is **institutional power.**

Personal power seekers were looked upon as a *negative condition* by McClelland, as he felt that people who sought power for their own needs were probably not the kind of people you would want to invite to dinner. Those who strive for power don't care who they hurt to get there. The *I win, you lose* mentality. That's fine when you are in friendly competition in a sporting event or you beat someone in a board game. *HAHA I win AGAIN!* Then it's okay. This type of person would be chronically competitive and seek to replace their manager just to see whether they can. I wouldn't be surprised if you know someone like that or recognize that trait in some of our world leaders. There wasn't much advice from the theory on how to deal with this type of person, other than avoidance if possible.

People who have a need for **institutional power** are those that seek higher positions in an organization for the good of the organization. They want to be leaders, managers, presidents, and CEOs, and they seek promotion. To help motivate this type of power-seeker, you can provide them with more responsibilities, a lateral title change, or help them get promoted. I always felt that I couldn't move up or move out until I had someone effective to replace me. Not every manager feels that way, but I always tried to help my people get promotions or better positions within or outside the company. One thing to keep in mind is that people who have a need for institutional power have an exceptionally low need for **affiliation power.** Institutional power people could lay off employees during the holidays because it was good for the corporate bottom line and then sleep fine that night. Affiliation-oriented people would never sleep again.

The need for affiliation

People who have affiliation needs just want to be around people, they seek acceptance from the group and they want people to like them. These are those bubbly types at work that notice your new haircut before your significant other does, who ask you about your weekend, and want to know where you shop for your clothes. They are happy, chatty, and people-oriented people. The fastest way to demotivate affiliation-oriented people is to put them by themselves, in a dark bottom-floor room with only a red stapler to keep them company. If you have seen the movie, then you know what I'm referring to, if you haven't, that's okay too. It's important to know that to motivate affiliation-oriented people, they need to be told that people like them, that their team appreciates all they do, and that they are doing a fantastic job. They need a pat on the back, a lot! They will also be very gracious once they receive kudos for superior performance and most likely say they couldn't have done it without their team.

Have you recognized yourself in any of the examples? How about your team members, could you list out their main motivating need or factor? If so, you are well on your way to a tailored approach to motivate your team members individually.

Peter Drucker's management by objective (MBO)

Peter Drucker was a large influencing factor in organizational development as a management consultant. In 1954, based on a book he wrote, Drucker created the SMART mnemonic. That may be familiar to you if you have attended any management training courses. It was a big deal in the 1990s when I was going through my management training at a large software company, and I'm still writing about it today. The reason setting SMART objectives is so important is because as a manager, you are working together with your team members to help them be successful. Even though this isn't necessarily a motivational theory, it is highly rewarding as a coach or team member to see success occur and to meet goals that may have seemed unattainable prior to the objectives being set. In *Figure 7.6*, you will see the SMART mnemonic:

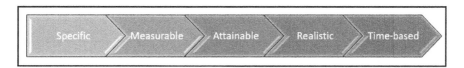

Figure 7.6 SMART mnemonic

Specific

Setting specific goals is the first step in attaining those goals. I read an article that stated that most people who make New Year's resolutions never keep them. This may be why the workout facilities and gyms are full in January, but totally empty come March. This is because the resolutions were not specific. *I want to travel more, I want to get healthy, I want to make more money.* These are wishes not goals, and that is the reason why they are impossible to meet. There is nothing quantitative about the statements and thereby no path to follow to get where you want to go. I had a boss who loved to say things such as, *You all need to do a better job.* Umm okay... at what? Nothing specific means nothing can improve.

Measurable

To track progress, it is important to know how what the goals are and how to measure those goals. This is where even milestones are an effective way to measure progress. Typically, once you have a specific goal in mind, you can determine how to measure the progress toward that goal. Instead of *I want to get healthy,* the specifics could be *I want to lose 10 pounds.* Then we can start to look at how to measure that. *I want to lose 10 pounds in 4 months, and that means I want to lose 2.5 pounds a month.* That is something that can be measured. Did you, or didn't you?

Attainable

This asks the question of whether it is even possible to meet that goal. In my example of weight loss, people do it all the time! Not me, but you know *people.* Is it something that the team member can do, and if not, there may need to be an adjustment to the goal or they may need some training, mentoring, or coaching to get them there. This isn't a race, so make sure when you are setting measurements that you take the time it will take to attain the goal into account. If they can't do it, they will become demotivated and deflated, so we as managers need to make sure that they have or can attain the skill sets to meet the proposed objective.

Realistic

Realistic may sound a lot like attainable, but in this case, we are trying to determine whether this is something they should be working on right now. Is it a realistic goal to be pursuing right now or at all? Maybe not. If I have a team member who is my schedule coordinator (yay!), it may not be realistic to pull them away from that and help them attain the goal of doing my budget for me or losing 10 pounds for me.

Trust me, if I could hire someone to do that for me I'd be a happy, happy thin person. My point is this: if what you are trying to attain isn't realistic at the time and it is pulling the team member away from things they need to be focused on right now, then it isn't realistic. If it's a skill they want to attain, it's something you can work with them on at another time if it isn't realistic right now.

Time-based

All goals must have a finish line, or we would never reach them. If you like to procrastinate, then you know what I'm saying when I describe no finish line. I have at least 20 years left on my mortgage to clean the garage, so I can put it off indefinitely is a good example of this. 20 years is too far out. Even though it has a finish line, it's too much time and any skills learned could be lost. It's important to have a deadline to goal-attainment or at least to see how far the team member has come at the time-based deadline. *I want to lose 10 pounds in 4 months, and that means I want to lose 2.5 pounds a month.* After 4 months, the goal was to lose 10 pounds. If at month four, I step on the scale and have lost four pounds, which is highly likely, then it could be my original goal wasn't attainable, but I have made some progress. It's important to celebrate those achievements, even if the goal wasn't met. Please say we are celebrating with cake!

One thing about setting SMART objectives is to work with the team member on their goals. You are not dictating to them, you are working with them to set those goals. Most people know their limitations and what they want to achieve, they may just not know the road map to achievement and that is where you come in. Help them help themselves. Another rule of thumb I follow for myself and when coaching other people is that I don't set more than three objectives to meet at any given time. This isn't a laundry list of improvements or goal-setting. Keep it SMART.

Ability and **willingness** is also something I keep in mind when setting goals with my team as a group or as individuals. I ask myself and the person whether they have the ability to do the work being asked of them. Saying, *Do a better job,* when they don't have the ability to improve is the single worst coaching tactic you can use. They will be demotivated and still not be able to achieve what you are asking. At that point, it is up to us to get them some training and help mentor and coach them to success. That is so much easier than a willingness issue. If your team member isn't improving because they simply don't want to, or they are pushing back because change is being asked and they have always done something a certain way, you may be in for a battle of wills.

If the team member doesn't have the willingness to improve or change when being asked, it may be time to have a serious conversation. Typically, this type of personality situation ends up in the HR department or with written warnings. It may be best to remove this person from your team (if possible) because they are negative, and not helping the team be successful. Lack of willingness and personality problems are few and far between. For the most part, we are all adults and professional people so hopefully that isn't what you are experiencing. Those are also the types where your X manager personality may show, and if nothing works, it may be time to call the game because of rain.

Rewards and recognition

The ability to reward and recognize is an important skill in management. How you go about doing that depends on your team and your organizational culture. If your organization doesn't already have reward and recognition built into their culture or their budgets, it may be time to get creative. There have been many times in my career where I reached into my own pocket and bought my team lunch or brought coffee or candy bars, and even let my team go early on a Friday if they had worked hard that week meeting a deadline. It's not that you are creating an expectation that every time they work hard they will get something. You don't want a team demotivated because they aren't rewarded the way they think they should be every single time. Setting good expectations and SMART goals and then sticking to your side of the bargain is a good place to begin. It's tough to motivate until you truly know your team on an individual level, but it is a good thing to keep in mind that certain personality types do not like public displays of recognition. How would you feel if you were pulled up on a stage in front of everyone and given a reward for good work? Would that make you uncomfortable? Would you think twice before doing that exact thing again? Sure, you would! Still, others on your team may crave that recognition and wonder where the heck the cake is. Sometimes the best way is a simple thank you for your arduous work on XYZ and keep doing what you are doing. The best practice for the exam states that a formal system of reward and recognition is a large part of human-resource planning, and if you have the bandwidth to create a system and the support of the organization, then it's easier. The other best suggested practice is to allocate money in the project budget for reward and recognition. I'll pause here for virtual laughter...

Conflict resolution

Conflict isn't about if, it's about when. Remember, all teams go through storming and even though most conflict will be considered functional conflict, there could be some dysfunctional conflict going on as well. Much like I couldn't tell you how to motivate your team of individuals specifically, nor can I give you exact resolutions for conflict on your unique team. The only way to address conflict-resolution is by presenting categories of strategies and which work better than the others.

Certainly, we would love it if every conflict was resolved in a solution-oriented manner where everyone walks away happy, but that is rarely the case.

What would you say is the number one cause of conflict on your team?

- Lack of communication?
- Personality issues?
- Unclear expectations?
- Work styles and habits?
- Being behind schedule or over budget?
- Lack of resources?
- Scope creep?
- Unexpected risk events?
- All of the above?

There are a variety of reasons why a team would have a conflict situation. Sometimes, it's just a couple of people, sometimes the whole team is trying to work through a situation. Remember, during storming, you oversee guiding your team through conflict resolution, the hope being that the team will eventually figure out how to play nicely together so you can stop parenting. Other times, the team stays in storming or the project itself is a bit of a nightmare and everyone is cranky about it.

 You will get questions on the Project+ exam that describe a conflict situation and how it was handled, and you will need to select the best resolution that matches the situation as presented. You may also be asked whether a resolution is win/win, win/lose, or lose/lose.

There are six categories of resolution for conflict; as you review them, ask yourself which resolution strategy you prefer:

- Confrontation and problem-solving
- Compromise

- Smoothing
- Forcing
- Avoiding
- Negotiating

Confrontation and problem-solving

This resolution strategy is considered win/win and the best, longest-lasting way to manage a conflict situation. This is because it is solution-oriented. The team or individuals will discuss ways to resolve the conflict and agree on the solution. This is a bit of perfect-world conflict resolution and is easier said than done. In fact, this is the most time-consuming of all solutions because it may take some time and effort to get everyone on the same page and reach an agreement. This strategy is best used when there is a disagreement in the way a functional conflict should be managed. We are behind schedule and one team member thinks if they just had more help they would move faster, and the other thinks fast-tracking is the way to go to protect the budget and not involve more people. In that case, both parties will be heard, and decisions can be made. If the disagreement is based on something personal and each party feels strongly about it, a solution may not be attained. Imagine someone trying to convince you that your favorite sports team was the wrong choice. Yeah... no.

Compromise

Believe it or not, compromise is considered a lose/lose strategy because both sides must give up something to reach a conclusion; it is, however, useful. This is especially the case when a decision or resolution needs to be made quickly, and if each party feels they gave up the same amount to move forward. If one party feels like they gave up more than the other party, there may be some residual conflict that shows up later in the project. Until then, compromise is a typical strategy. Lose/lose, but useful, especially if confronting and solving the conflict isn't possible.

Smoothing

Smoothing is considered win/win, but a short-term fix to a conflict situation because its focus is on commonalities between the parties and not the differences. I look at this like smoothing ruffled feathers. The parties may feel good about things in the short term and then go home and think about it or perhaps talk to their people and realize they are still not happy about it and that nothing was resolved.

The next day, they may come back with the same issues. That is why smoothing is best used in combination with collaboration and compromise. It just may be necessary to calm the situation down to do so.

Forcing

Forcing should be used sparingly because it's the equivalent of telling your children to knock it off and stop fighting with each other. This is a win/lose strategy and can breed more hostility and conflict if used too often. It may be necessary upon occasion, on your team as with your children, to lay down the law – especially if there is a compliance or regulatory need a team member disagrees with. That's a, *Too bad, so sad, do it anyway* conversation. It also may be necessary if a very quick decision needs to be made and you must make it. We are fast-tracking instead of crashing; end of story, let's move on and get it done.

Avoiding

I don't know many people who enjoy conflict, although there are those who enjoy drama and wreaking havoc. You know who they are, and you avoid them at all costs. When it comes to conflict though, avoiding is considered lose/lose. Trying to get away from the conflict doesn't make it go away – it only makes things worse and prolongs the issue. There are situations though where something called strategic avoidance is necessary. This could be because of a very heated or dangerous escalation of conflict. Another way to utilize this strategy is if you are all sitting around a conference room table and nothing is getting accomplished; everyone is cranky and tired – let them all go and shelve the conversation for another time when everyone has had some rest and downtime to consider the alternatives. I'm self-aware enough to know I am very avoidant of conflict in general and try ridiculously hard not to stir the pot or create drama or conflict, but it does occur on teams and it does need to be handled. Therefore, I need to pull my head out of the sand, be solution-oriented, and face the music. Conflict simply cannot be avoided sometimes in our chosen profession.

Negotiating

The last technique is negotiating. I mentioned that this is considered an aspirational skill, and the one that I work on the most. It may be that to truly get through the conflict, some negotiation is necessary for true resolution. Usually this is combined with compromise. Negotiate to reach a compromise. The other time you see this is in procurement, when there is a disagreement to terms and conditions and an alternative dispute resolution is needed. This technique is considered win/win if the conversation is facilitated effectively on personal conflict. In functional conflicts it is a necessary skill to hone as it may be used more often than not. The best course of action is to negotiate when you understand your side of things, listen actively to the other party, and reach a win/win agreement.

As we wrap up this part of the chapter on human motivation, team development, and conflict-resolution, just know that if you are new to your position, things will happen, and you will learn from them. Nobody ever enters this role for the very first time knowing exactly how to manage a team of people. It's best to get to know them on an individual level, see what makes them tick, and what their works styles are, and then you can begin to craft your style. It's always a work in progress, it's always an aspirational skill all managers strive to improve upon if we are good at our position and want to improve. You'll get there if you aren't there already.

Monitoring team performance

As we move further through the project and begin to monitor project performance, you'll see that there is a big focus on the constraints of scope, time, and cost. But how is your team performing? If you have a core team you work with all the time, you may oversee their performance reviews. On the team level, it is important to keep an eye on how they are performing as a team. We know they will go through the steps of forming to performing and we know that we must motivate, reward, recognize, train, mentor, and coach, but how is all of that going? Are your strategies working? Is your team responding? It's never a bad idea to stop and take a pulse throughout the project to see how your team thinks they are performing and how you view the team's performance. Coaching is necessary, and even if you are setting SMART goals, things on the team level may not be in sync. That doesn't always mean your project is going sideways, it may just mean you have to get out of your office and practice observation and conversation with your team. Step away from the Gantt chart! I was always incredibly happy to do that and hang out with my team. There are numerous templates on the internet that can help guide your team performance assessments. You may find it helpful to create a **Resource Breakdown Structure (RBS)**. This will help you allocate your resources across work more specifically and visually.

Much like the work breakdown structure shows the scope of work broken down to the work-package level, it's sometimes helpful to do the same with your resources to make sure they are where they need to be and allocated appropriately. If you are having team performance issues, this is a good practice to do with them, so they can see what everyone else is doing as well. Something else to keep in mind is that when we move to the next chapter and discuss risk, you may hear of a RBS. The acronym is the same and the visual breakdown is similar, but the RBS for risk would be categories of risk to help determine specific identified risks, rather than resources. You will know whether the question is about risk or resources on the exam, and most acronyms are spelled out unless they are testing on the meaning. In *Figure 7.7*, you will see a simple RBS:

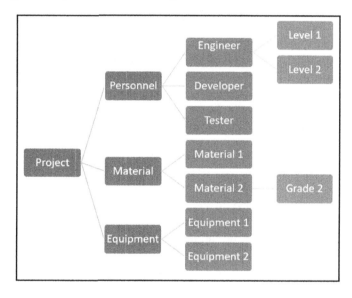

Figure 7.7 Simple RBS

Monitoring team performance is as important as monitoring scope, schedule, and cost performance. Remember, you may have people you have acquired from other departments or have team members via procurement. Keep an eye on how they are all doing and adjust as needed. Provide training, coaching, and mentoring, and be transparent about communication.

Communication considerations

We spend 90% of our time as project managers communicating. My guess is the other 10% is spent on seeking a quiet room to eat lunch in, but the fact remains that we communicate a lot! Whether it's via email, conference calls, meetings about meetings about last week's meeting, Skype, WebEx, or performance reporting and informal communication with our coworkers, we are constantly communicating. The larger the group or team, the more communication channels you will be working through. I look at this as how many ways my message can go horribly, horribly wrong. There isn't just one channel of communication, there is a feedback loop in which we hope our message was understood and the other party or parties respond with what they think they understood, and around and around it goes. For example, if I use the communications channels formula of $N(N-1)/2$ where N represents the amount of people I will be communicating with and then you subtract 1 because the person communicating is already considered, you will see the number of channels of communication. Running this formula will give you a specific number of how communication travels through channels or people, and the possibility of perception issues increase with the number of channels. Now you can see that the more people, the more channels and the more planning for communication.

Let's say I have 20 people on my team including stakeholders. Then the communication channels would look like this:

$$20(20-1)/2 = 190 \; channels$$

If five more people are added, then the channels go up exponentially:

$$25(25-1)/2 = 300 \; channels$$

That is a lot of ways a message can be misinterpreted, because we already know that perception is reality.

You may not be tested on the communication channels formula, but it is a good eye-opener when you have a large team. The greater the number, the more you need to plan for communication.

Much like everything in this chapter, communication is an aspirational skill. We work to improve upon our communication. An effective way that I have learned to improve my communication is mirroring. Mirroring means that you are copying the style of the person or people you are communicating with. This is more difficult face-to-face because of body language and things we do without even knowing, but over email it's remarkably effective. Are you a bullet point writer or a paragraph writer in emails? Are you more casual or more serious? How do you sign your emails? Do you use emoticons/emoji? If I receive an email that is written in a bullet-point format, I respond using that format. If someone sends me a paragraph with a smiley face, I return the in kind. If someone signs off their email with regards, you guessed it, I sign off with regards as well. The only two I won't use regardless of what the sender used is *thanks* and *cheers*. In a lot of cultures, signing your email with *thanks* is seen as dismissive:

> **I'll need that report by 5 PM**
>
> **Thanks**

Instead, try *thank you* or add an exclamation point after to at least show you are grateful for their hard work. I try never to be dismissive, and people know me well enough that if they see a straight up *thanks* on my email I am in no mood for discussion. *Cheers* is the other I don't use and there is an exceptionally good reason for not using it. I am simply not cool enough to do so. I really wish I were though! Other than those two anomalies, I try to mirror communication, read and re-read my emails for tone considerations, and do my best to be clear and concise – not that you would see that side of me in this student guide. Concise is tough, but I'm working on it.

A large part of communication is making sure that you have the right information, in the right format, for the right people, with the right impact, at the right time. That may need to be planned for, so everyone knows how and when to expect reports, meetings, and other communications. I typically let my team and other stakeholders know what to expect on the formal communications level, so I get the right data to update reports and distribute them accordingly.

Kick-off meeting

One of the very first big communications you will enter is your kick-off meeting. This is the meeting where everyone starts to learn about the goals and vision of the project, ask and answer questions, and get everyone's buy-in before work begins. There are a variety of versions as to when the appropriate time for a kick-off meeting is. CompTIA and PMI® would typically recommend that you hold the kick-off meeting after all planning is completed and before you being to execute work. Others may have the kick-off meeting before any planning is done and directly after the project charter has given you authorization to begin project work.

Personally, this is the time I prefer to hold a kick-off meeting because part of my job is to do a benefit analysis on the proposed project and let management know whether we are headed in the right direction before any planning is accomplished. I also believe that a lot of planning can be done in a kick-off meeting. When we go through Chapter 10, *Formal Project or Phase Closure and Agile Project Management*, we'll review some agile best practices and discuss a planning meeting that tends to be several hours long to plot out about a month of work. Kick-off meetings are formal communication but that doesn't mean they aren't collaborative and informal during discussions.

I find it best to have an agenda that I create and send out a couple of days before the kick-off is scheduled to occur. I do this for several reasons. First, if I missed a topic that needs to be discussed, someone can alert me to the need, and I can update the agenda. The second reason is so that anyone I assign to present information is prepared and ready to go. I am not the expert on everything and should not be the only person talking in a kick-off meeting. Therefore, the experts need some time to get their information, presentations, or hand-outs together. This way, they know when they are presenting and for how long. I like to put time frames into my agenda as well, so we don't end up sitting there talking in circles for hours. It's also important to invite any key stakeholders or customers, if possible, to understand their vision of the result and their expectations.

There isn't a wrong way to do a kick-off meeting and how it's done usually is influenced by the organization and the type of project. Best practice states that you have an agenda, you have other speakers and experts, that your team has time to ask and answer questions, and that everyone walks out with a good understanding of what is expected and buy-in is achieved. Remember that if you have any remote or virtual team members, the kick-off may be a bit more difficult, so all considerations for effective communication should be made in advance.

Considerations for virtual teams include the following:

- Time zone
- Language differences
- Lack of body language without video or webcams
- Slang or jargon that may not be understood by customers, or slang that is used locally but not understood in other countries
- The technology you are using
- Lack of buy-in since they can just mute the meeting and check their email

You can see that there are a lot of considerations for the human side of project management and it's an important piece. Without a motivated team who has the skills to achieve the goals of the project and without effective communication up, down, and sideways, the entire project could fail. It doesn't matter how good your schedules, budgets, or scope of work is. Without the human side working well together, the odds of a project being successful are slim. If your organization offers management skills training, take them up on it – you won't regret it!

Summary

In this chapter, you reviewed some common resource management concepts and reviewed how organizational charts and position descriptions can help allocate your resources and determine any gaps in your resourcing needs. Using a RACI chart, or something similar, and RBS, can help you determine how to allocate and whether the allocations are working efficiently for the project. Then, we reviewed several of motivational theorists' beliefs about human behavior as well as categories of conflict-resolution. Monitoring team performance is making sure that your team has what they need. If not, you can provide it to them through excellent communication. We wrapped up this chapter with communication considerations and kick-off-meeting management.

In Chapter 8, *Budget and Contingency Plans for Risk*, you will review how to define the project budget and identify risks to create contingency plans to manage those risk events.

Questions

1. You are the project manager for a large development project. You realize that you will need to acquire another developer from elsewhere in your organization. Which of the following techniques will you use to do this? Choose all that apply:
   - A RACI chart
   - Communication
   - An RBS
   - Negotiation

2. You are a project manager of a large project spanning several departments as well as your customer's organization. What would be the best document to help you get everything documented so protocols are followed for chain of command?
   - Project schedule
   - Project calendar
   - Project organizational chart
   - A RACI chart

3. You and your team are plotting out what tasks need to be done by which resource. Bill is a seasoned team member and wants to know what he will be responsible for. How can you demonstrate to Bill and the rest of your team the tasks and responsibility by team member appropriately?
   - RAM
   - RBS
   - Calendar
   - Project organizational chart

4. One of your stakeholders is asking you to provide a RACI chart to them. What does RACI stand for? Check all that apply:
   - Reasonable
   - Accurate
   - Attainable
   - Consulted
   - Individual
   - Informed
   - Responsible

5. According to Maslow's hierarchy of needs, among the answers given, which of the following is highest of the hierarchy?
   - Social
   - Esteem
   - Physical
   - Safety

6. You have just taken over a team in the middle of a project and after working with your team for a day or two, you recognize that there are some underlying problems and some conflict. What stage of Tuckman's ladder is your team in?
   - Forming
   - Norming
   - Performing
   - Storming

7. You are a team member working on a new project as a borrowed resource. Your project manager seems to delegate a lot of work, and use rewards and punishment as motivation.
   - A SMART manager
   - A *Y* manager
   - An *X* manager
   - A Z manager

8. As a manager, you feel it is especially important to motivate your team at the level they currently are in their hierarchy of needs. One of your team members is struggling at home and is having trouble paying their bills. What level of Maslow's hierarchy of needs is your team member on?
   - Safety
   - Esteem
   - Social
   - Physiological

9. Sam is one of your best team members. He is always on time and very precise in his work. Sam also prefers to work alone rather than collaborate on projects. What is the best way to motivate Sam based on McClelland's theory of needs?
   - Help him work better with the other team members
   - Try to get him promoted as soon as possible
   - Provide specific feedback and training for new skills
   - Give him a raise

10. Lisa is one of your main go-to resources and she is always the first in the conference room setting up chairs and bottles of water. What need is Lisa expressing based on McClelland's Theory of Needs?
    - Personal power
    - Institutional power
    - Achievement
    - Affiliation

11. According to Herzberg's theory of hygiene, which of the following is considered a satisfier?
    - The work itself
    - Recognition
    - Promotions
    - Money

12. Keenan and Abdul are in the conference room discussing different strategies for overcoming a risk event. Keenan disagrees with every suggestion Abdul is adamant about. At first glance, they seem to be having a heated discussion and conflict situation. When you walk in the room you overhear them working through each variable and discussing the best way to fix it. What kind of conflict-resolution strategy are they using?
    - Compromise
    - Smoothing
    - Avoidance
    - Confrontation

13. Ben dislikes conflict and has found himself in a situation with Kali, who emphatically disagrees with Ben's opinion. The problem is that they are arguing over something that has regulatory compliance; Kali disagrees with the process and Ben is trying to convince her to move forward. As a project manager, what type of conflict-resolution strategy should you implement?
    - Forcing
    - Avoidance
    - Confrontation
    - Smoothing

14. Two of your team members are hanging out in the break room discussing last night's news reports on politics. They seem to be a bit heated in their discussion but nothing too serious. What conflict-resolution strategy do you use in this situation?
    - Avoidance
    - Compromise
    - Smoothing
    - Confrontation

15. Your project has been given the green light via a project charter and your team has done some initial planning. You are ready to have a meeting in which everyone gets together to discuss how the project will go. What is the one thing that you should do before that meeting occurs?
    - Invite everyone
    - Create a presentation
    - Send out an agenda
    - Assign people to present

16. You have 12 team members, 4 stakeholders, and 1 customer. How many communication channels do you have?
    - 140
    - 136
    - 16
    - There isn't enough information to answer this question

8
Budget and Contingency Plans for Risk

In this chapter, we will be reviewing a lot of information on cost estimating and how including quality management and risk into your estimates will provide you with a comprehensive, time-phased budgetary baseline. We will also cover tracking the performance of costs and schedules, using the earned-value technique and the formulas that can be used to discover variances from your baselines. Then, we will review risk management and how to identify and manage risks by creating a risk register. We will then review how discovering the *price tags* of potential risks can help you make better project decisions. Lastly, we will review several response categories for managing risk events on your projects.

This chapter will cover the following topics:

- Estimating costs
- Quality management and the cost of quality
- Quality gates and governance gates
- Creating the project budget
- Tracking and reporting cost/schedule performance
- Earned value
- Risk management planning
- SWOT analysis
- Creating the risk register
- Qualitative risk analysis
- Quantitative risk analysis
- Expected monetary value
- Creating risk responses for threats

Estimating costs

The good news about this section is that everyone is aware of money and how budgeting works for their day-to-day lives. It's entirely possible that you will not be managing a budget for your current projects, and if you are, it may only be for the acquisition of materials and equipment.

The CompTIA Project+ exam assumes you will be doing some budgeting for project work and that you will be tracking budgetary performance throughout the project.

Estimating costs is not just about what things cost but whether there are alternatives that can be discovered for the good of the project. This means if one thing costs more than the project's budget, is there an alternative we can use to help protect the budget? This can be a dangerous game though, if you have ever cut corners on costs and received exactly what you have paid for. That dance is consistent in cost management and is also present in procurement management as well.

What does your organization value most? Time, scope, cost, or quality? Many organizations answer that question with cost. Because of that, it will be imperative to do your research, trust in your experts, and come up with a budget your project can probably meet. It's also realistic to assume that many project managers are given a set budget and then have to allocate that budget appropriately across project work. This could very well lead to fluctuations in the quality of work and cuts in scope or schedule. It's important to understand that cost estimating, like duration estimating, isn't always as accurate as you might like it to be. A variety of techniques will need to be used to narrow the gap a bit.

The wonderful thing for you is that the same tools and techniques we discussed in estimating durations are the same for estimating costs:

- **Analogous**: Lessons learned
- **Parametric**: Mathematical
- **Three-point estimates**: PERT

Bottom-up estimates will be the focus here, because using the work breakdown structure to estimate durations and costs is the most definitive way to estimate, since it deals with the specific scope of the work. The scope of the work plus the materials, equipment, and human resources will determine your budget.

This is because the costs are attached to your resources, which are attached to the schedule activities, which are connected to durations, dates, relationships, and constraints, and use materials and equipment to get the job done. That is why it is important to use the WBS to help you plan. Bottom-up estimates work from (you guessed it!) the bottom of the WBS at the work package level up to the main level deliverables. This is instead of a top-down or analogous estimate, which is essentially what the business case provided you with in the project charter. It's much easier to estimate effectively when you are working with smaller packages of work and aggregating all costs together into one sizeable number. This is essentially what your software is doing, if you attach price tags to resources.

Estimating costs isn't an exact science though, and there is always room for error and improvements. A lot of the success depends on how well you plan for scope and estimate your resources. At the beginning of the project, there is only the predicated result, the assumed ROI, and what is happening in the market at the time a business decides to invest in a project. Because of those influencing factors plus the top down estimate, it stands to reason that the margin for error could be exceptionally large. This would be considered a **Rough Order of Magnitude**, or **ROM**, estimate. The fluctuations in how wrong a ROM estimate could be waver between -50 percent and +100 percent. Of course, I don't know how your organization budgets, but if that was how I presented my budget to my sponsor and expected them to accept it, that could result in an **RPE**, or resume producing event!

Now, if there is a distinct business case with stable requirements, some historical information, and expert judgment, then that gap could narrow a bit, to -10 percent to +25 percent. This is better, but it is still not that good. That range of accuracy is also very typical in the chartering phase. Therefore, it's important for us project managers to do our own cost/benefit analysis, if possible, to make sure the numbers are matching up with what we know today. That could be when you ask the business analysts where they came up with *that* number. Remember, they love that question! No, they really don't, but ask it anyway.

Therefore, the bottom-up estimates are the best, because we have moved from the initiation and business-case part of the project to the real scope of work, with real resources and schedule estimates. This allows the estimates to get as close as possible to reality at -5 percent to +10 percent. Many budgets fluctuate and bounce between those numbers during execution of project work. I would say that 10 percent is usually my tolerance level for being over/under budget. Anything over that tolerance lets me know that I need to take corrective action to fix the issues causing my budget to wildly fluctuate.

You may be wondering why being under budget is so bad in a project environment. In many organizations, it's a wonderful thing. The problem is that if actual performance is too far under budget without the removal of scope or resources, it appears that you have padded your budget. Remember, many organizations are allocating money across multiple projects, and they typically budget their projects a year in advance. If you stack your budget higher than needed, that money isn't around for other projects. Well, until it's discovered and it's too late to do anything about it. That doesn't look good. Don't get me wrong, I do add some buffer money to my budgets for potential risk, especially if I'm not offered a **contingency amount** to handle those risk events that can be managed with money (or time). A best practice would state that the organization provides +/- 10 percent for threats and opportunities, but unfortunately many PMs don't have that luxury.

There is also the fact that many long-term projects must be planned using rolling-wave planning. This means we can budget in the short term definitively, but the future is fuzzy. Even though we are again working in the easier- said-than-done department, estimating costs is difficult, due to indirect costs that may need to be considered. **Direct costs** are easier. We can budget for them, but **indirect costs** fluctuate, which is always why we have a range of estimates, rather than one hard number.

Indirect costs are like your electricity bill: it's never the same every month. In the summer, it goes up as you use more air conditioning; in the fall, it goes down as the weather cools, and then it goes up again in the winter, depending on where you live in the world. When we get to Chapter 9, *Monitoring and Controlling Project Work*, we will review procurement more in depth. For now, it's important to know that different contract types carry different cost risks for the buyer (us) or the seller (them, supplier, contractor). If we have a firm fixed price agreement, then that's great for us; it's fixed, and we can budget for it. What if we need some scope flexibility, though? Then we need a more flexible contract, and with that comes variable costs that are tougher to budget for. Procurement and resources are not the only considerations for budgeting; we need to make sure that we are meeting quality requirements as well. It costs a lot less to budget well and to make sure we do it right the first time than it does to fix defects after the project is being executed. Therefore, the **cost of quality** is part of the estimation process.

Quality management and the cost of quality

Failure to meet quality requirements can have serious negative consequences for any or all of the project stakeholders, your schedule, and your budget. Quality is very tightly integrated with the scope of work, because both must be correct for the product, service, or result to be accepted. Therefore, it is important to make sure that requirements for quality are collected and met. Because scope and quality are so tightly integrated, it is sometimes difficult to tell them apart on an exam.

Quality is correctness, and the results are fit for use, and scope of work is the features and functions needed via requirements. Remember, we need to build the right thing (scope of work) and build the thing right (quality management).

To explain this, let's look at something tangible. I like to use a bicycle as an example. Remember the scope statement? That is where we describe what we will and will not create for the scope of work to keep the assumptions and risks to a minimum. Let's say you have finished the 12-speed cherry-red bicycle and you call the customer so that they can come and check it out and inspect the result. They will ride the bicycle around the block, check the brakes, shift gears, steer, and so on, to make sure everything is working. If the brakes work a little too well when used, they could flip the bike. Customers don't like that too much, by the way. If the chain falls off or the gears don't shift, that's a major quality problem. Don't even get me started on the bell that doesn't work. All those things are related to mediocre quality. Conversely, the bike could be of the highest quality but the wrong color. That would be a scope issue.

Both the quality and scope planets need to align for the customer to accept the result. This is precisely why we need to create a quality management plan, collect the right requirements, and practice excellent quality assurance and quality control to meet requirements. All that, of course, costs money.

We have all probably experienced throwing good money after bad. That typically happens to me when I attempt to do house projects and repairs myself. The same applies in the arena of quality management. Doing things right the first time is far less expensive than having to do it again.

There are two types of quality costs: the **costs of conformance** and the **costs of non-conformance**. Pay it now, or pay it later. The costs of conformance are what we will allocate for in our cost baseline and will include prevention costs, meaning the money we spend to avoid quality failures. Costs of non-conformance include defect repair, rework and, on the most expensive side of things, lost business, paying out warranties and bad reputations. All these things are expensive in more ways than one.

When we consider the cost of quality in our budgets, we are at least attempting to have the money to perform work right the first time. Is that process infallible? Not at all. Sometimes, we will have defects that need to be fixed but the hope is there are as few of them as possible. Even Six Sigma, which is a proprietary quality management process, expects 3.4 defects per million. That is about as close to perfect quality as a company can get.

Not all the costs of quality will come out of your budget though. Much of the prevention cost can be attributed to soft costs or organizational costs, such as having good working equipment or paying to train employees. Still, other costs *are* part of our budget and are used to acquire high-quality materials and equipment.

Other considerations for cost estimating are, of course, the scope of the work, resources, and potentially **contingency reserves** for identified risk events. This bucket of money would complement our project budget and be used for identified risk events that can be managed with money. We will review risk later in this chapter, but for the cost side of things, we would include that contingency money in our cost baseline, and it would be ours to manage accordingly.

Quality gates and governance gates

Quality gates are created when you are developing your schedule. This is because they are like milestones. Many projects are run in a phase-oriented manner, which would include a checkpoint at the end of a phase to make sure everything is running effectively.

Remember, the cost of quality can be awfully expensive if defects are missed and not fixed; therefore, quality gates are set up to make sure that things are correct before they are too far gone and become more expensive to fix. The quality gates may not even correlate to a project phase that has ended as many companies have specific requirements or even regulations they need to meet and if these checkpoints are not established defects could be missed. These gates *do* need to be formally scheduled though, and typically a trained inspector would be auditing the quality process and the output of the deliverables. If not, it's realistic that the organization would provide checklists for project teams to help with inspections or templates that are used over and over, so it's easier to effectively manage and control quality outputs.

Governance gates

Governance gates are like quality gates, but rather than just checking for quality, these checkpoints may include sign-off processes or approval points to move forward. Many times, these gates are used to make a *go / no go* decision. If I own a chocolate chip cookie factory and I'm inspecting one out of every one hundred cookies, they darn well better have chocolate chips in them. No chips? No go! Having a formal signature during a governance gate shows approvals throughout and a paper trail of documentation. Who is signing off on the approvals could vary, but this is typically the customer, internal management, or the overall legislative approvals, or some combination of the three. Putting in place legislative gates is a formal process and can help provide adherence to the quality, the schedule, and making sure agreements are following the law.

Governance gates are not necessarily all quality focused, so there may be a combination of both quality gates and governance gates throughout a project. Governance gates would also happen at periodic points in the schedule but may not be scheduled according to your project timeline. They may be scheduled according to the higher-ups who perform them and can often mean a long day at work for you and your team.

The goal is to do it right the first time and prevent mistakes rather than discovering them during inspections and to make sure that we collect the right requirements to meet the goals. Perfect-world project management would state you have tons of time to plan, but often we don't have that luxury. If you oversee budgeting your projects, try to etch out some time for quality considerations as well as scope, because they are tightly integrated and work together toward a successful result. No matter what the process is that your organization uses when you are creating your budget, you are considering multiple inputs. Scope, schedule, resources, procurement, risk, and most certainly quality. Once we have all the price tags of the individual aspects of project work, it's time to get the sizeable number approved as a baseline and keep track of expenditures throughout.

Creating the project budget

Many times, estimating costs and budgeting is a singular process. Because we all use software of some kind, it makes sense that as we add costs to project work, the software is adding them all up together and giving us an aggregated total project budget. That doesn't mean, however, that everyone will be happy to sign off on that sizeable number and except it outright. In many cases, the business case or a contract is driving the budget from the beginning. If you are given budgetary constraints to work with upfront, then you will spend your time splitting that sizeable number into price tags, rather than the opposite: estimating first, and then budgeting. Either way, the budget and inevitable baseline are time-phased. More money is spent during the execution of project work than it is during planning. Changes are easier to adapt to during planning and less expensive to make than during project execution. The cost baseline when represented visually in a chart is low expenditures at the beginning, rising in the middle, and tapering off again at the end.

The goal of any baseline is to allow for tracking of performance throughout the project, but we also need a living breathing budget, so we can update actual expenditures and then compare them to the baseline. Basically, the cost baseline is a formal, approved version of your budget, much like your schedule and your schedule baseline. Although you may think you have the greatest budget ever created and happily skip to your sponsor's office to prove it, it's likely you'll be walking out of the office dragging your feet after being told to cut the budget in half but still get all the scope of work done. Sigh! The joys of project management.

Keep in mind that the business case is an analogous top-down estimate and that you have the definitive budget in your hands. Sometimes, that is where the disconnect comes from. If you were told that your vacation to your favorite place was a particular amount one minute, and then the next minute it was double that, you may not take too kindly to that. Your sponsor may be feeling the same way.

This is an appropriate time to bring up risk management again at an elevated level. Risk is broken into two categories: **threats and opportunities**. Threats cost money; opportunities save or gain money for the project. If you have identified a risk event that could cost the project money but there isn't any way to handle it without throwing money at it, then it may be that you need contingency money as part of your baseline. Usually, contingency is +/- 10 percent of the estimated total project budget. If your organization takes that into consideration, then you may be able to push your budget through approvals without a lot of grumbling.

The assumption is that you get your budget approved, add the 10 percent contingency, and that equals your cost baseline. It's yours to manage. On top of that, there is a magical bucket of money called management reserves for risks you couldn't have possibly accounted for and that management can afford to use this money to help manage an *unknown/unknown* threat event. This is a unicorn, folks. It rarely happens. If you do happen to live in this magical project management land, then your *budget + your contingency reserves + management reserves* would be the entire project budget, the *big* number. You would only be responsible for allocating money from the baseline itself. Project budget and your contingency will be yours to manage accordingly.

Much of that responsibility ties to expenditure tracking and reporting in real time as the project work begins. Typically, weekly is how often you will be reporting on cost performance on projects, but, like everything we review, it depends on the size of the project and how often your stakeholders want updates. Using software, mostly, you will put together how the cost performance is going, what your **burn rate** is, and create project cost performance reports to communicate to your stakeholders.

The *burn rate* is how quickly you are *burning* through your project budget. If you do this too quickly, you may find that the project is over budget. Typically, the burn rate is tracked to make sure that venture capital isn't spent above and beyond the income capabilities of the organization. This can apply to projects as well, because they have determined project pay-back periods and net present values. Too much out and not enough in is a bad position for projects to be in.

Your organization may also have what is called a **funding limit reconciliation**. I remember this, as I must admit that I have a limit to my funding. Jeez! Story of my life, right? That same principle applies to project budgets. Organizations don't want too much out and not enough in, and they are paying for other projects, salaries, building rentals, power bills, and the like. This means that a project budget may be approved but they aren't writing you a check on day one of the project for the entire amount.

Instead, the disbursement will occur over time and may have limits attached that don't meet your budgetary expenditures, as they are currently scheduled. For example, if my project budget is 1.5 million and my schedule baseline is set at one year, then the organization may say *In Q1, we will allocate 250 thousand for your project work. In Q2, we will allocate another 250 thousand. In Q3, we will release 500 thousand,* and so on. You may be thinking, *I need 500 thousand in Q1.* But you won't get this, as you must now reconcile that there is a limit to your funding and find ways to adjust your schedule, resources, procurement, and other project costs across the project's life cycle.

Typically, this is either a widespread practice and you are aware of the limits, or you will know it through the business case up front. Still, at other times, it's a surprise or a shift in project priority. It's never an enjoyable time to find it out, but it's better that you do at the beginning of the project than after you have suffered through task sequencing! The bottom line is that once you get your cost baseline approved, it will become a static document that can only be changed through **formal change control** processes and typically is due to an addition or subtraction of the scope of work at some point during project execution.

That brings us to tracking performance. Both schedule and cost are tightly integrated, so your costs become a time-phased baseline that is working with your schedule to pay for executed work. While it would be nice to think all things went the way of the baselines, it's probably better to assume they won't. Since you are responsible for reporting on the performance, it's important to know ways to do that effectively. This means that we will cover both schedule and cost performance together using a handy technique called the **earned value technique**. A word of warning: if you are mathematically challenged (I just pointed to myself), then this section may seem a bit overwhelming to you. If you like, you can blame the United States **Department of Defense (DoD)** who created this technique for losing the next hour of your life, because I certainly will! I'm just kidding! (No I'm not). Let's get to it and get through it together.

Tracking and reporting cost/schedule performance

What is the time value of money? That is essentially the question we are trying to answer as well as what is the money value of time. Delays on your schedule can affect your critical path and cost the project money to fix. Spending more than has been allocated will affect your project budget negatively. This is a moving target all the time. Just because you are behind schedule doesn't mean you are also over budget. In fact, many times, being behind schedule makes it look as if you are under budget because you haven't yet paid for the work that needs to be done. Your variables will fluctuate. The goal is to keep a close eye on your baselines versus actual performance, because, trust me, your sponsor, and customers, certainly will.

I always expect some level of fluctuation and am typically very aware of what my tolerance levels are. By this, I mean how far over/under budget and ahead/behind schedule I am. There is a visible line that, once crossed means it is time to figure out how to fix things. Just like the cost and duration estimates have a range, so do the results. Bounce outside of that range and it's time to take corrective action.

Earned value management (EVM) looks at the scope completed and compares it against what should have been done at this point in the schedule and looks at what was paid out of the budget for the work. The hard part is thinking about time in the context of money. This was difficult for me at first, so I'm both empathetic and sympathetic to those of you that could be confused as well. I think it's best to give you each concept and then jump into the formulas you could see on the exam.

Remember, you will have a calculator and something to write with and write on. As soon as it was time to begin my exam, I wrote down all the formulas. I knew I would blank on them when I got to a formula question. My brain and math don't mesh very well. If you are the same way, then take a minute and no more to jot down what you need to remember. It's worth the short amount of time, if it saves you math angst during the exam. This exam is also not totally math oriented. It will take you longer to read this information than the number of questions you will get. I think I had about 15 formula questions. Many of the earned value questions will be based on your understanding of what the result of the math is telling you about your projects rather than rote memorization of formulas.

All EVM formulas are algebraic and contain acronyms. It's easier to remember the formulas using those acronyms but necessary to understand the terms and what the acronyms relate to first before we cover the formulas themselves. The first variable to cover is **budget at completion (BAC)**.

Budget at completion (BAC)

Unfortunately, this acronym is the opposite of what you might think it is. It sounds like the amount of money spent when the project is over, but it's actually the amount of money you get approved as a baseline during planning. It's the *assumed* amount of money you will spend on the project. Remember that the goal of this is to compare planned versus actual. So, we need the total planned budget to begin this process. Think of it as your **budget and cash**. In *Figure 8.1*, you will see a spreadsheet that portrays your BAC:

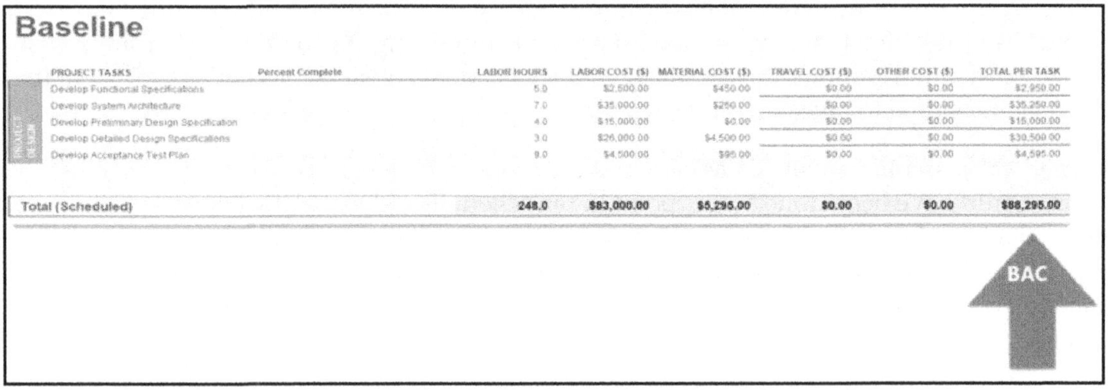

Baseline

PROJECT TASKS	Percent Complete	LABOR HOURS	LABOR COST ($)	MATERIAL COST ($)	TRAVEL COST ($)	OTHER COST ($)	TOTAL PER TASK
Develop Functional Specifications		5.0	$2,500.00	$450.00	$0.00	$0.00	$2,950.00
Develop System Architecture		7.0	$35,000.00	$250.00	$0.00	$0.00	$35,250.00
Develop Preliminary Design Specification		4.0	$15,000.00	$0.00	$0.00	$0.00	$15,000.00
Develop Detailed Design Specifications		3.0	$26,000.00	$4,500.00	$0.00	$0.00	$30,500.00
Develop Acceptance Test Plan		9.0	$4,500.00	$95.00	$0.00	$0.00	$4,595.00
Total (Scheduled)		**248.0**	**$83,000.00**	**$5,295.00**	**$0.00**	**$0.00**	**$88,295.00**

BAC

Figure 8.1 BAC

From this, you see all the project tasks and labor hours, plus the costs of the labor and materials. If you aggregate all of those numbers together, you get your baseline, or your BAC. This is a key place to begin, because we now need to look at actual performance on the project work and see how much of that work has been accomplished and what that work is worth in money. Once that baseline is approved, it is set in stone, unless a formal change is needed to adapt that number. Otherwise, it is static and used to track planned versus actual budgetary performance. Notice that each task has its own price tag attached and the hours that it should take to complete at that price point. This is key for calculating earned value.

Earned value (EV)

Earned value is basically the amount of work that has been completed and what that work is worth based on the price tag assigned to it. If task number two is worth 35,250 US dollars at its completion than when it's halfway complete or 50 percent completed, it's worth 17,625 US dollars. The goal of the earned value is to see how much work is completed and its current value. The formula to use to calculate earned value is *BAC * % complete*.

In *Figure 8.2*, you can see the earned value represented on this spreadsheet:

Baseline

PROJECT TASKS	Percent Complete	LABOR HOURS	LABOR COST ($)	MATERIAL COST ($)	TRAVEL COST ($)	OTHER COST ($)	TOTAL PER TASK	EARNED VALUE
Develop Functional Specifications	20.00%	5.0	$2,500.00	$450.00	$0.00	$0.00	$2,950.00	$590.00
Develop System Architecture	15.00%	7.0	$35,000.00	$250.00	$0.00	$0.00	$35,250.00	$5,287.50
Develop Preliminary Design Specification	10.00%	4.0	$15,000.00	$0.00	$0.00	$0.00	$15,000.00	$1,500.00
Develop Detailed Design Specifications	25%	3.0	$26,000.00	$4,500.00	$0.00	$0.00	$30,500.00	$7,625.00
Develop Acceptance Test Plan	0	9.0	$4,500.00	$95.00	$0.00	$0.00	$4,595.00	$0.00
Total (Scheduled)		248.0	$83,000.00	$5,295.00	$0.00	$0.00	$88,295.00	$15,002.50

Figure 8.2

Let's say you have hired someone to paint your living room. You have four walls in that room and the painters have told you the cost for the entire room is two thousand US dollars, equally distributed across all four walls. This means each wall's worth is 500 US dollars. Half way through the project schedule, you check on their progress and are expecting them to ask for some money based on the work completed. You look around the room, and two walls are done. What have the painters earned? One thousand US dollars. That is the earned value. Does that mean they are on schedule? Nope. Does that mean they are sticking to the budget? Not at all. What it means is they have completed one thousand worth of work. The earned value can be calculated for each task or on the project level. If the project is 50 percent complete or if a task is 50 percent complete, they each retain their original value that was planned. That would be the only way to tell whether things were not working out as planned. But, to do that, we need to review a couple more variables. The next variable will allow us to determine schedule performance using planned values.

Planned value (PV)

Remember, your entire baseline is comprised of individual price tags for the work, that when rolled together equal your BAC. The BAC is a timed-phased budgetary baseline that we will use to pay for work that will be done on the project. It makes sense that each task has a value that could include resources or procurement or the simple costs of working the plan. The **planned values** (PV) are the distribution of your BAC across time and could be considered the budgetary costs of work scheduled. Going back to my wall example, we determined that if all money is distributed equally across work (which it never is), then each wall's worth is 500 US dollars. Now, let's say the schedule the painters gave us was four days, meaning it will take them four days to complete all four walls and all four walls are worth 500 hundred US dollars each. If I look at my schedule, I would say that each day, one wall should be done, or 500 US dollars a day worth of work should be completed.

OK, well, let's check on their progress at the end of day three. In *Figure 8.3*, you can see their progress at the end of day three:

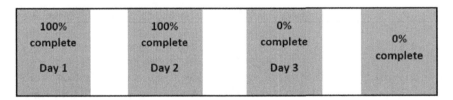

Figure 8.3

If I were going to pay them for the work they had accomplished or their EV, then I would write them a check for one thousand. But it's the end of day 3! I should be writing them a check for 15 hundred. Am I happy with my painters? Yeah...no. Why? Because the planned value of work I expected to be completed was 1500, and they did one thousand. Hmmm... so they are 500 behind schedule. Planned values are determined by the original budget spread out over time and assigned to each task. If you don't use an EV, you may say instead that the painters are one day behind schedule. That day is worth 500. Does that mean they won't get all four walls done on time? Not necessarily; they may get it all done on time and on budget, but right now it looks as if they are not working up to the full schedule potential, and I must report that.

There are three ways to report on schedule performance and all provide a different kind of performance review. The first are schedule variances.

In *Figure 8.4*, you can review the spreadsheet with the planned values:

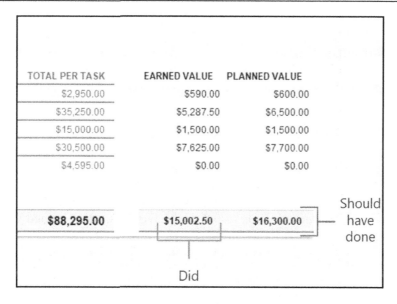

TOTAL PER TASK	EARNED VALUE	PLANNED VALUE
$2,950.00	$590.00	$600.00
$35,250.00	$5,287.50	$6,500.00
$15,000.00	$1,500.00	$1,500.00
$30,500.00	$7,625.00	$7,700.00
$4,595.00	$0.00	$0.00
$88,295.00	$15,002.50	$16,300.00

Should have done

Did

Figure 8.4

Schedule variance (SV)

Variances allow us to see whether there is a difference between planned and actual variance for both schedule and cost. If there is a big variance on one side or the other, corrective action may need to be taken. You can run the numbers on the entire project or look at individual work packages, and sometimes you can tell exactly where the schedule problems are and target a correction to the right tasks.

For your exam, you will most likely be asked to calculate the schedule variances or other formulas for schedule and cost based on the entire project. Also, watch out for positive and negative results for variance formulas. Negative bad; positive good.

The formula for schedule variance is as follows:

$$EV-PV=SV$$

Basically, my painter's performance shows their EV, 1,000. Their PV is 1,500, so their schedule variance = - 500. That tells me that they are behind schedule. Any time the amount of work completed is less than planned, it will result in a negative variance. What we really want to see is a zero variance. That means we are right on track. A positive variance means we are ahead of schedule, which isn't so bad, within reason.

Schedule performance index (SPI)

The **schedule performance index** (SPI) is a formula that can provide you and the team with a rating of your schedule efficiency. You'll notice that we are using the same data for the formula. EV and PV. However, we are changing the mathematical operator. This time we will divide.

The formula for schedule performance index is as follows:

$$EV/PV = SPI$$

In this case, I'm trying to figure out the percentage of efficiency of my painter's performance. If I take the earned value (what they have done)/the planned value (what I thought they would do), I can see they are not performing well at all.

1,000/1,500 = 0.67 is the result, if I were to follow normal rounding procedures. Basically, that tells me that my painters are working at 67 percent efficiency when I expected 100 percent. **Anything below *1.0* is behind schedule**, and **anything above *1.0* is ahead of schedule**. If the result is 1.0, then my painters are exactly where they should be.

 Follow normal rounding procedures on your exam, but if you don't see your answer and you know you did the math correctly, then round up. Most results will include two decimal points.

Schedule variance and schedule performance index give you the money side of time and a percentage of efficiency based on scope of work completed versus what you expected to be completed. If there is a variance or a difference, it may be time to apply some corrective action to get back on track. This would be done during formal change- control procedures, since you can't just change your baselines whenever you want to and without approval from the powers that be. The last formula steps away from time as money and looks at the earned schedule versus the planned schedule.

Earned schedule (ES)

The **earned schedule theory** is an enhancement to the other earned value formulas that have been around since the dawn of time. In fact, this is a new formula. It's so new that you most likely won't see it on your exams, but may want to use it.

The formulas are as follows:

Earned Schedule (ES) – Actual Time (AT) = Schedule variance.

Earned Schedule (ES) / Actual Time (AT) = Schedule efficiency metrics.

This way, you can calculate using time and your schedule, especially if you don't do budgeting for your projects. This is yet another way to put together performance reports on your schedule and your project's progress. Now that we have compiled the schedule information, we can then turn our attentions to cost performance.

Cost variance (CV)

When we look at costs for the project, we are now looking to see exactly what was spent during the work being executed. Remember, we have a baseline, and now we are going to be collecting information about **actual costs (AC)**. Actual costs include all expenditures for work in the process of being executed. It is the actual amount being spent. When we compare the work that has been done (EV) again, and the amount of money spent on it (AC), we can begin to get a clearer picture of whether our budget is working out the way we planned.

The formula for cost variance is as follows:

earned value (EV) – actual costs (AC)

Essentially, we are comparing the amount of work completed against the amount of money spent on it. If the earned value is **less than the actual costs,** that means the team got less work done and you spent more on it. You are over budget. If your earned value is **greater than your actual costs,** then the team got more done and you spent less on it. If the variance is zero, then they are right on target. Remember, being behind schedule doesn't automatically mean you are over budget. Even though we are viewing time as money it doesn't reflect on your budget. Only actual costs compared to earned value can give us true budgetary information. If I asked my painters how much they spent on supplies and they say 5 thousand, I'll probably first flip out because I realize they are way over budget. But how much? Let's look at the numbers again.

The painters at the end of day three: **one thousand completed**

What the painters spent on three days' worth of work: **five thousand**

Right now, my painters appear to be four thousand over budget, and even if they were on schedule, which they are not, it stands to reason that the actual cost number could go up. Even if the five thousand number remains and the total amount spent stays the same *and* they complete two thousand worth of work on time or otherwise, they will still be over budget by a large amount. Right now, during my assessment, this is the result I'm getting. Two walls completed; five thousand spent:

$$1,000 \; EV - 5,000 \; AC = -4,000$$

There are no real ways to compress your budget like fast-tracking a schedule. When your project is over budget, it's almost impossible to regain that money without cutting scope or begging management for their reserves. The next formula is considered the most important metric since it tracks cost efficiencies.

Cost performance index (CPI)

The reason the **CPI** is considered the most critical metric on a project is because it looks at the earned value and the amount spent to give a percentage of budgetary efficiency. This can give us information on the past to present performance and be used to forecast future performance if the way the project is going now remains the same in the future. The question of how much will this project cost is always asked, at every meeting with your sponsor or customer. You must show that future performance is just as good (hopefully) as today's and conversely if performance is not good today, how you plan to fix it.

The formula for the cost performance index (CPI) is as follows:

$$Earned \; Value \; (EV) \; / \; Actual \; costs \; (AC)$$

If I look at my painter's efficiency rating for cost then, right now, today, the CPI is this:

$$1,000 \; EV \; / \; 5,000 \; AC = 0.2$$

0.2??? 20 percent efficient???? RPE! That is unrecoverable money and an exceedingly long walk to your sponsor's office. I give you the extremes, because anything lower than 0.5 CPI is typically unrecoverable, and if we used the information to forecast forward, it's not looking good. Now, imagine a mega project that spans years and billion and billions of invested monies. You can imagine how that wouldn't go over well. Granted, my painting project isn't being funded by sponsors, but it's still irksome to be drastically over budget.

In *Figure 8.5*, you can see the spreadsheet after running all the data. See if you can tell how the project is doing based on the results of the analysis:

EARNED VALUE	PLANNED VALUE	ACTUAL COSTS	SCHEDULE VARIANCE	COST VARIANCE	SCHEDULE PERFORMANCE INDEX	COST PERFORMANCE INDEX
$590.00	$600.00	$300.00	-$10.00	$290.00	0.98	1.97
$5,287.50	$6,500.00	$350.00	-$1,212.50	$4,937.50	0.8	15.11
$1,500.00	$1,500.00	$3,600.00	$0.00	-$2,100.00	1.00	0.42
$7,625.00	$7,700.00	$7,700.00	-$75.00	-$75.00	0.99	0.99
$0.00	$0.00	$0.00	$0.00	$0.00	0	0
$15,002.50	$16,300.00	$11,950.00	-$1,297.50	$3,052.50	0.92	1.26

Figure 8.5

Hopefully, it was easy to tell that this project is a bit behind schedule and under budget. Even though the schedule performance is a bit low, it's still darn good. Considering our tolerance levels are usually +/- 10 percent before we start adjusting, this project is doing fine. Also, when we catch up on the schedule's performance, our budget will adjust also, but we still won't be over budget. Remember, this is all a moving target. We are updating this information weekly and trying to accommodate risks and issues and keep everyone on the team's eyes on the prize. It's a balancing act and an EV technique can help you see where the areas are for improvements and what to leave well enough alone.

Here are just a few tips and tricks to remember to help you with these formulas for the exam:

- Earned value is first in all formulas.
- Planned value is for schedule questions.
- Actual cost is for budgetary questions.
- For variances, negative results are bad. Over budget, behind schedule.
- For indexes, below 1.0 results are bad. Over budget, behind schedule.
- Variances are subtraction.
- Indexes are division.

I promised I would help the mathematically challenged with an uncomplicated way to remember these formulas. Here it is. I memorized all the formulas straight down, instead of across, like this. First, on my scratch paper, I would write down EV, since it came first in all formulas:

$$EV$$

$$EV$$

$$EV$$

$$EV$$

Then, I knew variances were subtraction and indexes were division, so I wrote those next to the EV, like so:

$$EV -$$

$$EV -$$

$$EV /$$

$$EV /$$

Then I knew PV was for time and actual costs were for costs, so I added that to the mix:

$$EV - PV$$

$$EV - AC$$

$$EV / PV$$

$$EV / AC$$

There you go, and here's the thing: if you say it in the same way, there is a bit of a little rap song spin you can put on it. EV, EV, EV, EV, MINUS, MINUS, DIVIDE, DIVIDE, PV, AC, PV, AC. You can dance too; nobody is looking. Hopefully that helped with those formulas!

Forecasting

There are forecasting formulas that help you to calculate what would happen if performance remained the same and give you results that will answer these questions.

How much more will we need to spend to get this project completed (*estimate to complete, ETC*), and how much do we think this entire project is going to cost (*estimate at completion, EAC*)?

Many times, the **estimate to complete** (**ETC**) is based on expert judgment and an idea of how work is performing today. **Estimate at completion** (**EAC**) is merely taking that estimate and adding it what has been spent to date. I'll give you the formulas, but honestly you probably won't see them on your exams (insert happy dance here)! The formulas are a bit like the which comes first question: the chicken or the egg, but it depends on who's asking for what information and what information you must provide:

$$EAC = ETC + AC$$

$$ETC = EAC - AC$$

The following table will give you all the formulas in one section, and feel free to use them with your practice questions at the end of this chapter or any other practice exams you take. There is no shame in taking questions open book, and nobody expects you to absorb everything all at once:

Meaning	Formula
CV	EV-AC
SV	EV-PV
CPI	EV/AC
SPI	EV/PV
EAC	AC+ ETC
ETC	EAC-AC

Phew! We are through that section and now get to jump into another big section: risk management.

Risk management planning

Risk is the trouble maker in a project and can wreak havoc on baselines, deliverables, the team, and pretty much any area of a project if you leave the project susceptible to threats. Typically, when I'm teaching risk management, my classes fall on one side of the extreme or the other. They either comprehensively manage risk with documentation and meetings designed just for risk assessments or they fly by the seat of their pants and put out fires when they happen. A lot of that depends on the industry and the organization. It's safe to say that in IT you will have a lot of technical risks on the hardware or software side of things. Cyber security is a massive concern these days. Every time I take a cyber security class I'm am freaked out more and more about what is happening in the world of tech. It's our job to stay on top of those threats as much as possible. It's a lot to manage, but possible. If you set up the project for success right from the get go and keep a fire extinguisher there too just in case, then hopefully you can get in front of the threats and stop them in their tracks. Easier said than done? For sure.

Throughout this section on risk, you'll be reviewing some best practices to identify risks, analyze them, and to create responses for them. Those responses are much like motivational theories or conflict resolution in the sense that they are categories of responses rather than a step-by-step guide on dealing with all risks to an IT project. Remember, projects are unique, and even though some risk events are expected to happen over and over, there will be some that are unique to your specific project. Those are the risks we really need to plan for because there isn't any historical information or lessons learned to refer to.

Risk management is an iterative process and happens throughout the project until the deliverable is accepted, and the project or phase is closed out. That is why it's a promising idea to have a process in place during planning that can be followed throughout the project, only adjusting or adapting that process if it isn't working.

The other thing to consider with risk is nothing is 100 percent. Mostly we are dealing with **known/unknown** risk events, meaning we know it could happen, there is a probability attached, and if it does happen, then the impact is mostly unknown. It's subjective analysis and we can guesstimate and plan, but we could also be totally wrong.

The other thing to consider is that your stakeholders have a variety of risk tolerance levels. Some stakeholders are risk takers and others are risk-averse. Others could be risk-neutral. Worse yet, the stakeholder's tolerance levels could change during the project depending on what is happening. An effective way to find out the tolerance levels of your stakeholders is to ask. I like to use extreme questions such as *Would you ever swim with sharks?*, *Would you go on the scariest roller coaster in the world?* If their answers are *Sure, I'd do that!* I know they are a risk taker. If their response is *Enter the food chain??? Nope, nope, no way; no how!* then I know they aren't. If they say, *Sharks no; roller coaster yes*, then I know I have a stakeholder who can be convinced to take a risk as long as it is a calculated risk, and they fall into the risk-neutral category. I'm totally risk-averse in life and in business. I used to be more of a risk taker when I was younger, and some would have looked at my life and where I have traveled by myself and said, *Yep, she's a risk taker.*

It's perception of what is considered risky and what isn't. That is why it's important to get everyone involved in the risk management process. Make it a formal thing. People who do the work know the risks, people who pay for projects know the cost risks, and people managing the project need to cover all their bases. We'll start by going over some best practices for identifying risks. It may seem we are going in a linear fashion, such as schedule management, because we are covering one thing at a time and progressively building out our plans for risk. Instead, in the real world, it is a cycle of continuous focus.

I find that it is best to get everyone on the same page when it comes to classifying risks. I say this because risk takers and risk-averse folks may disagree as to the severity or probability of a risk event occurring. There is also the need to determine how risks will be accounting for probability and impact. Some teams use a 1-5 scale. On this scale, 5 is a high probability or high impact and 1 is low. Other teams will use red, yellow, green, or high, medium, and low. There isn't a wrong way to classify risk, but it is important to get everyone on board with what a red is, what does 1 mean, and what exactly is medium. If I'm a risk taker and I identify a risk, I may classify it as yellow. If I'm risk-averse, I may think it should be red. Of course, there is room for discussion, but I think it is best to lay the ground work prior to the execution of the project work.

The most typical way to do so is to classify based on the big constraints. If a schedule risk has been identified and determined to impact negatively at 20 percent, that is a 3, a medium, or a yellow, depending on your classification system. Over budget by 30 percent is a red, a high, a 5. Once everyone agrees on the scalable system, then it's consistent when risks are identified by a variety of stakeholder risk tolerances and far easier to identify, classify, and move on to response planning. In my world, this is part of a **risk management plan,** and once that plan is approved by the powers that be, it is what it is. That is, until it no longer serves the purpose it was meant for, and then we would go through formal change control to update it. Typically, the scalable system is used as a template for future projects as well. If you don't have a strategy and are dealing with probabilities and impacts, you could find yourselves dealing with risk instead of executing work in a timely manner.

Because you will be iteratively identifying risks throughout the project, it's best to set this up as early in the project as possible. Remember, the first place we see risk (if we are lucky) is in the project charter. The sponsor, customers, and the powers that be, have already assessed cost risk in the business case and have some ideas as to the major categories of risk. Whether they have been clearly expressed depends on your organization. To identify risks on a regular basis, it's important to realize that some brainstorming may need to occur. This is due to working with things that *could happen* to negatively impact the project.

SWOT analysis

SWOT analysis is brainstorming using categories to help with focused thought. Although the origins of SWOT analysis are a bit fuzzy, this technique has been used to identify risks since the early 1960s, and allows for compartmentalization and identification.

SWOT stands for these things:

- Strengths
- Weaknesses
- Opportunities
- Threats

Make sure you know what SWOT stands for by the time of the exam, so you can answer questions effectively if presented with this technique in a question.

In *Figure 8.6*, you will see a quite simple SWOT diagram and then we'll go through how to use it for risk identification:

Figure 8.6

The reason why SWOT is so helpful is due to the forced focus on each quadrant.

For strengths, we want to look at things that are going well for us now. Effective team? Well-known product or service? Being first to market? All these things can help counteract the bad.

Weaknesses identifies the challenges we are dealing with at any point in the project. During planning, we want to transparently identify potential problems as soon as possible. Not enough resources to meet a schedule constraint? Sellers who provide less than satisfactory products or services? A slim budget without contingencies? All are weaknesses that can create problems in the long run.

Opportunities are what could go well in the future. People lined up around the block to buy our latest and greatest? New customers who have signed a long-term agreement with us? Better quality in our deliverables? These aren't guarantees, but they are possibilities that we can strive for.

Threats are the terrible things that can impact our projects. Being behind schedule, over budget, inferior quality, scope creep, not being first to market, losing customers due to inferior quality results, and so on.

It would make sense that strengths could produce opportunities and weaknesses could cause threats, but I also like to look at things on the diagonal as well. What strengths have we identified that if not leveraged could cause a threat in the future? Conversely, what weaknesses can be overcome to produce opportunities in the future?

People who do the work, know the risks. The project manager is not responsible for identifying every single risk event nor should we. We are *not* the best resources for individual identified project risks. We work on the 50-thousand-foot overview or total project risk. Be careful about the possibility of your team experiencing analysis paralysis though. You could really get into the weeds with brainstorming about risk, so it's important to facilitate well and stay out of any brainstorming pitfalls. Nobody wants eight-thousand-line items of project problems to deal with, much like an eight-thousand-line-item schedule is tough to manage.

Another consideration is to identify the **root causes** of risk as much as possible. This would be the reason why a risk event would occur. Root cause identification is a practical conversation because the closer you get to the actual reason why a threat event would occur, the better able you are to prioritize and create responses that are effective. This isn't about getting through yet another best practice; this is about making sure you have everything possible to plan accordingly. Many times, the root cause is the most obvious. Our schedule risk is due to lack of resources. But in some cases, there is something deeper lurking. It could be an intermediate cause that is less obvious but more impactful or an organizational cause that is tough to identify, control, or respond to. Either way, you want to identify the causes as much as you identify the risks. We use something called the **five whys.** This technique was created at Toyota to identify the actual root cause. If you ask "why" five times, you will get to the real root cause. It's an interesting way to get to the bottom of things.

You know this if you have small children, or if they have now grown up; you remember those *why* conversations.

Why is the sky blue?

Why do I have to clean my room?

Why is Johnny always on the swing?

Hey, you get to act like two-year olds, and that's fun! Clearly, the reason is to ask enough questions to get to the root cause, so you are better able to prioritize and plan responses.

Another way to get to the root cause is to use a **fishbone diagram.** The fishbone diagram was created by Dr. Ishikawa to target categories of problems and then work backwards from the effect to the root cause. If you can draw, it looks like the head of a fish, which represents the effect, or the risk event, and the bones of the fish represent categories of reasons why the event could occur. Much like SWOT analysis, it gives the team a visual way to determine root causes. The fishbone diagram has several different names. You'll most likely see it on your exams as a fishbone:

- Ishikawa diagram – I remembered this as a *FISHikawa* diagram!
- Cause-and-affect diagram
- Root-cause diagram
- Fishbone diagram

The fishbone diagram was created mostly to determine problems in product quality, and the original categories of potential causes were typical to that of the manufacturing industry. These days, it is used for root cause analysis in a variety of industries for both quality issues and for risk assessments.

No matter what technique you use to identify risks the immediate goal is be as clear and concise as possible and begin the process of documenting identified risks in a living, breathing project document called the **risk register.**

Creating the risk register

The risk register will contain all of the information you discover throughout the project about threats and opportunities. At this point in the process the register will contain all identified risk events and possibly some responses. The reason for that is there are just some things that happen on every project, and you already know how to deal with them, or you think you do anyway. It may not be necessary to drill down any further with analysis techniques if you already know how it will play out. That would be analysis paralysis! For other risks, you may need to delve a bit deeper to analyze probability and impacts as well as responses to update your risk register. As part of identifying risks, I like to compartmentalize risks into categories such as scope risk, cost risk, schedule, and quality risk. This is because they are the big constraints, and typically a risk to one is a risk to them all. If I can create categories to help identify risks, then I can certainly use those categories to stay organized. As we work though this section on risk, we will be updating the risk register with the latest information we need through analysis and response planning. Remember, this isn't a linear thing in the real world. When you identify a risk, you will analyze for root causes, probability, and impact, and determine responses all at once. To update your risk register with additional information, you will need to analyze those risks accordingly. That brings us to qualitative risk analysis.

Qualitative risk analysis

Qualitative risk analysis is about qualifying the information you have collected about risk and getting it organized by category. Then you will determine probability and impact based on the set process you created with your stakeholders for a scalable system. High, medium, low. Red, yellow, green. 1 through 5.

Once the risks have been analyzed for probability and impact, you can begin to sort them by priority. I like to use a spreadsheet program such as Excel for my risk register because I can sort, filter, color code, create tables, and have a lot of columns or tabs available for text and documentation. Most **project management information systems (PMIS)** don't do risk very well, because they don't have separate sections specific to risk management. It's mostly scope, schedule, and budgets.

It's also entirely possible that you would use a **risk breakdown structure (RBS).** Much like the RBS the risk breakdown structure is based on the identified categories of risk and used to break those categories down to more specifics. The RBS, like the WBS and any other breakdown structures, is a hierarchical representation of project risks, starting from higher-level categories and breaking them down to finer-level risks.

In *Figure 8.7*, you will see another tool that can be used to work through identified risk events. The **probability** and **impact matrix** define identified risks events, the category, and a scoring model. The assumption is that once you qualify the information, you can identify the risk score by *multiplying the probability by the impact*. Once the score is determined, you can prioritize the risks. The matrix is only showing financial losses in the example, but it could be schedule, scope of work, and the like. You will cover financial impacts later in this chapter under quantitative risk analysis:

Impact Scale Example:		
Level	Impact	Description
5	Severe	Financial Losses greater than $$$$$
4	Higher than Average	Financial Losses between $$$ and $$$
3	High	Financial Losses between $$$ and $$$
2	Moderate	Financial Losses between $$$ and $$$
1	Low	Financial Losses less than $$$

Risk Assessment Example:		
Risk Rating	Description	Action
16-25	Severe	Financial Losses greater than $$$$$
12-16	Higher than Average	Financial Losses between $$$ and $$$
8-12	High	Financial Losses between $$$ and $$$
4-8	Moderate	Financial Losses between $$$ and $$$
1-4	Low	Financial Losses less than $$$

Figure 8.7

If I have a risk event that has been classified as near term with a high probability and impact, then that is something we need to work on first. Its proximity to the project is close and needs to be managed quickly. You can't do that if it is way down the list of risks and could be overlooked. The qualitative risk analysis process is designed to review identified threats, assess probability, and impact, and then prioritize. Some risk events could be considered watch-list items and be placed further down the list. Still, others will be high priority and move up to the top of the list. I find this to be a second vetting process as well as determining the quality of our risk information, especially from very risk-averse stakeholders. Flying dragons in the office conference room is probably not going to occur unless it's a new script being written for a fantasy-themed movie. This is of course an exaggeration, but, believe me, some risk-averse people can go off the deep end when addressing risk. No, not me, but you know people. It's best to keep it as clear, concise, and simple as possible but with enough information to make the best decisions. Otherwise, you'll spend all your time updating your risk register, which could lead to sleepless nights worrying about the state of your project.

Not every single risk event will impact your budget or schedule at a deep level and those you can address with qualitative risk analysis and then move right to creating responses for it. Still, others may need some further analysis, especially if they may impact your budget or schedule in such a way that could dramatically affect the entire project. If that is the case, you will need to look further at those risks and make the best decisions you can. That process would be considered **quantitative risk analysis**.

Quantitative risk analysis

Having a probabilistic analysis of a project's risk and determining the impacts in a financial way can sometimes shift stakeholders in the direction they need to go to pursue the best responses to risk. This is also an effective way to apply a **price tag** to identified threats. Trust me when I say most stakeholders aren't scared of the number five; they *are* scared of number 50 thousand, especially when that is what you calculate as a potential project loss due to a threat event. Quantitative risk analysis is statistical and mathematically focused. There are numerous techniques that can be used to quantify objectively, even when using subjective information but the most commonly used and tested on is the **expected monetary value (EMV)**.

Expected monetary value (EMV)

EMV is a way to look at the probability of a risk event and the monetary impact if that risk were to occur at 100 percent. Here's the thing though: nothing is certain where risk is involved, so we must use the information we currently have available to make the best decisions we can at the time. The way the formula is presented is still *probability * impact*, as we saw in qualitative risk analysis, but instead of using a 1 through 5 scale, we will use percentages and money.

The EMV formula is:

*probability (%) * impact (currency costs at 100 percent)*

If I identify a risk to my project such as reworking quality due to defects, I could say there is a 20 percent chance we will have defects outside of normal control metrics, and if that occurs, it will cost the project 50 thousand. Of course, if it does happen at 100 percent, then it will cost 50 thousand, but right now we are trying to determine the impact at the percentage we have identified to create the best response. In this case, the expected monetary value of that risk event is *20 percent * 50 thousand = 10 thousand.* You would have to determine if that impact would drive a response. I could add 10 thousand to my budget, as the cost of quality to eliminate the probability and be no worse for wear, or I could decide that result is an acceptable risk. If it does happen, it will cost 50 thousand. Remember, threats cost money, and opportunities gain or save money. If there is a 20 percent chance it will happen, then there is also an 80 percent chance it won't. These are the decisions you will have to make. Do we look at that as low probability and high impact? If so, what response should we implement to stop it from happening?

Even though you aren't dealing specifically with the full impact, you are getting an idea as to how much a threat could cost the project and then determine the best direction to go. Some people will combine this formula with **decision tree analysis** to pick the best "branch" to follow when making tough decisions without a lot of information.

An organization may be trying to decide whether to build a brand-new high-tech data center or update the one they currently have in place. Each decision carries risk in both the threat and opportunity column. Is the threat larger than the opportunity? That's what expected monetary value helps you figure out.

In *Figure 8.8*, you'll see a simple decision tree using expected monetary value. There would be multiple branches and leaves on an actual decision tree, and the odds are good enough that analysis paralysis will occur as well. You would need to decide how far to analyze your decisions to make the best ones:

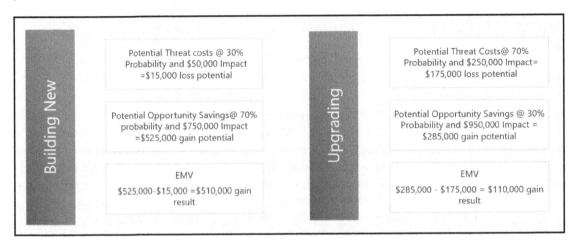

Figure 8.8

In *Figure 8.8*, you can see that when we analyze the potential losses and potential gains of both decisions, we can see that building new is the best decision for this project. There is more to gain and less to lose. Now, the organization may eventually decide that upgrading is less disruptive to the organization and consider other variables for choosing that branch. That is why the example isn't formally fleshed out. There are other considerations for sure. However, if this is what we must work with and need to make a quick decision that is monetarily focused only, then building new looks to be the best decision. Where did the money numbers come from? Expert judgment. Same with the probabilities. You are taking subjective information and making it mathematical or objective. Sometimes when stakeholders see the price tags and impacts they may decide that five is a scary number after all. In this example both choices result in good outcomes. That is not always the case.

I used EMV and the decision tree with my sponsor once, to explain why we should choose one vendor over another. He wanted to go with the least expensive option, and I wanted to prove that we would get what we paid for. Money wasn't the only consideration, because I had a very stringent schedule constraint. I needed to make sure my vendors delivered quality results on time or early. I interviewed other project managers who had worked with both and they resoundingly agreed the more expensive vendor was the best choice due to time and money lost going with the less expensive choice. My tree was poorly drawn but made an impact. Consequently, we chose the more expensive vendor and closed out the project on schedule. Could that be the first time that vendor delivered late? Of course. I would then be subjected to many versions of "I told you so" from my sponsor. It's better to be on the delivering end of that message rather than the receiving end of that message. Expected monetary value and a decision tree can help you do that.

 You will most likely get a question on expected monetary value. You may not see decision trees, but they may be helpful in the real world.

At this point, we would be updating our risk register with any information we can use after we quantified our data. For most of us, the act of quantifying our data is multiplying probability and impact to get a **risk score**, and that's OK. Most of your identified risks will be analyzed that way. A fair few may need some deeper dives into the data, but typically expected monetary values are used to help make decisions about responses or a change in direction. No matter what, your risk events are going to need responses. Next up are the categories of responses and some key phrases to recognize each on the exam.

Creating risk responses for threats

Since many of the risks you will be dealing with fall under the threat category that is where you will spend most of your time creating responses to manage them. It's tempting to slap the response entitled **mitigate** on everything. Mitigate is a buzz word, jargon, and a one-size-fits-all response. It isn't the only response though, and as you review these responses, watch out for the key words; they can help you answer correctly on the exam. As tempting as it may be to select mitigate on every response question or even contingency which another familiar risk term is there is more to the story than that. In *Figure 8.9*, you'll see the threat responses and the key phrases that define them:

Response	Description
Avoid	Change PM Plan through Integrated Change Control
Transfer	Involves Procurement Agreements
Mitigate	Reduce Probability and Impact
Accept	Passive: Do nothing Active: Spend Contingency

Figure 8.9

Avoid

This response category makes it sound like you narrowly escaped something, but it is taking extremely specific steps to remove the risk from your path by **changing the project management plan through formal change control**. Here's the deal: remember the project management plan is your list of YouTube videos for how to do things in each knowledge area. If you have a scope risk, you want to avoid you may need to change your scope, cost, and schedule baselines, depending on the impacts to each. You can't just update your baselines to avoid a risk. You also need to make sure that you don't create another problem. I call this the domino effect. On any risk response you run the risk of creating a whole other problem. These could be **secondary risk events** or **residual risk event**.

Secondary risks

This is when you implement a risk response and create a whole other risk event you didn't plan for. I hate it when this happens. You think you have created the best way to avoid a schedule risk by fast tracking and, oops!, you messed up your quality! Surprise! Now you need a fallback plan, a workaround, a plan B. Someone grab a fire extinguisher because it's about to get hot in here—the domino effect.

Residual risk events

These types of risk mean that whatever response you created didn't get it all. You will also need a fallback plan because typically this residual risk is not at an acceptable level. It is still impacting your project in a negative way and needs to be dealt with quickly.

The reason I bring these up here is any time you are changing anything in your project management plan you will need to assess the impact of that decision on the other constraints before creating a response or solution. Thus, we are making sure these surprises don't happen as often as they could.

Transfer

This response involves using procurement or other agreements to protect the project by placing the brunt of the impact on a third party. These include warranties or letting someone from outside your organization be the experts instead of winging it on your project. Mostly, transferring involves insurance. Health insurance, car insurance, and business insurance. It still costs money, but the impact is lessened.

Mitigate

Ahh, the risk buzzword! It's the placeholder for all risk responses in the real world, but it is only the reduction of the probability, the impact, or both. You would take specific actions to reduce the full probability or impact from the project. Now, you might be thinking to yourself, *Yeah, but changing your project management plan could be reducing the probability and impact because you just said there could be secondary and residual risks. Mitigating by using contracts sounds legit as well.* You would be correct in theory, but remember this is an exam prep guide, and those key phrases will help you answer questions correctly. If you want to toss around mitigating risks at work, have at it! The risk management police aren't showing up, I promise. Just make sure you keep a close eye on the questions and what they are asking before you *yeah but* the exam. With regards to the exam, mitigate is reducing probability and impact only.

Accept

Difficult day at work? Things didn't quite go the way you had planned? Yep, it happens, and sometimes we can do nothing but accept it. Mostly **passive acceptance** involves an identified risk event that really doesn't impact too much and/or trying to implement a response would take more time, effort, and money than it is worth. Sometimes, we must sigh, roll our eyes, and move on with our day.

Active acceptance is where your contingency money comes into play. This response is for those threat events that can be solved with money. Behind schedule? Need to crash? Spend the contingency allotted for that event. It's part of your cost baseline. It's yours to manage. Not everything can be fixed with money though, and you aren't working with an endless supply of it either, so use this response sparingly and only for risks you can respond to using money.

You will see in the following table a cheat sheet on the differences in the responses and key phrases to be aware of:

Avoid	Changing the plan through formal change control
Transfer	Procurement
Mitigate	Reducing probability and impact
Accept	Passive: Do nothing Active: Spend contingency

Contingent response strategy

Another response used for threats is a **contingent response strategy**, which is only used under extremely specific circumstances and is usually determined by the organization. If this happens, do that. You will see this in action but may not even notice it in the world. If you have ever seen the plaque on the back of a hotel room door everywhere in the world, you may have noticed the check-out times, the rates, and what else? It's certainly not where the ice machines are located, that's for sure! It's the fire escape route. That is used in the case of a fire or other risk event, so you know how to get out of the building safely. You also see it happen on airplanes. The exits are here and here (with the appropriate hand flourish), and here's how to use a seat belt. Seat belt? Anyone not know how to use one? This is doubtful, but they do it anyway. Why? Because in the case of a risk event, you need to know how to put your seat belt on and where the floatation device is, and the like. It's contingent on something bad occurring whether you use it or not. Well not the seat belt, because turbulence I could without, so I always wear my seat belt. I'm risk-averse, remember? No matter what, your organizations have measures in place and responses to use under certain threat circumstances. You may know what those are, or you may not. It depends on your organizational processes.

Opportunity responses

Opportunities are typically harder to identify specific to project work. The entire project may have been chartered due to an opportunity but the specifics of that opportunity or others may not be considered during planning. So, unless you have the bubbly, optimistic coworker who constantly reminds you about the greatness of life, you probably don't take the time to identify or document opportunities. If you do, having good response categories is a clever idea. You will notice that these responses are the opposite of the threat responses but utilize the same key phases.

You are more likely to get questions on threat responses rather than opportunities but it's a promising idea to know the terms and that they use the same key phrases.

In *Figure 8.10*, you'll see the responses for opportunities:

Response	Description
Exploit	Change PM Plan through Integrated Change Control
Share	Involves Procurement Agreements
Enhance	Increase Probability and Impact
Accept	Passive: Do nothing Active: Spend Contingency

Figure 8.10

Opportunities may be few and far between on your projects, but if they are identified and you can plan for them and seize those opportunities, then your project will benefit greatly. I totally understand being so focused on threats though as it is tough to see the forest through the trees. Most of my risk register is unwelcome news the team must deal with.

Risk triggers

To have a comprehensive risk register, it's important to document risk triggers as much as possible. Triggers let you know the risk event is on its way and it's time to implement the response. Unfortunately, triggers are usually discovered after the fact. Hindsight is 20/20 vision. Either way, we want to document them. They are lessons learned and a new red flag to watch out for on future projects. If you can document triggers in advance, then your risk owner knows it's go time!

Risk owners

Owners are the ones who implement the chosen risk response. People who do the work know the risks and they are the best people to suggest responses and to implement them. As you execute work and responses are implemented, it's important to update your risk register with the result of that response. Was there secondary or residual risk? Did the response look good on paper but didn't work as executed? Was the response great and the owner's implementation flawed? This is all essential information, because you and your team will be reassessing risk until the project is formally closed. Identify, qualify, quantify, response.

That brings us full circle to the **risk register**. The register is updated after every step and more information is added as it is discovered. In *Figure 8.11*, you will see a simple risk register I hand out to my classes to use. They can change it and so can you. It's not going to hurt my feelings. This is your project, your risk, and your way of documenting. This is merely to give you an idea of what one looks like, so we can exit theory and look at reality:

Risk Category	Description of risk	Risk Owner	Impact (1-5)	Probability of Occurrence (1-5)	Risk Score	Rating Color Code	Risk Priority Number	Risk triggers	Preventative Strategy/Action(s)	Mitigation action(s) (actions to be taken if risk occurs, Activated by Threshold)	Action plan implementation Status and effectiveness of action
Scope											
			3	4	12		◯				
			1	2	2		◯				
			5	5	25		◯				
					0		◯				
					0		◯				

Figure 8.11

Risk management is a big undertaking, but imperative for the success of the project. Depending on the size and scope of the project, your need for intense risk documentation may adjust. In smaller projects, it may be enough to know what to expect and handle it in the way you always do. If the project is longer than a month, I would highly suggest you get into the practice of documenting your risks, so you stay ahead of the curve and enjoy fewer sleepless nights.

Issue logs

There is just one more aspect of the risk world to consider and that is an **issue log**. An issue is a risk that has been realized. It's a surprise! Issues carry a bit less of a wallop than an identified threat event, but they still make the day longer than it could be. An issue would be five of your team members calling out sick who were working on critical activities. A risk would be five of your team members quitting and you don't have anyone else.

The issue log is also updated on a regular basis, like the risk register, and all stakeholders will be communicated with regarding issues as well as risks. Typically, the issue log is a document used for communication and to keep track of things that go sideways on a project. Many project teams have an issue log and not a risk register, and some use both. It depends on your projects. You'll want to make sure the issue is documented, who brought up the issue, who is assigned to help fix the issue, the date is was resolved, how it was resolved, and any additional information necessary. Issues can cause conflict on a project team as well, so it's important to keep on top of the surprises as well as the threats and opportunities.

Summary

This was a large chapter with a ton of information in it. You covered many topics in cost and in risk, and it's OK to feel a bit of a headache coming on. See how you do in the practice question section, and as needed, go back through this chapter again to brush up on the information. Much of what we covered is highly testable, so this chapter is an important one to understand. First, we covered estimating costs and in addition to estimating for resources and scope of work we included quality management and the cost of quality into those estimates. Then, we covered the importance of quality gates and governance gates, to make sure we are getting what we paid for on the quality side of things and determining go/no go decisions and formal sign-off.

Then we covered creating the project budget and aggregating costs and risk reserves together to gain approval on the cost baseline, and then we reviewed tracking and reporting cost/schedule performance using earned value technique and a variety of formulas to do so.

Then, we left cost and went to risk management planning, including SWOT analysis and the beginnings of the risk register. This was followed by analysis techniques such as qualitative and quantitative analysis. In quantitative risk analysis, you learned about expected monetary value and decision tree analysis. Once that analysis is completed, we can then create responses for those risks and update our risk register iteratively throughout the project. Finally, we covered issue logs to track the surprises that can cause problems on your projects.

In Chapter 9, *Monitoring and Controlling Project Work,* you will review some additional techniques to make sure that the project is running smoothly, including quality control charts and graphs, formal change control for projects and for organizations, key performance indicators, and scope validation, as well procurement management processes, including contract types and the seller section process.

Questions

1. You are the project manager for a large development project and are discussing budgeting with your sponsor. The sponsor is asking for a definitive estimate from you to properly allocate funds for the project. Which of the following estimating techniques will give you a definitive estimate?
   - Analogous
   - Parametric
   - Bottom-up
   - Three-point

2. Which of the following could be considered the costs of quality? Choose all that apply:
   - Training
   - Appraisal
   - Resource rates
   - Scope creep
   - Formal change control
   - Prevention costs

3. You and your team have reached a milestone on your project, and your senior stakeholders will be signing-off on the quality of the work and the project's progress. These formal processes are known as which of the following?
   - Quality gate
   - Phase gate review
   - Governance gate
   - Go / no go decision

4. As a project manager, your responsibility is to put together a comprehensive budget that will be approved as a cost baseline. Therefore, you need to incorporate several considerations into the total number. All of the following are included in your cost baselines, except which one?
   - Funding limit reconciliation
   - Contingency reserves
   - Cost of quality
   - Scope of work
   - Resource rates

5. It's week four of a 30-week 40 thousand US dollar project, and you are collecting work performance data from your team to determine your cost and schedule performance. Your team reports that it is about 10 percent complete and that it has spent 15 thousand dollars of the total budget. What can you tell about the cost performance of this project?
    - The project is currently over budget
    - The project is currently under budget
    - The project is right on budget
    - There is not enough information to determine budgetary performance

6. You have compiled your performance reports and are about to have a meeting with your sponsor. Your current performance information shows which of the following:
    EV = 30,000; PV = 32,000; AC = 28,000
    What will you be reporting to your sponsor about the project schedule and budget?
    - Behind schedule and over budget
    - Ahead of schedule and under budget
    - Behind schedule and right on target for the budget
    - Behind schedule and under budget

7. One of your team members comes to you and states that their current CPI is 0.8 and their SV is -12,000. How is this part of the project performing?
    - Over budget and behind schedule
    - Under budget and ahead of schedule
    - Over budget and ahead of schedule
    - Under budget and behind schedule

8. Which of the following is the correct formula for earned value (EV)?
    - EV-SV
    - BAC * SPI
    - BAC * % complete
    - EV/BAC

9. You have received approvals for your four thousand US dollar cost baseline and have scheduled the project work across four weeks. Which of the following could be considered the planned values of each week?
    - Two thousand
    - Four thousand
    - One thousand
    - There is not enough information to answer this question

10. Your project team is in the process of beginning to identify risks, and you have set up a facilitated brainstorming session in which the team can focus on categories of risk. Which of the following tools may be helpful in this process?
    - Risk register
    - Qualitative risk analysis
    - Quantitative risk analysis
    - SWOT analysis

11. Jill is one of your best team members, and she is excellent at identifying and managing risk on your team. Jill is concerned that an identified threat on the project may impact your budget more than your project can handle. What technique could you use to determine the price tag of the identified risk event?
    - Earned value
    - Expected monetary value
    - Cost variance
    - Cost performance index

12. Keenan and Abdul are in the conference room discussing different strategies for overcoming a risk event. Keenan feels the best course of action is to change the project management plan through formal change control and adjust those items that are creating the potential risk event. What risk response is Kennan suggesting?
    - Avoid
    - Mitigate
    - Exploit
    - Transfer

13. Ben is a member of your team and is the risk owner for one of the big impactful risk events on your project. When the risk occurred, he implemented the response but then quickly noticed that another risk had occurred elsewhere in the project due to the response he implemented. This is an example of which of the following?
    - Residual risk
    - Mitigation
    - Secondary risk
    - Contingent response strategy

14. Two of your team members are discussing the best way to update the risk register to make it more effective and you mention that adding categories of risk events may be helpful. Which of the following risk processes suggests categorization?
    - Identify risks
    - Quantitative
    - Qualitative
    - Response planning

15. You and your team are in a meeting discussing risk, and Jamal is concerned that one of the risk events could impact the project financially. His estimate puts the impact at 35 thousand US dollars. The team discusses the identified risk and agrees on the impact and determines the probability of that event occurring is around 20 percent. What is the expected monetary value?
    - Seven thousand
    - 35 thousand
    - 35,020
    - Six thousand

16. As a project manager, you are collecting work performance data from your team and need to process the data through variance analysis. Your data includes the following:
    EV = 42,000; PV = 41,200; AC = 42,200
    What is your SPI and your CPI on this project?
    - 1.02 and 0.99
    - 0.99 and 1.02
    - 800 and - 200
    - -200 and 800

Monitoring and Controlling Project Work

9

In this chapter, you will be reviewing multiple best practices to monitor and control your projects. You reviewed some of those best practices in `Chapter 8`, *Budget and Contingency Plans for Risk*, but this chapter is focused on additional knowledge areas. You will review scope creep and the validation of deliverables, as well as quality control best practices and some of the charts and graphs used to track progress. You will also review formal change control and the reasons changes may need to occur across the project and the organization. Then you will review procurement best practices, from determining procurement needs, selecting sellers and contract types, to making sure all terms and conditions are being followed to avoid a breach of contract.

This chapter will cover the following topics:

- Quality control
- Validate scope
- Integrated change control
- Procurement management

Quality control

Quality control is imperative to the successful acceptance of the deliverable. In the last chapter, you reviewed quality gates and governance gates that are scheduled to check for quality and to make go/no-go decisions. It is also realistic to assume that scope of work is being inspected as well to approve that the requirements have been met. Scope and quality are like peanut butter and jelly. They just go together. When reviewing quality gates, I mentioned that the inspection of the deliverable is necessary. Riding the bike around the block or checking for chocolate chips is all part of the inspection process of quality control.

Quality assurance is making sure our team is following the steps of the process, and quality control is making sure the result is fit for use and that it works. To track that performance, it may be necessary to utilize visual charts and graphs to monitor trends in performance. Mostly, quality control best practices began in the manufacturing industry, in which it was necessary to set up random samples or statistical sampling. This was because checking every single result is costly and time-consuming. Although, in the case of the chocolate chip factory, I'd love to give checking every result the old college try!

These days, quality is important in everything we do in IT. We may not be sampling, but we may be running tests on our hardware or software. Software developers do integration testing to make sure their code works and that the result functions the way it should. We all care about the quality of work, and even though you may not use these charts or graphs, it stands to reason that there must be a way to track quality performance, regardless of your industry. Therefore, in most IT project management environments, we are more likely to use **Gantt charts**, **dashboards**, and **status reporting,** as well as **knowledge management systems** such as SharePoint or the like. Still, others with virtual or remote teams will utilize real-time updates on intranet and internet sites, Wiki pages, or collaboration tools such as WebEx and Skype to monitor day-to-day work and project progress. **Performance measurement tools** are usually driven by organizational processes and your enterprise environment, so keeping track of project performance can vary.

The goal is to have a scorecard for scope, quality, cost, schedule, and other project aspects that are tracked and communicated on regularly. In earlier chapters, I brought up **key performance indicators (KPI)**. These are the items that indicate whether our performance is up to scratch. Typically, this would come in the form of baselines or other targets for performance, as well as governance gates or phase-end reviews. Our goal is to stay as close as possible to the plans, and track to any irregularities and communicate those transparently. Having a balanced scorecard is the goal, but things don't always work out as planned. That would be the very reason for formal change control that is integrated across all knowledge areas, meaning change can happen in any knowledge area, and often if one aspect is affected, then so are several others. We'll cover formal change control later in this chapter, but right now we are trying to figure out how our project performance is going, and specifically quality and scope performance.

Many times, if we find defects outside of normal limits or tolerance levels in our quality control inspections, the result points to a problem with the way, in which we are executing the work, or our process is flawed. There is always human error to consider, but if your results are consistently riddled with defects, then your process is most likely the problem.

Going back to my fictional cookie factory, let's say my process was to use a cup of salt and half a cup of sugar. My team gets to work and follows that recipe to the exact measurement. Then, when we inspect one out of every one-hundred cookies for quality, we notice that they don't taste particularly good. But why? Too much salt? Not enough sugar? My recipe is flawed somehow. My team's performance is fine, but the process is out of control. That inspection gave a heads up that something is amiss, but what?

There are numerous ways to review your process and your results in a visual way. Most teams create a **process flow diagram** during planning, so they have a checklist to follow. This is also immensely helpful when trying to figure out what is wrong with our process. You are certainly not going to scrap an entire process, because we don't know yet what is wrong. It can't be everything! Plus, we spent the time to plan out the process and execute the work. We can't go all the way back to the drawing board now; we have cookies to bake.

A process flow diagram allows us to look at the process visually, and often process flow diagrams have decision points. Did this happen? Yes or no? If *yes*, go in this direction; if *no*, stay the course. Process flow diagrams can be quite simple or quite complex depending on your output. Even if you create a process flow diagram *after* defects are found, it's a good tool for communicating with your team and a balanced approach to finding out the reason the defect occurred. Too much salt? That would be fixed with a defect repair using formal change control to update our process, and then we can begin to execute it again.

Remember, not every defect is cause for panic, and scrapping an entire process is costly in a lot of ways. Some defects are expected, and if they are within normal limits then it's considered an anomaly or human error, or it's time to update the machinery. If there are too many defects, we would use root cause analysis (FISHikawa!) and try to figure out what is causing the defects to occur and then work to fix them.

The other thing to consider is there may not be just one thing causing problems. Maybe the cookies are overcooked, which is a machinery problem. Maybe there aren't enough chocolate chips in the cookies because I'm eating more than I'm putting into the dough, which is a human error (sorry, not sorry!), and a variety of other issues could occur that would need investigating. Therefore, just reviewing your process flowchart may not be enough. We would need to focus our inspections on a variety of potential issues and document them accordingly.

Histograms

One way may be to use a simple bar chart that tracks the number of defects compared to when they occurred or where they occurred. Your stats are your own to track, but it's always good to have something visual to review and to communicate with. In *Figure 9.1*, you can see a simple histogram for tracking quality and defects:

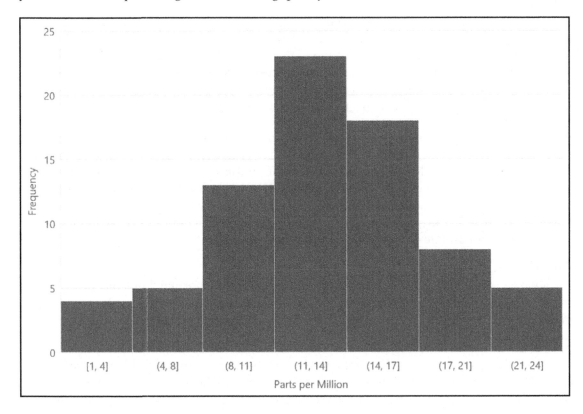

Figure 9.1

Without getting too statistical on you, most histograms will show a bell curve or normal distribution. Six Sigma is based on the concept that there are six standard deviations between the customer's specification limit and the mean of the process. Process variations can be reduced by correcting the process itself until it is almost perfect. Fewer than 3.4 defects per million is the goal of Six Sigma processes. Six Sigma, as a concept, is described as a **highly disciplined process** whose focus is on developing near-perfect products and services:

- Six Sigma is a statistical term used to measure any deviations from a perfect result the process is causing.
- More deviation equals more defects.

In *Figure 9.2*, you can see the variables, as they are presented in a bell curve (typically presented in a bar chart or histogram), and the sigma variables:

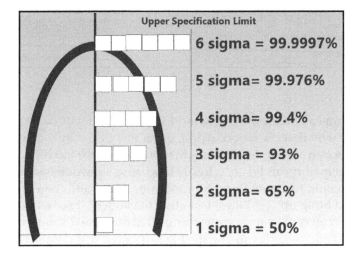

Figure 9.2

If all outputs of our process fall within six standard deviations from the mean, we will have satisfied our customers almost all the time. If we have one million customers, only 3.4 will experience a defect.

If that flew squarely over your head, do not despair; you will not be tested on anything Sigma-related or statistical in nature on the Project+ exam; it's just another way of showing your data visually and a focused attack on preventing defects. Too many defects = the cost of non-conformance.

Fishbone diagram

Remember this guy from the last chapter? It is used for root cause identification based on several categories. In *Figure 9.3*, you can see an example of the fishbone diagram in action:

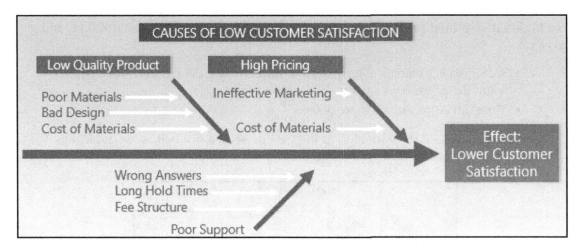

Figure 9.3

The **fishbone diagram** can be used for risk and for quality to focus or target our conversations about why defects are occurring, or, in this case why we are getting too many low customer satisfaction survey results. Is it that our prices are too high, and if so, why? Is our product lower in quality, and if so, why? Is it because someone had to sit on hold for two hours while listening to a poor excuse for elevator music and internally seething, only to be transferred and hung up on? Yikes! Is it all of the above? If so, what is impacting us the most right now? You can't change everything all at once, so it's important to determine what you can fix first and what is causing the biggest impacts and defects. That is where another chart can come in very handy. That chart is the **Pareto diagram**.

Pareto diagrams

First, a little history on the Pareto diagram. Vilfredo Federico Damaso Pareto was a man with a large name and brain and clearly hailed from Germany (just kidding). Pareto was an Italian engineer, sociologist, economist, political scientist, and philosopher—busy guy! He is also most credited with the 80/20 rule, or **the Pareto Principle**, created in 1906.

Pareto was studying the distribution of wealth in Italy, and determined that 80 percent of the country's wealth and land was owned by 20 percent of the population. He was also credited with the study of economic principles such as income distribution. Pareto was also responsible for the term *elite* becoming a popular way of describing the rich. Now that you have had the history lesson and are craving Italian food, let's look at the theory in the context of quality. The theory postulates that 80 percent of the output from a given situation or system is determined by 20 percent of the input.

We are looking at displays of results and trying to determine the relative importance of the defects and then direct improvement efforts to those areas. The biggest impact for the good of the result and achieved for the least amount of money is a pretty typical way to begin. Although the cost of quality is a pay-me-now-or-pay-later concept, we sometimes must pay later to fix the main causes of defects.

The Pareto principle was not originally created for quality management; it was more a theory on economics. But a quality guru named Joseph Juran came along later, and, in 1941, implemented the principle as a way of discovering what the 20 percent of causes of defects are and make plans to fix those first. By the way, Joseph Juran spent his entire adult life working in quality management as a speaker, a writer, and influencer in both Japan and the United States, and from all the research, I can conclude he was an all-around nice guy as well. Juran was often quoted as saying *the vital few and the useful many.* What this meant was focus on the big 20 percent of the causes of defects and work on those first, but don't forget the other 80 percent either.

There is only so much we can do to check things ourselves before we wreck ourselves or our product, service, or result, so focused efforts and continuous improvements are the core tenants of quality management. In *Figure 9.4*, you will see a simple Pareto diagram:

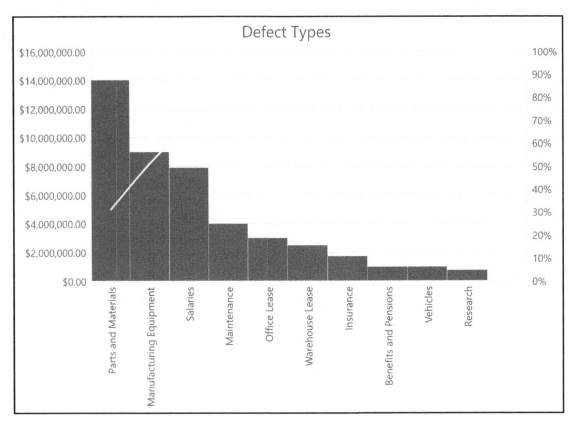

Figure 9.4

To read a Pareto diagram, you'll see that the visual is a combination of a bar chart or histogram and a line graph. The values are in descending order, and the cumulative total is represented by the line. So, if you read this to determine the biggest cause of defects, it would be parts and equipment. Then we would focus our efforts on fixing that problem first, and before moving on to manufacturing equipment, and so on. This is easier said than done, for sure! What this chart is lacking is a timeline. When were these defects discovered across time? Is there fluctuation in the results at different points in time? This is where a run chart can be helpful.

Run chart

If you can remember back to when you were about six or seven, you may have done a school science experiment to track the weather and temperature every day for a month. Just me? I'm still running that experiment on the East Coast of the United States, and I'm here to tell you the results are grim. For the love of Pete, please stop raining and snowing! Sorry… weather tangent. My point in asking the question is that using a run chart can help plot out results during a specified check-in across a specified length of time. Every day at noon, I will log the temperature over the course of one month and see whether there are any wild fluctuations or whether things are standard across the board. In *Figure 9.5*, you will see a basic run chart. It is also a line chart, and they are typically quite simple to create and to read:

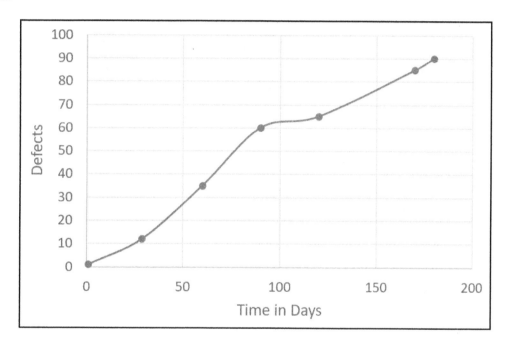

Figure 9.5

Our last chart will be used to compare two different variables to see whether they are working together to create a problem, or whether we have two separate problems on our hands. That is called a **scatter chart**.

Scatter charts

As mentioned, scatter charts allow us to compare two separate inputs to see whether they are working together to create a defect. It's possible that two things working together could be creating a problem. I'm eating too many chocolate chips; therefore, the chocolate chip shooter isn't getting enough chips into the cookie dough. Sorry about that! In *Figure 9.6*, you will see a quite simple scatter diagram. The key word that represents this chart is **a relationship**. Is there a relationship between the two variables shown below?

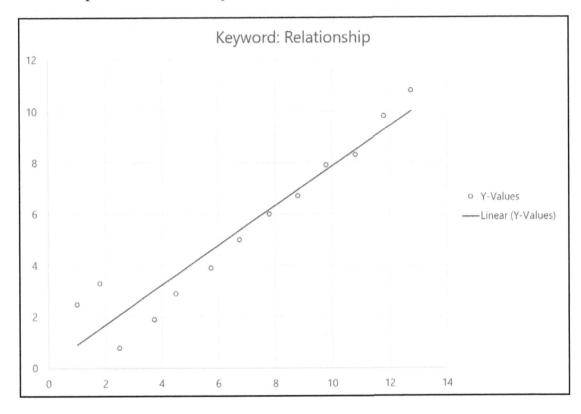

Figure 9.6

The way to determine whether there is a relationship is by looking at the scatter. The closer the results are scattered together around the mean (diagonal line), the closer the relationship is. The further away the scatter is, the less of a relationship there is. This means there are two separate issues causing the defect, and now you will have to look at each individually to decide what to focus on first.

You may be asked to recognize these charts and graphs visually or to identify them based on a description in a question.

Managing quality and controlling defects is a constant game of whack-a-mole. As soon as one problem is fixed, another one pops up somewhere else. That is why proprietary quality control processes are so popular, such as Six Sigma or the **International Organization for Standardization (ISO)**. They set the standards for quality in certain industries. For the rest of us, we are just trying to create the best product and service we can, and in IT that is tough to quantify. We must keep our eye on the prize, and in many cases, that is inspection first and, hopefully, the quality and scope of work are accepted as fit for use and correct.

Validate scope

Just like during the governance gates a signature is necessary to move on, the same applies to the scope of work. In fact, to close out your project, it is usually necessary to get the final signatures. This does a couple of things: it provides formal acceptance of the scope of work, and it provides the necessary documentation needed to begin project closure procedures. Not every organization has formal sign-offs on the scope of work, but I find it is an important step. After all, you did all the planning and execution and monitoring and controlling, and you would like to feel validated for all that hard work, darn it.

There is a cadence to project management. This is the reason for everything else we do to plan and execute and monitor and control effectively.

That process includes the following:

- Producing the deliverable during execution
- Verifying quality via inspection
- Validating scope via inspection
- Formal closure of the project or phase

That's it! The entire reason for every best practice we cover outside of those processes is to support that trajectory, from deliverable creation to a closed project, with full acceptance, without any adaptations. Does it always work that way? I think you know the answer to that question—nope, nada, no. In Chapter 10, *Formal Project or Phase Closure and Agile Project Management*, you will review a variety of reasons why projects may not reach the finish line. It's the goal, of course, but best-laid plans don't always go the way they should.

It may be that scope validation doesn't occur because the scope of work is not correct, the bicycle seat isn't right, the color is off, and who the heck added that bell? The dreaded **scope creep** strikes again!

Scope creep is unauthorized, uncontrollable changes to the scope of work without regard to constraints or formal change control. It happens. Often. A lot. Every project. You get my point. The thought is that if you have a formal process in place for change control then scope creep won't happen. I'm officially rolling on the floor, laughing out loud! For the millennials in the house: ROTFLOL! Why is it so funny? Because it doesn't matter how good your change-control procedure is or how well the team understands it, there will always be tweaks and adjustments made without regard to requirements. Your team may think it is helping, but adding scope outside of requirements is a big no-no.

 Keep in mind the process of deliverable creation, verified quality, validate scope, and project/phase closure—not because you will be tested on the process, but because it helps you see the big picture as to why these formal processes are necessary, and could help you answer questions on your exam.

The inevitable goal of any project is to produce the result to spec and requirements, make sure it is fit for use, gain the appropriate approvals, and then transfer the result to the customer or end users. Without formal acceptance and validation of scope, that can't happen, so scope needs to be controlled, and scope creep needs to be kept in check. As we move on to change control, keep in mind that this is all formal. Quality control is formal, validate scope is formal, and change control is formal.

Integrated change control

Change happens, and when it does, it's good to have a set process in place. Many organizations have a very formal change control procedure, and others do not. It's a lot like risk management that way. It may be because projects are smaller, and the project manager or sponsor can approve changes or make project decisions on the fly, and still other projects are much larger in size, scope, and costs, so making sure changes are formally approved and communicated may be necessary.

 The assumption on the exam is that the projects are larger and formal change control would be necessary.

There are many reasons why changes could occur on a project.

The most obvious changes include the following:

- Timeline change
- Funding change
- Risk event
- Requirements change
- Quality change
- Resource change
- Scope change

These are the normal changes on most projects. The one major thing to consider, though, is that if scope or requirements change, they typically drive changes to other areas such as quality, schedule, and cost—the domino effect. On the risk side of things, remember avoiding and exploiting risks as responses for threats and opportunities? Those responses include changing the needed aspects of the project management plan to make sure the threat doesn't occur and that the opportunity does. All the potential changes are for extremely specific reasons and affect the project in multiple ways. If you could place all potential changes into categories, there would be four that describe the reasoning behind why changes would be necessary.

Types of change

These are the major categories for change:

- Corrective action
- Preventative action
- Defect repair
- Scope changes

Corrective actions

Corrective actions are any actions taken to bring performance **back in line** with the original plans and baselines. You are trying to fix something—not something that didn't go according to plan, but because someone took a shortcut and left the plan. Much like if you plug in an address to your GPS in your car and you are going along following directions and all of a sudden decide you are going to take a shortcut and turn off route.

The genuinely nice person on your GPS suggests you make a U-turn as soon as possible. It's because you have left the planned route. I was convinced my GPS was saying make an illegal U-turn as soon as you can, and I made a few; I'm not going to lie. There will be no illegal U-turns in corrective actions. We will need to recognize that we have left the plan and correct our direction by determining what needs to change and then go through formal change control to get back on track. That's not to say that every single plan is perfect, and if things go sideways, it's because we didn't follow the plan. It's a category of change that suggests things *would* have worked out if we had stuck to the plan.

For example, you are installing software patches across multiple departmental systems. In the middle of it, you go to lunch and come back and skip a department by accident. Oops! Now you will need to correct the action as soon as you figure out it was missed. Days could have gone by when you discover it. If that task was on the critical path, you have now pushed out the schedule and affected the scope of work. Those changes would need to be formal because of the impact to other areas of the project. Corrective action would be necessary.

Corrective actions are reactionary. Something has happened that needs to be fixed as soon as it is discovered.

For the purposes of the exam, stick to the thought that corrective action is bringing performance back in line with the plans due to a deviation.

Preventative actions

In this case, your team sees something lurking and the team has determined to avoid it at all costs by changing the project management plan in a preemptive strike. Much like the avoid category of risk responses, the team has discovered something in the plan that hasn't been executed yet and won't work out no matter what they do. The action is taken to prevent something from affecting the project management plan in the future. We are actively taking steps through formal change control to stop something negative from impacting our project. This decision could come from hindsight or foresight. We learned something earlier and we can't have it happen again, or we have peeked into the Matrix and discovered a potential problem that we can't have occurring in the future.

Defect repair

Defect repair is mostly a quality fix through formal change control. We have identified a defect in our product or service and we need to remove the cause of it from our process and our plans. We are trying to correct something that isn't working. Once we go through the inspection of our result and determine that there is a defect outside of normal limits of acceptance, we would have to determine why it was happening and how to fix it. That is where quality assurance and quality control work together. Execute the work, audit the process, and inspect the result.

If inspection shows defects, then you would perform root cause analysis on your process flow to see which decision point was incorrect, then take steps to fix the defect. In all changes that are approved and implemented, we would need to validate that the change worked. Or in this case, fixed the defects.

I want to stop here for just a moment and address quality management as an entire entity. Because we go in such a linear fashion with these concepts, I think it's important to tie some of these processes together. Quality is repeating cycles of **plan-do-check-act**, or what is known as the **Shewhart cycle**, which was made possible by another quality guru: W Edwards Deming.

I am going to give you a quick history lesson on Deming, because he was super-influential in quality management in both the United States and Japan, especially right after World War II. Deming's experience looks a lot like Pareto's in the respect that he had experience in multiple arenas. Deming was an American engineer, statistician, professor, author, lecturer, and management consultant, and an all-around nice guy too! Deming promoted the work of Walter Shewhart, including statistical process control and types of operational definitions, which were credited for helping Japan rebuild its economy after the war.

Deming implemented the **plan-do-check-act** cycle (**PDCA**) in quality management best practices. He always referred to it as the **Shewhart Cycle** (see, nice guy!), even though Deming was credited for utilizing PDCA to practice continuous improvement. Why does all this matter? Because quality management is a *cycle*. First you plan, then you execute, then you monitor and control. Oh, wait, that is project management! Hmmm... There is a distinct correlation between quality management and our process groups in project management. Project management is messy; it's two steps forward, one step back, and it's a process of continuous learning and improvements. On the quality side, I like to explain the planning, assurance, and control as a cycle as well.

In *Figure 9.7*, you will see the processes of quality management:

Figure 9.7

To bring defect repair back into the conversation, let's assume you put together your plan for quality and listed out the process, the acceptable tolerance levels for defects, and even a **process improvement plan**. If you want to use a fun term at parties, we call process and product improvements **Kaizen.** It's the combination of two Japanese words: *Kai = continuous,* and *Zen = improvements,* which mean a focused approach to improving quality in a continuous fashion via improvement plans. There isn't a set process attached. Each organization would need to determine what that might look like to the organization. As a team, we would then begin to execute project work using the quality plan and processes. During that execution, we would audit the process (QA) to make sure we are following the steps, and then inspect the result for defects (QC). Even though a Kaizen sounds very relaxing, it is a very intensive-focused approach to improvement in overall organizational quality.

Referring to *Figure 9.7*, we are essentially performing those processes going in a clockwise motion. If defect repair is needed, then we begin to go counter-clockwise. If a defect is discovered, we would have to perform quality assurance audits, look at our process and determine the root causes of defects, and then process a change request to update our quality management plan. If approved, we would update the plan and begin going in clockwise order again:

- **Plan**: Create or update the quality management plan
- **Do**: Execute according to that plan
- **Check**: Quality assurance and quality control
- **Act**: Change control for defect repair

The last category of change can also impact your quality, your schedule, your budget, your contracts, and your sanity. Scope changes impact everything.

Scope change

Scope changes are quite common, especially with external customers. The problem is that we have created a very front-loaded, predictive project management plan with baselines. Even if it's the smallest change in scope, we must look at everything that changes will impact. Domino effect. There are a couple distinctions to be aware of with scope changes, and what is considered a small change in scope versus a project ending change in scope.

Let's say that bicycle project is about halfway through and the customer asks for that darn bell; we would have to determine how that addition in scope affected the rest of the project and then create a solution that is approved both, through formal change control and by the customer. But what if the customer says, *you know, I've been thinking* (no phrase will strike fear into the heart of a project manager more than those words!) *I've been thinking, I'd rather have a motorcycle.* Really? We are half way through the project, and now you want a motorcycle? What would we do in that case? Would we process a change request, or is that a totally different project? If you thought that is a totally different project, you would be correct!

The scope of work is now so different than the scope of work planned and completed to date on the bike project that there is nothing else to do but start from scratch. We would need formal sign-off or scope validation to whatever form of completion the bike is, and the project would be formally closed out. Then, a new business case, a new charter, a new project would need to be created.

Watch out for questions related to a scope change versus project closure due to a massive change in scope of work.

Otherwise, scope and other changes are quite common, and all will need to be managed formally. It's just a part of day-to-day project management and a way to prevent (not stop) scope creep from happening.

Change control process

Most large organizations that fall under a strong matrix or project-based dynamic will have both a **project management office (PMO)** and a **change control board (CCB)**. A CCB's only job is to deny all your change requests. Wait... sorry. A CCB's only job is to review all change requests and approve or deny them on the organizational level. They are overseeing multiple projects, programs, and portfolios, and making the best decisions for the good of the organization. If you are asking for more time or money, they must look at the allocation of resources, funding limit reconciliations, management reserves for risk, and the like. They will be very thorough, I promise you that. Therefore, it is important to go to the change control board with solutions and not problems.

While some change requests can be approved by the sponsor, or even by you, for smaller change needs the CCB is the final authority on big changes like the scope of work, defect repair, corrective, or preventative actions. That is why having a process for change can be extremely helpful. At a high level, the process for formal change control is comprised of about nine steps. They are as follows:

- Identify and document
- Evaluate impact and justification
- Identify approval authority
- Obtain approval
- Implement change
- Validate change/quality check
- Update documents/audit documents/version control
- Communicate throughout as needed
- Validate scope

There may also be a time when you've made a mistake and must reverse an approved or implemented change. This would be known as a face palm moment in project management. Where you take the palm of your hand and smack yourself in the forehead. It's okay; it happens. There are projects in which I have had a permanent palm print right in the center of my forehead. Listen, even with formal change control, nothing is guaranteed! These changes are called **regression plans** (reverse changes). If you are lucky, your forehead will escape without casualty and your changes will all fix whatever problem your project is facing. Therefore, the second step is so important.

Evaluate impact and justification is probably the biggest influential time to prevent a regression change in the future. The impact of the change on other variables is important to investigate, and not on your own either. The people who do the work know the work, and they are the people who are requesting changes and are in the trenches, so they know the impacts to their piece of the project. You do not have to be the authority on everything, but your job is to look at the big picture and determine if their assessment is correct on the project level, and then help create solutions for implementation. After approvals happen, it's necessary to make sure the change was implemented effectively and validate that the change worked.

It's also your job to communicate the approvals or denials of the powers that be to your stakeholders. I keep a changelog for just that purpose. What the change was, who requested it, whether it was approved or not, how the change was implemented, documents that were updated, and whether the result was validated. Much like an issue log, this is good information for the present project and future lessons learned.

The easiest way to remember this process for the exam is this:

- Assess the impact of the change on every other constraint. If we add a bell to the bicycle, how will that affect the schedule and the critical path? How will our budget be affected? What quality requirements do we need to put in place? Do I need an experienced bell resource?
- Work with the team to create solutions for implementation.
- Find the right power to sign off on the solution, usually the CCB or sponsor.
- Get the customer's approvals as well. This is an important step because the customer may view your solution as not probable. *Wait! How much does a bell cost? How long will it take? Never mind, I don't need a bell.*
- Then update your documentation, communicate to stakeholders, implement the solution, cross your fingers, and validate it worked.

This is the typical process for project changes, but there are other forces of change where the influencing factors are coming from outside your project and outside your control.

Other causes of change

Changes in business happen all the time on the organizational level. Sometimes they feel like a big surprise, and other times the rumor mill is working overtime. Organization changes are painful. I know; I speak from experience, having survived three major mergers and acquisitions. It happens. When a change occurs on the organizational level, it may impact your ability to effectively manage your projects. Organizational changes usually fall into several categories. They are as follows:

- Business merger/acquisition
- Business demerger/split
- Business process change
- Internal reorganization
- Relocation
- Outsourcing

There is not a single situation on that list that results in good news for your projects, and that is because change is painful. Nobody likes organizational change, even when it is necessary. Well, except for wet babies; they like changes. Adults do not like change at all, and when an organization is making decisions for everyone, it can be a very harrowing process. Especially a business process change.

Every change is painful, but when an organization decides to change the way they are doing things, chaos ensues. This painful experience is quite elegantly represented in a model created by Dr. Virginia Satir, who, as a family counselor, created the **Satir model** for change within a family dynamic. Her view was that everyone is working within their normal behaviors, then a change is forced. Chaos will occur until the new normal is integrated and accepted. Chaos is the biggest factor.

I see this all the time in organizations which are trying to improve their processes. As a management consultant and instructor, I'm usually the one trying to convince them that change is needed to improve their business. The organizations that embrace the chaos as a normal condition and work their way through it are always successful. Too often, though, chaos is blamed for a process not working, and the organization will scrap the change and try to go back to the way things were or implement something else that is new. Consequently, those organizations are always in a state of chaos and never get out of it. Something to keep in mind. Chaos is a necessary force of change.

I bring this up here because if you and your team decide that you are going to implement some of the best practices you have read about in this guide, keep in mind it will be new. People, yourself included, will make mistakes, and it will feel uncomfortable. Push through it, see the value in what you are trying to do, perpetuate the vision of better results, and get your team to the new normal. My best advice is do not try to change more than *three things* at once. That is the tipping point for most process changes. Get to the new normal and then change three more things. Even with defect repair, the focus is on the most impactful items. Fix those and move on to the rest. The same thing goes for organization process changes. Control what you can and live through the rest.

Procurement management

Procurement management is a big topic, and for many of you working with procurement, this may be a very surface-level thing. Perhaps you have contractors that work on your team, or you have reviewed some procurement documentation to make sure the equipment you need is correct. There is a variety of levels possible for a project manager to be involved with in procurement for the project. As we move forward through this section, there are several assumptions that are made in exam questions. Mostly, this is to keep things out of the gray areas and to focus on concepts. These concepts or assumptions may not align at all with that you do now, but may later in your project or careers. Procurement is also represented in a very surface level way without getting too deep into terms and conditions and legalese. The very first assumption on the exam is that you have a procurement administrator, legal department, or procurement administrator that is helping your organization and project fulfill procurement needs. These would be stakeholders on the project, and would be the people who oversee all procurements. You, however, understand the scope of work and know what is necessary from outside the organization for resources. Your job is to make sure that everyone is on the same page with the scope of work, and that you create and maintain good relationships with any stakeholder derived via procurement.

Another assumption that is made is that project managers cannot legally or contractually bind their organization to that of another because we are not attorneys, and nor are the procurement department/coordinator/administrator. Those are all terms that may be used to represent the people who negotiate and manage procurement from the legal side of things. That is not to say that you are off the hook where contracts are involved. Oh no, you will have to make sure that you are following the letter of the law and protecting your organization from future costs, arbitration, mediation, and litigation. I believe that is why this section is both comprehensive and scratching the surface. It is comprehensive because you will need to know the roles and responsibilities and all the jargon involved in procurement, and it is scratching the surface because we are not expected to know all the ins and outs of the legal side of the business.

With that caveat in place, let's start with why you might need to enter into a procurement agreement and what your role will be.

Another assumption is that we are the buyer because we are paying out of our budgets for goods, services or staff. That the contractor/vendor/supplier or sellers are external to our organization. This also keeps things out of the gray areas on the exam. Most questions are written from the perspective of the buyer (us), unless otherwise stated in the question.

If we are considered the buyer, then it stands to reason that we will need to understand the scope of work, what we are lacking, and what can be obtained via agreement. Keep in mind that the term agreement isn't always a set, formal, legal contract. It could be an email or a handshake. The majority of what you will cover for the exam, though, is contracting types and a variety of other documents that are formal and very legally inclined.

What you would need to procure for your project depends. Do you need to augment your staff? Do you need materials and equipment from outside our organization? You will need to do what is a called a **make-or-buy analysis**. Can we make it if we gain the right parts from outside the organization? Can we just buy what we need outright? Rental decisions can be made as well. Should we rent computers or buy them? Should we rent warehouse space or buy a warehouse? These are questions that need answers before anything is determined. You may be wondering why we are talking about planning for procurements in the monitoring and controlling section of the guide—excellent question! The reason is that procurement can happen at any time in the project, and not just during planning. Sometimes, a project kicks off with a contract, and the last thing we do is close out our contracts before the project or phase can be considered closed as well. Keeping a close eye on procurement by monitoring and controlling is important to protect your organization and to make sure the work is being done the way it needs to be. Controlling procurement is making sure breach of contract or other legal issues do not occur throughout.

It may also be that as you monitor and control project work, you discover that you didn't order the right amount of parts or equipment in advance, and now, as a corrective action, you will need to go through the procurement process to get what the project needs. There could be multiple sellers involved in large projects. They don't all start on day one, and they don't all stay throughout. It's a cycle, as is everything else.

Your organization's process assets typically drive procurement processes, as well as the types of contracts that are used. You may need a variety of different types of procurement depending on the needs of your project. It's best to understand the contract types first, and then the process by which we select our sellers, the documentation to solidify the contract, and who does what, when, and where.

Contract types

There are typically three flavors of contracts, and they include the following:

- Fixed price
- Cost reimbursable
- Time and materials

The fixed price and the cost reimbursable have a variety of different characteristics, depending on what the project needs. Sometimes we need to protect our budget and we know the scope of work implicitly, and sometimes we are not totally clear on scope of work in the future and need some flexibility. It's a good idea to understand who carries the main cost risks on each contract type in case you get a question on it or are in the process of working in the realm of procurement now.

In *Figure 9.8*, there is a quick cheat sheet to keep in mind, and then we'll cover each individually. Also, keep in mind that the world of procurement isn't so cut and dried, of course. These days, the trend is more about shared cost responsibility, especially when there is something the seller can't control affecting costs, as well as specific terms and conditions that are written into the contract:

Agreement Type	Scope of Work	Risk Bearer
Fixed Price	Well known	Seller
Cost Reimbursable	Known but not clearly defined	Buyer
Time and Material	Not well known	Shared

Figure 9.8

Fixed price

Fixed price contracts are great for us because we are the buyers, and if we can fix the price, we can budget for it. It's static, and it just is what is; unless the scope of work is changed, that is. For now, let's say we know the scope of work involves obtaining three thousand licenses for software. We know the cost of each and can calculate easily what the costs will be. It's fixed, and scope of work is well known. That would be known as a **firm fixed price agreement (FFP)**. It just is what it is. That's great if it's that easy, but remember that money isn't everything. Sometimes we want to offer other incentives to the sellers to deliver on time or early, or to provide us with expert staff, but we still want to keep costs from getting out of control. In that case, you would use a variation of a fixed price contract.

Fixed price incentive fee (FPIF)

The FPIF contract is based on target prices and applies financial incentives for finishing under budget or before schedule due dates. Basically, an incentive means if you do it, you get it, and if you don't, you don't. Specific terms and conditions would need to be documented, and it will be important for you to track their performance. If they meet all the incentive requirements, make sure they get paid, or at least the procurement department knows they met their goals for incentives, so they receive them in a timely manner.

Fixed Price Economic Price Adjustments (FPEPA)

With the global project market growing every single day, there may be a need for a structured agreement that accommodates inflation, currency exchange rates, costs of living, mega long-term projects, and the like. A FPEPA contract provides a level of flexibility in specifications when the project will span many years or be influenced by the other factors I mentioned. Let's say the contract states that you will pay a certain amount for oil needed for your machinery. If oil prices rise by five percent, you will pay five percent more, and if they drop to five percent less, you will pay five percent less. This does a couple of things: it allows you to still budget using a fixed price contract, and it also protects both parties from fluctuations outside of their control. It becomes a fairer type of agreement for all parties involved.

Cost reimbursable

In a perfect world, we would always know the true scope of work, we would always because to sign fixed-price agreements and budget according. As we know, we are not in a perfect world, and there may be some scope needs that need to remain flexible to accommodate changes. This flexibility is good for the scope of work and progressive elaboration, but can wreak havoc on our budget if not set up correctly. There are several types of cost reimbursable or cost-plus agreements.

None of these are exhaustive list; they are just the most common types of each. You may see a variety of these represented in the question, so make sure you understand each and the be aware of their acronyms as well.

This involves payments or cost reimbursements to the seller for actual costs incurred, plus a fee representing the seller's profit for completed work.

Cost plus fixed fee (CPFF)

The seller is reimbursed for all allowable costs for performing contract work and receives a fixed fee, based on a percentage of initial estimated project costs. If the seller states that they will charge 100 thousand for the work, that essentially covers their costs. At the time of negotiation, the seller may say our fee is 10 percent of the total estimated costs for our product or service. The total price of the project would be 110 thousand. If scope changes then it will still be 10 percent of whatever the new price is. At least we can budget for the fixed fee. It makes sense that the seller would want to make a profit on what they are providing.

Cost plus award fee (CPAF)

Remember that with incentives if you do it, you get the incentives? In a CPAF contract, financial awards are granted based on milestones met, and the seller's fee is based on performance and the decision of the buyer. This is an interesting contract type, simply because whether the sellers get the award or not is based on the buyer's perception of their performance.

We could easily say, well, I don't believe you did everything we were expecting and therefore we will not give you the award. Not everybody gets a trophy just for playing, not in the procurement world anyway. The United States Department of Defense (there they are again!) uses this type of contract a lot. The carrot versus the stick. If you do this, we'll give you that. It may be costlier, but at the same time money may not be everything. In some cases, quality is more important.

Cost plus incentive fee (CPIF)

The CPIF contract is probably the most common. In this type of contract, the seller is reimbursed for performing the work and receives a pre-determined incentive fee after achieving certain performance goals. There is also a caveat to this: if the seller saves us money from the original estimate, then we will share some of those savings with them. If the final costs of the project are less than or greater than the original estimates, both the buyer and the seller share the costs. The share costs are from a pre-negotiated cost-sharing formula, usually an 80/20 split over/under target costs. The 80 is us, and the 20 is them. It is our money after all. Let me give you an example of how this works:

- **Price quote**: 100 thousand
- **Incentive fee**: 20 thousand
- **Share ratio**: 80 us/20 them

The seller comes to you after their work is completed and says not only did we finish early to gain our incentive, but we did the entire thing for 90 thousand. Everyone gains some money back. You get some money, they get some money, everyone gets money!

This is how it would work out for them and for you:

- **Price**: 90 thousand
- **Incentive fee**: 20 thousand
- **Share ratio**: 10 thousand (saved) * 20 percent (share ratio) = two thousand
- **Total price paid to the seller**: 112 thousand
- **What would have been paid if no cost savings occurred**: 120 thousand
- **What we saved**: eight thousand

And that is why the CPIF contract types are popular. We are incentivizing for schedule and quality performance and for costs.

The downside to this type of agreement is if something goes sideways, we must pitch in and help take the brunt of the cost risk. We pay 80 percent and they pay 20 percent. That's a typical share ratio. It could be 50/50. Just depends on the negotiated structure of the terms and conditions. The last type of contract is a bit of a hybrid between fixed price and cost reimbursable, and that is time and materials.

Time and material (T&M)

T&M contracts are typically used when a specific scope of work isn't as clearly defined as in a fixed price contract, and are mostly used for experts to augment your staff and other outside support. They can also be for materials. I need a specific number of widgets and may need later.

T&M contracts typically have a ceiling price; in fact, many of these contract types do as well. At some point, the project bank must close. It's much more typical in this case, and both the buyer and seller share the cost risk. I was a contractor for many years, and I owned my own business. When I was hired as a contractor to consult or teach, it was typically for one year with re-sign possibilities in the future. I charged a certain amount per hour. My hourly rate was fixed and could be budgeted for up to one year. That was the ceiling. If I had signed up again for another year, it would have been the same thing. The reason this is a shared risk is the contract could have been terminated at any time, like if the project fell through or if I decided to do something else. The risk to me, the seller, was they wouldn't re-sign me again or the project would be canceled, and the risk to the company was that I could cancel at any time if I got a better offer. If everyone stayed happy, the ceiling was the most they would pay and the most I would make from that company. If anything had changed, it could fluctuate over time on either side of the agreement.

The roles in procurement

Now that you have a good overview of the contract types, keep in mind that a lot of what types are used is up to your organization. It's important to understand what your role is versus the procurement administrator. In *Figure 9.9*, you'll see a simple cheat sheet overview of the roles at a high level. We'll then break it down more specifically into who does what:

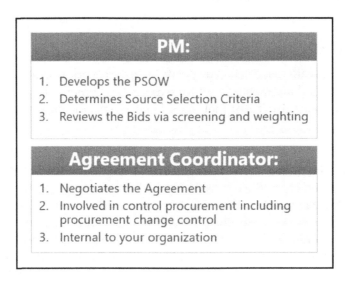

Figure 9.9

The project manager and procurement

I mentioned earlier that you have some responsibilities when it comes to procurement, and the first step is to do the make-or-buy analysis. Once that is done, it is time to reach out to prospective sellers/vendors/suppliers and let them know your procurement needs so they can respond accordingly. The **procurement statement of work (PSOW)** is sometimes referred to as the **statement of work (SOW)**, but, in general, a SOW is an input to the project charter. It comes from a customer who is asking your organization to do something for them that they outline in the SOW. It's their version of the needed scope of work. From there a contract could be signed launching the project charter into existence. The PSOW is similar, except now it's your organization reaching out to prospective organizations that can provide the people, materials, or equipment needed for the project.

Since you and the team know the scope of work, it will be up to you to construct a document that describes your procurement needs. This can be time-consuming because you may have several different procurement needs, each with its own scope of work. You may need to create a PSOW for the potential widget sellers, a PSOW for the prospective licenses sellers, and possibly even for contractors or staff to extend your team. This may be something you will need to make room in your schedule to do. You may very well have the procurement administrator looking over your shoulder to make sure everything is legal and documented correctly, but it is typically the job of the PM to create a statement of the scope of work for procurement needs. Each PSOW will be tailored, so there isn't a one-size-fits-all approach to this, and much of this responsibility is delegated by your organizational process assets.

The other thing that you will be responsible for, in most cases, is to determine how you will select your sellers. You will need to put the wish list in place, and this is called **source selection criteria**. Or the criteria by which you select your seller. Think of it this way: if you were going to lease a big-ticket item such as a new car, you may have a few things in mind that are must-haves to seal the deal. That may be price, color, whether it has heated seats, make or model, and so on. There are some things that are more important, and as you go to a test drive you'll be looking for your must-haves. You would be willing to give up heated seats for a price adjustment, but you cannot give up the *pearlized* black color for anything. You have your priorities, of course! This is the criteria by which you will select the vehicle to lease and enter into contract negotiations. The same thing can be said for prospective sellers.

What is most important to your project?

- Capability and capacity?
- Product and life cycle costs?
- Delivery dates?
- Warranties?
- Technical expertise and approach?
- Specific relevant experience?
- Adequacy of the proposed approach?
- Qualifications/availability/competence of proposed staff?
- Financial stability of the organization?

If this is your wish list, it will be important to make sure you know what is most important and what you can live with or without. Once your prospective sellers respond to your requests, you will need to know how to review their responses. Typically, there is a scoring and weighting system attached to keep any nefarious procurement activities to a minimum. As in, I know a guy, so we don't need to look any further. Let's keep it legal.

Once you have the PSOW written out and the source selection criteria, you will also need to send out specific procurement documents.

Those can include the following:

- **Request for Information (RFI)**
- **Request for Proposal (RFP)**
- **Request for Quote (RFQ)**
- **Request for Bid (RFB)**

It will depend on your level of knowledge about the prospective sellers as to what you would send out with your PSOW. It also depends on your organization and what they use the most. Most organizations I've worked with use an RFP. It is the function of asking for prospective sellers to review your PSOW and provide a proposal for how they will execute upon the request. An RFI is used when we don't know a lot about them and are looking for some background information to help make an informed decision. A RFQ is typical to money being the only consideration, and an RFB also falls under that category as well. That's not to say money is the only request, but it's up there. That may be due to having worked with them before, and you know what they can do and just need to see what they may charge for said project need.

It's not unusual for some industries to hold bidder's conferences, in which every potential bidder replying to the same scope of work gets together in a room with the procurement administrator and the project manager to ask questions and get them answered. That way, everyone hears the same information. This, then, allows the seller to make informed decisions when they respond to the request. This prevents collusion and conspiracy as well. It's important for the PM to attend because they have a deeper knowledge of the scope of work and can answer questions accordingly. I do this with potential students and organizations deciding about whether we are the right vendor for them. Mostly salespeople are doing the talking because they create and work on the procurement side of things. I'm there to answer questions about content or how I run classes. I'm giving product knowledge, but have nothing to do with contracts or pricing. Same thing for you in bidder's conferences.

There may also be some situations in which there isn't a bevy of sellers out there that can provide you with what you need, either because your organization has already chosen a seller or there isn't a lot to choose from.

Single source

In the case of a single source situation. you will be working with only one seller because your organization has already vetted, approved, and signed a contract with them. They are your source. That doesn't mean negotiations won't occur or that you won't be providing them with scope of work documentation; it just means you only must do it once.

Sole source

In a sole source situation, there is only one seller that can provide you what you need for your project. This can be a difficult situation because they haven't been vetted, but they are your only option. That can make quality and scope hard to determine in advance. I always use the example of an Intel® Pentium processor. Remember when every single computer manufacturer had to have the Intel® inside? Who did they get it from? Intel®. They could charge what they wanted, make whatever deals they wanted, and put their sticker on every single computer out there that they wanted. They were, and still are, the sole source of the Intel® Pentium processor.

Conducting procurement

Remember that procurement could be happening throughout the project. During week one, you need widgets, and by week 15, you need the staff to join the project, and so on. On large projects, it isn't unusual to have multiple sellers. That means that, as each proposal or bid comes in, you and your team, working with the procurement administrator in most cases, will select your sellers using a screening and/or weighting system.

Screening system

This is easier said than done, of course, but a screening system is essentially the yes/no piles. Did they meet our price? Yes? Then that proposal moves into the scoring and weighting process. No? It goes in the trash. This is easier said than done, but it is a quick way of vetting the proposals. Is it or isn't it?

Weighting system

Remember your source selection criteria? Each criterion will have a weight attached to it. If price is most important, it will carry the most weight. Let's say price carries a weight of 20 and being on schedule carries a weight of 15. As you go through each proposal in the yes pile, you will score the proposal using a 1 through 10 scale.

In the following table, you can see three vendor bids and how they are scored and weighted. Essentially, the one with the highest score wins:

Vendor	Price Bid Score	Price Weight	Price Final score
Vendor 1	4	20	80
Vendor 2	7	20	140
Vendor 3	10	20	200

It's clear that Vendor 3 has the highest bid score and the highest overall score. Now add to that the entire list of source selection criteria and follow the same process. *Score * weight = final score*. That way, you have shortlisted the top several high scorers. They will then enter into the room with the contract administrator as selected sellers to negotiate the contract.

Just as a side note, in the real world, the highest score on price doesn't *always* mean that seller wins. Remember, we may have a long wish list of source selection criteria. Price is important, but may not be everything on all projects. There may be discussions about two vendors. One may have the right price but we know they have delivered late in the past. That may be a risk we aren't willing to take again, so the second highest bid may get the contract.

Contract administrator/agreement coordinator

The reason they have so many names is that different organizations call them different things. Either way, these procurement department people are the ones who can legally and contractually bind your organization to that of another. The assumption on the exam is that they are internal to your organization, and as the buyer the negotiations would happen for the good of your project. I realize that isn't always the way things happen, so read the questions carefully and ask yourself if you are the buyer in the question or the seller.

Their job is to negotiate the contract for a fair and reasonable price and explain the terms and conditions to you so you don't inadvertently breach the contract. Their job is to also make sure that if a change is necessary on the contract due to a change in scope or even a simple administrative change, that they are present in the decisions for solution implementation. It's essentially integrated change control with an attorney present. They are also there to support any alternative disputes and resolve them first with negotiation, and second with the other options available.

Another item to consider is that even though the legal folks are there, it doesn't mean that you are not in charge of creating and maintaining good relationships with the seller. It's your job to explain what could be a breach or the needs of the project. If you tell them to go speak with your attorney, those are fighting words! They are stakeholders, and it's your job to make sure that they are doing what they are supposed to do, and that you are doing what you are supposed to do as well.

Once the contracts are negotiated, the seller is contractually bound to the project due to mutually binding documents in the form of a formal agreement or contract. With that comes many terms and conditions specific to the contract and the buyer/seller relationship.

Partner-centric procurement documents

While there are several to consider, you may not be tested on all of them. I wouldn't be surprised if you are familiar with some of them already. These documents can cross the conducting procurements and controlling procurements processes we'll discuss in the next section. All are considered legal, and it's important to know, at least on the surface, what they represent:

- Letter of intent
- **Memorandum of Understanding (MOU)**
- Breach of contract
- **Service Level Agreements (SLA)**
- **Purchase Order (PO)**
- **Nondisclosure agreement (NDA)**
- Cease-and-desist letter
- Warranty

Letter of intent

During the negotiations of a potential contract with a selected seller, there may be some back and forth over terms and conditions until both parties agree on them. A letter of intent is drafted for both parties to sign and agree to before anyone signs on the dotted line in the form of a legally binding contract. Typically, this would be the job of the procurement department in the buyer's organization, who then negotiate on with the sellers until an agreement on terms and conditions is reached.

Memorandum of Understanding (MOU)

In some cases, a contract is unnecessary, or a formal agreement on terms and conditions cannot be reached. In this case, an MOU would be drafted. An MOU is like a contract in the sense that terms and conditions are outlined for performance metrics and product/service requests. It differs from a formal contract because it isn't necessarily a legal document like a contract is. If one party or the other doesn't meet expectations of performance, then neither party can take them to court. In contracts like fixed price, cost reimbursable, and time and materials, if a breach of contract occurs then a court date could be forthcoming.

Breach of contract

I'm sure we know what a breach of contract is. It's when one side or the other doesn't meet contractual obligations. There are two types to consider. A breach of contract doesn't always mean a court date. It also doesn't mean that both parties don't have to pay or do the work depending on who breached. They do. Much like if you leased a car and then left it on the side of the road because you decided you didn't want to drive it anymore, you would still be responsible for the payments and the welfare of that vehicle. A **material breach of contract** is egregious; a court date will be forthcoming, and damages can be awarded.

Service Level Agreements (SLA)

I would imagine SLAs are familiar in your world, since we see a lot of these types of agreements in the IT industry rather than full blown contracts. This would be an agreement that sets performance guidelines and expectations between two or more parties. Those parties could even be in the same organization and document how quickly your IT team will respond to certain tech issues and within a certain time frame—patch Tuesdays!

There may also be a **master service level agreement** (**MSLA**) in place, and this streamlines future agreements between parties because each party agrees to most of the terms that will be in place in future agreements. This allows for a faster negotiation and turnaround time for future interactions where the specifics don't need to be constantly renegotiated.

Purchase Order (PO)

If my team needed a certain number of monitors to help with business expansion and technical upgrades, it may decide to use a PO instead. The PO would be written by the buyer (us), and very specifically describe our monitor needs and quantities to the seller (them). Even though it's not a fixed price agreement, POs are legally binding.

Nondisclosure agreement (NDA)

Many organizations use NDAs when they hire from outside their organization. The nondisclosure agreement is signed by the seller, and states that they will not communicate trade secrets or internal conversations outside of the organization. You may have noticed a lot on the news lately about people being sued or prosecuted for breaking an NDA. That is because they signed a legal document stating they wouldn't do just that. It is how organizations protect themselves from their competition.

Cease-and-desist letter

This is exactly what it sounds like. A cease-and-desist letter is sent out when one organization discovers that another organization is using their trademarked content/products and re-creating them. You see these a lot in the entertainment industry, where artists of all kinds have trademarked their brand, their music, or their writing. If someone tries to duplicate their brand in any way, even seemingly, then an attorney will send out a cease-and-desist letter. If that letter is ignored, a lawsuit is forthcoming.

Warranty

A warranty is when you buy a new washing machine and they promise it will work for one year, and that if it doesn't the company will pay to fix it. One year and one day later it breaks! No? Just me? I joke. (Not really). Most warranties apply most to equipment, vehicles, manufactured goods, technology, and the like. Once the warranty period has expired, the organization is no longer liable for fixing the item.

That brings us to monitoring and controlling procurements, or just control procurements.

Controlling procurement

The controlling of procurement is a crucial step in the entire procurement process because it includes protecting your organization from breach of agreement, keeping track of the seller's performance, maintaining good relationships with your sellers, paying out of your budgets for contract work and incentives, processing formal changes as needed, and closing out any procurement documents once the work has been completed and approved. Your organization may also have knowledge bases just for your vendors, where in everything is kept and updated. I know we had to hold on to our contracts for eight years after they were closed to be compliant. Your mileage may vary. Another best practice we followed was seller surveys and procurement audits.

Seller surveys

The survey for your sellers is a key step, whether the results were great, terrible, or somewhere in between. If their performance was great and they got all their incentives and we were happy with the entire result, a survey can be a good relationship move for future work. They have been vetted and approved, and now other project managers and the organization know they have a stable seller to work with in the future. If the performance wasn't good, then we know who to steer clear of in the future. There isn't a set best practice for this, but standard templates are an effective way to go since each seller is graded on the same items.

Procurement audit

Remember, any time you see the word *audit*, it means you are reviewing a process. There may be quality audits, risk audits and **procurement audits**. In this case, the procurement audit is reviewing the procurement process internally. Did we do our due diligence when selecting our sellers? Did we use the right contract types? Did our sellers perform the way we needed them to? If not, could we have done a better job selecting our sellers? This process is formal and may include the procurement coordinator. It's your job to protect your organization from future costs or litigation on the current project, or by not taking your lessons learned and applying them in the future. It's always a promising idea to audit your processes to see whether they are working.

Closing procurements

The process by which contracts are closed out depends on the contract/agreement type, your organizational processes for procurement, and the terms and conditions stated in said contract/agreement. Procurement closure can happen at any time in the project, and this hopefully is because the work was done correctly and the seller's piece is completed. Early termination could also occur if the project is cancelled, or the buyer or seller breached agreement. Either way, the assumption on the exam is that contracts need to be closed out before the phase or project can be closed out. I know we had some payment structures that were met 30, 60, 90 days out past the work being completed. I'm not suggesting we wait around for all of that to happen before we close out a project and work on something else. Quite the contrary. We need to make sure all work has been completed and validated and all contractual obligations for both sides have been met. Many times, this is done with a **waiver**.

Waivers

When I was younger, I was a bit more of a risk taker and decided to jump out of a perfectly good airplane for fun. Consequently, I am now afraid of heights. Before I suited up and proceeded with this insanity, I was asked to sign a waiver. That waiver stated that the company could not be held liable for anything that happened to me, and I agreed not to sue them or have anyone in my family to sue them for the next 350 years. I think it was more like sue them never. That is a waiver. It protects the party or parties from future litigation. In the case of procurement closure, the buyer (us) would sign the waiver stating that the seller (them) had completed all the work they were hired to do. The seller would then sign the waiver stating that we had paid them everything they were due. Now both parties have protected themselves.

In the case of an **alternative dispute resolution** (**ADR**), the waiver would not be signed because one party disagreed with a change or an outcome and is not willing to let the other party off the hook. In this case, your procurement administrator would step in and try to negotiate an acceptable conclusion, and if that didn't work then arbitration, mediation or litigation would be considered. That's not good at all. I had a judge tell me once that I should never let a judge make a decision that could be made myself. The judge was a friend, not presiding over a court case, in case you were wondering. He was correct, and I never forgot it. That is something we project managers need to keep in mind. Create and maintain good relationships with your sellers, keep track of their performance, pay out incentives and other payments on time, follow the terms and conditions to the letter of the law and if you have questions or concerns then get your procurement department involved. They are, after all, there for that very reason. Auditing allows us to look back on our procurement decisions and relationships and make changes for the better, going forward.

Summary

In this chapter, you reviewed quality control and validate scope as ways to make sure that your product service or result is meeting requirements. Then, you reviewed formal change control and why changes may be necessary on the project and organizationally. Finally, you covered the entire procurement process, from planning for procurements, conducting procurements, controlling, and closing procurements. All these topics are large topics to cover, and change can happen anywhere, at any point, and in any knowledge area.

In `Chapter 10`, *Formal Project or Phase Closure and Agile Project Management*, we will wrap up everything with formal project or phase closure, final-lessons-learned meetings, and postmortems, as well as get a crash course on the other side of project management—the agile side.

Questions

1. After meeting with your end users, they have stated that they would like to perform an inspection on the quality and the scope of work before accepting the result. You let them know that would match up with your organization's best practices. In addition, you will want them to formally sign off on the deliverables. The customer agrees. Which of the following processes include formal sign-off on the deliverable?
   - Quality control
   - Close procurement
   - Validate scope
   - Quality assurance

2. Which of the following charts or graphs would be useful when trying to determine the main causes for defects in your quality?
   - Fishbone
   - Pareto diagram
   - Histogram
   - Scatter diagram

3. Project management has a cycle that is like quality's continuous improvements. Which of the following would be considered continuous improvements for quality?
   - Plan, check, and act
   - Initiation, panning, execution, monitoring, and controlling
   - Governance gate
   - Plan, do, check, and act

4. Bill is an expert on your team and he is typically very dependable. Today, Bill shows you something that he added to the deliverable outside of requirement and he is overly excited about the new functionality. What is the new functionality called?
   - Change control
   - Scope creep
   - Validate scope
   - Change request

5. It's week four of a 30-week, 40 thousand US dollar project, and you are meeting with your team to collect work performance data. Jamal states that he and Kellie were working on a large deliverable and needed to cut some corners to meet the schedule constraint, and consequently some of the quality of the deliverable has suffered. What type of change control is needed in this situation?
    - Defect repair
    - Scope change
    - Preventative action
    - Corrective action

6. Chris is one of your key team members for installing software, and he alerts you to the fact that he will be on vacation next week. You determine that the tasks will be impacted because another resource is behind schedule. Otherwise, Chris would have completed the work before he left on vacation. What should you do next?
    - Evaluate the impact of changing the plan to accommodate Chris's vacation
    - Create a solution such as fast tracking, and process a change request
    - Go to the sponsor for sign-off on Chris's vacation and your solution
    - Talk to the change control board to determine the category of change requests necessary

7. You are working with your procurement administrator and determining what the best contract type should be for acquiring the equipment you need. You are concerned about your budget because you are working with a funding limit and need to keep the cost risks low. What is the best contract type to use in this situation?
    - Fixed price
    - Cost reimbursable
    - Time and materials
    - Service level agreement

8. Your organization has used the ABC company for years to help with large installs of server upgrades in multiple locations, and Doug has been the resource assigned to your projects. You and Doug have a good working relationship, and you trust him to get the job done. The ABC company has signed a fixed price incentive fee contract and has stipulated that Doug will get his incentives when the customer validates scope. In the middle of the project, Doug comes to you and asks for his incentives early because he always gets his work done and he could use the money. What should your response be?
    - Sure, let me process a change request to see if we can get you some of your incentives early.
    - Sorry, Doug, I can't make that decision; you're going to have to talk to Larry, my procurement administrator.
    - Sorry, Doug, I know you'll get your work done and make your incentives easily, but that would be a breach of contract, and I can't pay you early. I'm really sorry about that!
    - Sure, Doug, let me write you a check for half of your incentives.

9. You and your team are trying to determine what you will need from outside sellers in the form of materials and equipment. During your discussions, you are attempting to figure out what can be done in-house and what can't be. This could be an example of which of the following?
    - Make or rent analysis
    - Make or buy analysis
    - Source selection criteria
    - Planning procurements

10. After a good hard look at your procurement needs, you have put together a document that clearly states your needs for that seller, as well as the requirements for the product you are building. What document does this best represent?
    - RPF
    - RFQ
    - RFI
    - PSOW

11. The project you and your team are currently working on needs an incredibly unique piece of equipment that only one vendor has. You will have to pay what they ask and can't confirm quality until the part is delivered. What kind of seller are you working with?
    - Single source
    - Sole source

- Vendor bid analysis
- Selected seller

12. You work for a large organization with multiple locations and departments. You and another IT team from another building are working together on a project. Both departments feel it is necessary to clearly outline each team's responsibilities and key performance indicators, but a legal contract isn't necessary. Which of the following may work instead?
    - Letter of Intent
    - Memorandum of Understanding (MOU)
    - Service Level Agreements (SLA)
    - Purchase Order (PO)

13. You have reached the end of the project and are wrapping up the close procurement process. You have drafted a document that both you and the seller will sign to remove liability from either party. This is known as what kind of procurement document?
    - Waiver
    - ADR
    - Audit
    - Close procurements

14. You have reached the end of a project phase and all procurements have been closed. You meet with your key stakeholders and your team to discuss how the phase's procurement process worked. This is known as which of the following?
    - Close procurement
    - Vendor survey
    - Control procurement
    - Procurement audit

15. Other than preventative actions, corrective actions, scope changes, and defect repairs, which of the following reasons would also involve change control?
    - Schedule change
    - Budgetary update
    - Internal reorganization
    - Scope creep

10
Formal Project or Phase Closure and Agile Project Management

In this chapter, you will review how projects or phases are closed out formally and what types of project endings you could be working with. You will also review how to obtain a formal sign-off of the deliverables, as well as administrative closure and lessons learned. Then, you will review an immensely popular agile framework called Scrum, and how having a more adaptive approach to your projects can help manage many changes. The tools and techniques you will learn can help you improve your agility.

In this chapter, we will cover the following topics:

- Project or phase closure
- Formal acceptance of the deliverable
- Administrative and team closure
- Lessons learned and final reporting
- Overview of agile project management
- Introduction to the Scrum framework
- Hybrid or tailored project management

Project or phase closure

All good things must come to an end, and projects must end as well. Hopefully, they will be closed out with good results and happy customers, but that is not always the case. There are many reasons why a project would go through formal closure and the hope is that they were completed successfully and the result was approved. Still other times, the project is canceled because the result is no longer relevant, or the money has run out. It may not even be your organization's influence that cancels projects but rather your customer's. Perhaps their organization merged with another, or they decided they want a motorcycle instead of a bicycle. It happens.

Phase closures also occur if your projects are run in any phase configuration. If you have a project running in **sequential phases** wherein one ends and the next begins, **overlapping phases** where there are different aspects of work happening at the same time or your project is being run in **Sprints** or iterations in an agile environment closure process could be very different. We will cover Scrum and agile later in this chapter and address how those iterations are closed with **reviews** and **retrospectives**.

No matter the reason for a project or phase closure, the same processes need to be followed to formally document the levels of completion, get signatures on the scope of work completed to date, close out procurements, and document your lessons learned before releasing your team onto their next project.

The four categories of project endings

There are four main categories that describe why projects end:

- Extinction
- Addition
- Integration
- Starvation

Extinction

This is the best-case scenario for project managers because it means you have finished the project successfully and it is now **extinct**. Gone but not forgotten, much like dinosaurs. If your project is completed successfully, chances are you will be transitioning your product, service or result to the customer and the product life cycle or operations will begin. If you installed and tested new servers for your customer, and everything is working, it's now in the customer's very capable hands to pick it up and use it from there. We always hope that a project will be closed out in this way, but unfortunately that isn't always the case.

Addition

In a lot of IT projects, **addition** occurs. This is an ending where the project you are working on develops into a functional department or contributes to the ongoing operations of the organization. Typically, this type of ending is a good one as well because your project has helped to contribute to better standards of operations in your organization or your customer's organization. As an example, let's say your project was to set up a help desk. Your team installed all the equipment, did the testing, trained the help desk staff, and stuck around to make sure they had everything done and then closed out your project. That help desk is now part of operations, but it took a project to get there. You see this a lot in functional, weak, or balanced, matrix organizations whose project goals are typically to upgrade organizational processes and business units.

Integration

Think of the word *integrate*. Everything is working together toward a common goal. Unfortunately, that common goal may not be the same as when you started your project. Perhaps the organization has decided that your people, equipment, and materials better serve the collective *we* by being moved to other projects. They are then integrated elsewhere. Maybe the functional departments are suffering due to all their resources now being part-time due to project work and they are less than pleased. Your project will need to be closed out in whatever state it was left because you simply don't have the resources or the project priority to support your project execution.

Starvation

This is a common situation in which people just steal all your resources! Because that never happens, right? There you are, working away on your project, things are going well, the output is as expected and all of a sudden, BAM! Resources get rescheduled to other projects and the project needs to be closed. Insert multiple exclamations of a negative variety right here! It's true, it happens all the time. It's the state of business these days, as we are already doing more with less.

A lack of resources is the number-one complaint from project managers globally. Now, everyone has scattered to the four winds and is working on other projects that have taken organizational priority over your project, or your customer decides they don't want or need the result anymore, or your organization decides they don't want to spend the money on the project anymore. Don't take it personally. Perhaps the organization has issued a hiring freeze and you can't hire the resources you need. Organizations are in the business of making money, and sometimes to do that they will need to shuffle things around. You would still go through your formal closure and hopefully have enough time with your resources to capture final lessons learned. Remember, resources aren't just people. Sometimes our equipment and materials are removed as well. That can make it difficult to get things done, even if all your human resources are still formally assigned to the project. Either way, the project is being deprived of resources and is therefore starving.

This sounds a lot like integration, right? I agree, but there are subtle differences. Integration means your people, equipment, and materials have been moved or assigned to other *more important* projects, and starvation means there are no resources, no money, no equipment, and no materials to complete your project.

Phase closure

Phase closures have similar formal processes to be sure that they are closed appropriately. Often, that process will be aligned with your organizational process assets and will include a phase gate review or governance gates to get that go/no-go decision. No matter whether the phases overlap, are sequential, or are agile, they will be closed out formally. Much like in project closure, there will be sign-off and a transfer to the next phase. There may be a hand-off to the next project manager if the phases are being managed by multiple project managers. You also may be entering a training phase or something similar. The production of the result has completed but now you need to make sure the transfer to the end users goes smoothly.

Formal acceptance of the deliverable

No matter the reason for a project being closed out, the need for formal processes for closure remain. In `Chapter 9`, *Monitoring and Controlling Project Work*, you reviewed the validate scope process:

- Produce the deliverable during execution
- Verify quality via inspection
- Validate scope via inspection
- Formal closure of the project or phase

To formally close out your project or phase, the validation or formal sign-off of the scope of work needs to be done regardless of why the project has ended. Even in the case of the bicycle customer wanting a motorcycle halfway through the project, the bicycle scope of the work would need to be validated or approved. You still have to get paid, right?

The same concept applies to phase closures. We reviewed quality gates and governance gates as check-points for approvals, go/no-go decisions, and formal acceptance to move on to the next phase. Many times, that phase-end review involves a technical transfer to the next phase, and documentation would be needed to do that formally.

Whether your sponsor is internal to your project or an external sponsor/customer, it is important for them to be part of the sign-off process. In fact, if there is a significant amount of sunk costs on a project (throwing good money after bad), the sponsor would be the one that calls for a project close-out, not the project manager. Even though you are assumed to be managing the budgetary baseline, the sponsor would make the project close-out call. What makes the process formal is obtaining acceptance of whatever state the deliverable is in at the time and getting a signature to prove it.

 Watch out for questions that involve a project being cancelled halfway through. You would still need to go through the process of formal closure, including getting signatures of deliverable acceptance.

The other item to mention here is procurement closure. We covered the process in `Chapter 9`, *Monitoring and Controlling Project Work*, but it's an important mention here as well. Contracts need to be closed formally before the project can be considered complete. Remember, it is our responsibility to protect our organization from future costs and litigation. Dot the *i* and cross the *t*.

Administrative and team closure

Even though administrative and team closure sound like they would be one and the same, they work together to make sure that everything is formal. On the administrative side of things, you and the team are making sure that all the project records are stored appropriately in your PIMS, having a final lessons-learned meeting, and making sure that all lessons learned and collected during the project are stored as well.

You are documenting lessons learned all the way through the project. During closure, you will be collating them and creating a final project report.

It's entirely possible that you and the team will have a lessons-learned meeting or a *postmortem*. Postmortems usually happen in the case of a project being closed before completion or terminated early due to one of the reasons mentioned earlier, specifically starvation and integration.

Some of the documentation may need to be transitioned to the functional department or customer so that they have records during the product life cycle. Specifically, any warranties that were negotiated and created, training materials, or other maintenance or support documents.

Lessons learned and final reporting

Even though lessons learned are documented throughout the project, it's important to have a lessons-learned meeting at the end of the project. This is the opposite of a kick-off meeting, in which everyone on the team gets together with whichever stakeholders are appropriate to attend and discuss what went well and what didn't go so well. A lot of my lessons learned over the years were based on surprise risk events, or issues, as well as changes that were or were not approved. All that information can be discussed and then submitted as historical information for future reviews. Remember analogous estimating from cost and schedule estimates? This is where that information comes from. Past projects that are now being used to estimate future projects. I also think it's important to celebrate success, even if the project was unsuccessful. Unsuccessful projects don't always result because your team wasn't performing, but rather because risk events, scope creep, issues, and changes were wreaking some havoc. It's important to give that pat on the back and be specific with your feedback, such as, *Thank you for all your hard work, I know a lot of you put in overtime to get the work done and were away from your families, and I want you to know how much I appreciate all your efforts.* Things such as this go an exceptionally long way. Even a simple thank you is important to the team.

Final reports will also be created and communicated to key stakeholders. Much like they created the charter at the beginning of the project, you will now return the favor with your final report. The final report is a summation of the successes, the challenges of the project, and lessons learned, as well as specifics on budgetary performance, schedule performance, reviewing the scope-validation process, and whether the final deliverables were accepted. If they were not, provide a clear reason as to why. Like all reporting, this could be driven by your organizational processes and your communication plan, which describes what information the stakeholders need and find important for you to report on.

The biggest takeaway from this section is that no matter how your projects are run and how your organization influences those projects, all projects must be formally closed. In fact, everything that you have reviewed in this guide is open to interpretation as to whether this or that document is necessary to create. The project charter and the project closure sandwiches all other decisions. They are the only two processes that are assumed mandatory. If you currently don't have these two processes on your projects, it may be the first recommended implementation of better best practices. From there, you can decide what is needed and what is not.

This brings us to the end of predicative project management best practices, and hopefully you have some best practices to take away to utilize on your projects, and the knowledge necessary to answer questions on your exams. Now we are going to step away from the world of predictive project management and step into the world of adaptive project management. Welcome to the world of agile!

Overview of agile project management

What exactly is agile? You may be familiar with agile frameworks due to being in the technology world. Ask any software developer what agile is and they will probably be able to explain it, but what if you aren't a software developer? Is this even something you can use? The answer is yes, yes you can. I wouldn't be at all surprised if you pull a couple of best practices from the Scrum framework and decide to use them on every project. Agile isn't just for software anymore.

You also might be wondering why any agile appears on the Project+ exam. Remember, the Project+ exam takes best practices from the Project Management Body of Knowledge, or *PMBOK® Guide*, which is currently in its sixth iteration. The Project Management Institute (PMI®) collaborated with the **Agile Alliance** to determine best practices that could be used in a predictive environment. Because of this collaboration, the **Agile Practice Guide** is now a companion document to the sixth edition of the *PMBOK® Guide*. There are now considerations for agile and project tailoring within the best practices for each knowledge area. Why? Not every single project last a year or longer, has a budget of $1,000,000 or more, and can be heavily preplanned. The value in having a lot of different tools and techniques to use is exponential due to all the technology and innovations going on today.

The benefits of using agile in industries beyond software development are many. To tailor approaches that better meet the rapid pace of projects today, it is important for organizations to be able to respond to the swift changes in technology, competition for products, services, and results, and changing requirements. Only recently has there been much of a collective understanding of agile frameworks, as it has been something of a well-guarded secret for only software-development projects. Some organizations attempt to implement agile best practices but are not using them effectively because it's the latest, greatest thing in project management and they rush into it. It is important for the effective implementation of any agile framework to practice the steps until proficient and to encourage others not only to internalize agile best practices, but to practice them regularly. The hard part is that a lot of organizations are used to their current process flow, and, even though it may not be working sufficiently, change is always painful.

One thing to keep in mind is that agile is just a label for multiple frameworks and processes that have been developed out of necessity. Some are designed specifically for rapid output of software programs (eXtreme Programming or XP) and others were designed to combat the challenges that waterfall project management created in the technology space.

One of the most popular agile frameworks is **Scrum**. I believe this is because the structure of Scrum is more distinct then some of the other frameworks and methods. There are some extremely specific rules and flow to Scrum. Organizations that have been practicing waterfall for years can see the value in utilizing the framework. Even though there are numerous things I want to write about agile to help you understand it completely, for the scope of the exam, the questions will be limited.

If anything in this section sounds cool or interesting, check out more information on it and pull in some best practices to see how they work in your environment. Remember, tailoring is one of the best skills to have as a project manager. This allows you to look at the unique project and decide what to use for the good of the result. It may include some waterfall and some Scrum. With agile (think agility), you must be malleable in the process to improve your best practices and products or services.

Introduction to the Scrum framework

Scrum made its first appearance in 1995. Think back to that time and think about what was going on in technology. Our computers weighed 80 pounds and used floppy disks, Internet Explorer had just been created, we were using dial-up, and once you finally got logged on you heard *You've got mail!* Look how far we have come. Think about the limitations to our technology and the necessity for large organizations to get automated with payroll and other business functions. Developers needed to produce results quickly and often. Front-loaded planning didn't work for that kind of project because they weren't able to fully predict the outcome. The developers would do what they thought was correct and then learn the hard way. They would shift gears and learn some more, and practice adapting and agility. This led to faster software design, and they would push out the updates to fix the bugs later. "Let's do the simplest thing that works" is the battle cry of most practitioners of agile methods.

Scrum was designed to be a framework, *not* a process, and while the framework is considered lightweight and simple to understand, it is inherently difficult to master. It takes years of practice and continuous improvement to truly master Scrum, but that doesn't mean that you can't use it in your projects daily and work hard to master all, aspects.

The Scrum theory was founded or based upon the Empirical Process Control theory, or *empiricism*. And much like many other agile frameworks, knowledge comes from experience and making decisions based on what is currently known about features, the customer value, and what the result looks like today. In Scrum, we call this the **definition of done**.

At a considerably basic level, utilizing Scrum allows us to review, adapt, and improve on an iterative level while producing something of value incrementally, as well as optimizing predictability in the framework or the way things are done. That will then reduce risk exponentially. Since the Scrum framework was created based on Empirical Process Control, the three pillars of Scrum theory are **transparency**, **inspection**, and **adaptation**.

Transparency

When you look at the agile methods, a common theme of openness and communication about value, processes, techniques, and even how to manage risks and issues, becomes very apparent.

The entire focus of Scrum is based on the understanding that everyone knows what everyone else is doing and how they are doing it. If someone makes a mistake, they own it and work as a team to fix it. Transparent and clear communication across all aspects of the Scrum framework sets the stage for effective production of completed increments and a team atmosphere of unity.

Inspection

Frequent inspection of the completed work and deliverables also allows progress toward the overarching goal and allows for identification of variances that would keep the result from being accepted. Frequent inspection of the increment or deliverable is a crucial aspect of Scrum theory, but if the inspections are too frequent, it will do the opposite. Too-frequent inspections will disrupt the work rather than promote effective execution of the work. There is a fine line and a balancing act that occurs between testing and inspections to consider the result totally finished or done.

Adaptation

The final pillar in Scrum theory is adaptation, and it is an apt description of all agile frameworks. Think of the words *agile* or *agility*, which describes the ability to adapt, pivot, and change direction when necessary. If, during an inspection, a result doesn't pass the tests or is deemed not acceptable, that points to a problem in the process and the execution of the process. If the process is deemed not working and affecting the result or increment, the process itself must be adjusted. Sounds a lot like quality assurance, right? It is. If the process is flawed, fix it. The difference is we can do that without change-control, and the Scrum team decides how to fix it rather than formal change-control boards agreeing or disagreeing with the strategy. Scrum and all agile frameworks are adaptable, but that doesn't mean you switch from Scrum to XP; it means that the process is not being effectively executed and it's necessary for the team to adapt or revisit best practices of Scrum and constantly check themselves to make sure that the process is working. One of the coolest things about Scrum is that we know *we need to fail to succeed*. Woah... failure is not an option in Waterfall! Empirical Process Control describes our ability to communicate transparently and inspect the results, and if they aren't working then change them. Lather, rinse, repeat.

All frameworks have core tenets or values they abide by, and in Scrum, those lean more toward the human side of project management rather than set processes. There are five values, and those values support the pillars of Scrum and Empirical Process Control:

- Commitment
- Focus
- Openness
- Respect
- Courage

Key Aspects of a Scrum Project

There are several key aspects of a Scrum project that may differ from a predictive project. Instead of a project management plan, there are different ways of collecting and documenting requirements.

The three main items to be aware of are:

- The product backlog
- User stories
- The sprint

The product backlog

The first thing I think is important to explain is something called the **product backlog**. Imagine a large list of features and functions that could go into a software program you are developing that edits photographs. You will probably have some core aspects that need to be in place before other features and functions work. For example, you would need to be able to upload your photograph into the program before you could edit it. That would be a priority at the top of the list along with other priority items. Then there would be a long wish list from a customer or the internal organization of cool features and functions they want done, as soon as possible. The priority of those items could fluctuate wildly as the software program begins to take shape. The customer may test the upload and realize they can only upload in JPEG not RAW images. Now they have a new wish list item that has become a priority before the other features can be built.

The key aspects of a product backlog are:

- Dynamic
- Constantly changes
- Exists if a product exists
- Lists all features, functions, requirements, enhancements, and fixes

User stories

The reason why stories are used instead of a long list of tasks or features is because they are easier to remember and understand. If you have ever tried to teach a small child their ABCs, you know you can't just say *Okay A, B, C, D, E, F, G. Got that?* Instead, you say things such as *A is for apple, B is for baby, C is for cat.* It's easier to understand that way.

From a project management standpoint, we probably hear and see a lot of requirements in lists. A story is easier to understand. User stories in come a variety of sizes, just like requirements. It will be up to the team to break them down to the point at which they can be executed. A good rule of thumb is that a user story is no larger than about three to four days' worth of work. Some stories will need to be progressively elaborated on, especially if they are stories for the future and are not quite developed yet.

The format for a user story is typically the following:

As a _____, I need or want _____ so that I can/so that I get _____.

> *As an end user of photographic software, **I need** to be able to upload in RAW format, **so that I get** the best results from my photographs.*

Now the team can ask questions about the story and work together to determine the requirements, and then decide **how** to execute on the work.

The sprint

Before we review what the team does, it's important to define another term in Scrum, called a **Sprint**. Think of the word Sprint and what it means: to run quickly, but not get extremely far. That is a very apt description for the phases that a Scrum team uses to manage their work. All agile frameworks accept changes without formal change-control because the product backlog is updated regularly. Sprints allow the development team to produce a usable, testable, and working increment at the end of each Sprint. Then they reset and start another Sprint. Sprints are typically one month long.

The Scrum team

If you are familiar with the sport of rugby then the word Scrum may be recognizable. A Scrum is a banding together of certain players on the team who work toward a common goal. They are much stronger together than they are apart. In all team sports, there are specific positions that are played. A Scrum team has three major positions:

- The **Product Owner** provides the information on *what* will be done
- The **development team** decides *how* the work will be done and how much they can handle
- The **Scrum Master** is a *servant-leader* who helps guide the Product Owner and the team

The Product Owner

Guess whose job it is to stay on top of and manage the backlog and write the user stories? Yep, the Product Owner. They communicate with stakeholders and the development team to make sure that the highest-priority items are worked on first. Some features will be larger than others, and in some cases, the Product Owner needs to say the all-important *no* to some features. Still others will be waiting patiently at the bottom of the list and never make it into the result.

The Product Owner has a tough job because they oversee the process of keeping the backlog organized and prioritized. Some items will be **must-haves**, some will be **should-** and **could-haves**, and others will fall into the **won't-have** category. We call this **MoSCoW**. It's a way to prioritize. Another thing to consider is that priorities could change when the result is tested, and the Product Owner will have to adapt.

Developing and keeping up with changes in the product backlog is a bit different from the define activities and sequencing process, and more like the development of your WBS. This is because all features and functions in the backlog will be written into *user stories.*

The Product Owner has a difficult job and must communicate regularly with stakeholders and the rest of the team.

The Product Owner maximizes the value and the work of the development team.

They are the sole party responsible for managing the product backlog, including:

- Explaining the features and functions currently in the backlog to the team and stakeholders.
- Prioritizing the work to provide the most value first.
- Working to make sure the backlog is clear and concise as to what work is next.
- Providing the development team with enough information about the backlog items so they can effectively plan.
- Owning **the product backlog**. Everyone must respect the decisions they make on priority.
- Communicating regularly and transparently to manage stakeholders' expectations.
- Validating the completion of increments or the work that has been completed.
- Writing the user stories.
- The development team is only **allowed** to work on requirements based on the Product Owner's decisions.

The development team – how

The team plans out their month using the priority user stories and produces something potentially usable or releasable at the end of each Sprint. Does that mean it always goes that way? Not at all! They have risk, schedules, and budgets, just like the predictive project teams, but the plan isn't front-loaded. The team uses an **emergent design** or progressive elaboration because the backlog could change or be updated with new information before the next Sprint.

During the Sprint:

- No new work is selected, and no changes are made after the work is selected.
- The quality goals determined will not be adapted or changed until the next Sprint is needed.
- It may be necessary to gain clarification on the scope of work and use negotiation between the Product Owner and development team as they learn more about the work.
- Sprints are like a mini project because they kick off and close out every month.
- Cost risk is lowered greatly due to having a shorter timespan to budget for.

Let's go back to my example of a user story of **As an** *end user of photographic software,* **I need** *to be able to upload in .raw format* **so that I get** *the best results from my photographs.* The team may be able to get that feature totally completed and ready for testing at the end of one month. They may also be able to accomplish four more user stories of a variety of sizes. It's up to the team to decide what they can accomplish in one month, because they are **self-organizing** and **cross-functional**. That means the team size can be smaller. Typically, there are about seven to nine team members who have multiple skill sets and can work on their own.

 There isn't a project manager role on Scrum teams, and the closest to that position would be the Product Owner.

The teams decide how much work they can do in one Sprint, and then they go about doing the work in a self-managed way. They delegate their own pace, and everyone accepts the pace they have chosen. The team is structured and empowered to organize and manage their own work.

Scrum Master – servant-leader

The Scrum Master is known as a neutral **servant-leader**. Their job is to make sure that the team has what they need to produce the working feature or result. The Scrum Master is responsible for making sure Scrum is understood and that the team adheres to Scrum theory, practices, and rules based on the Scrum Master's guidance.

The Scrum Master's role on the project is to:

- Help the Product Owner manage the backlog as needed
- Be a guide/coach for the development team
- Lead by example due to their experience and understanding of the Scrum framework
- Help remove problems and impediments to the team's progress
- Help the organization with the implementation of Scrum and the empirical process of product development when Scrum is not well understood
- Identify any causes of decreased productivity and help implement changes that increase productivity
- Identify ways in which the organization can improve their processes, which could mean working with other Scrum Masters to create and maintain the effectiveness of Scrum in the organization

The Scrum Master's entire job is to make sure that the Product Owner, the development team, and the organization practices the framework of Scrum effectively and maximizes value in all interactions.

Some of those facilitated events or interactions include Sprint planning and daily Scrums or stand-up meetings.

Sprint planning

Sprint planning lasts a maximum of eight hours for a one-month Sprint. That may sound like a long meeting for predictive project management, but imagine plotting out an entire month's worth of work in one meeting. That would practically eliminate the need for other meetings. Hmmm... sounds like project management nirvana, right? For shorter Sprints, the planning event is usually shorter. Best practice dictates two hours per weeks planned. *Four weeks = eight hours.*

Sprint planning involves the questions of:

- What can be delivered in the increment?
- How will the work be achieved?

The team would select the work they are going to do during the Sprint and create a visual view of the work/user stories they intend on doing.

The process of Sprint planning

Even though the Scrum framework is easy to explain, it is difficult to do. To be the most effective during every Sprint, there are specific planning best practices needed to achieve the Sprint goal:

1. The team works together to determine what the functionality of a feature should be and how to attain it.
2. The Product Owner explains the objective to the team and what the top priority items are to work on next.
3. The entire team collaborates on the work to gain an understanding of what the result should be.

4. The current product backlog, what was produced in the last Sprint, what the next Sprint could produce, and past performance are discussed.

5. The team determines how much of the priority backlog items can be worked on in the next Sprint.

6. The Scrum team creates a Sprint goal and decides how they will build functionality into the result.

7. The team will select work that may include different sized features, or levels of effort based on what they think they can achieve.

8. The development team works with the Product Owner to break down the first few days of work to get a clearer picture of the effort needed.

9. The team is self-organizing. Therefore, during Sprint planning, and as needed throughout the Sprint, they will determine how much work to do and how to accomplish the work.

10. The development team may renegotiate the selected product backlog items with the Product Owner if they feel that another aspect of the work needs to come first to make the result technologically accurate.

11. The development team could invite experts to the Sprint planning meeting when they need additional technical or domain advice.

12. By the end of the Sprint planning meeting, the development team will be able to explain how they intend to do the work to accomplish the Sprint goal. That goal will be visible during the Sprint.

There is much more information in this section on Scrum and agile than you will see on the exam. The types of questions you may see will be based on understanding team roles, Sprints, user stories the product backlog, and documentation at a very high level. If you do well on the chapter review questions, you should be just fine on the exam.

The team, having selected the user stories to work on during the Sprint, will create a visual way of keeping track of the work they selected and that work's progression through the Sprint. They will do this with a **Scrum board.**

A Scrum board

A Scum board uses the philosophy of a pull system to keep the flow of work moving in the right direction. When there are user stories that are completed, the team will pull new work in from the selected stories in the Sprint. A Scrum board is a big visual chart that can be posted in the team space or it can be a computer program. There are multiple programs that allow the creation of a task or Scrum board. For now, I want you to imagine a big whiteboard with lines or swim lanes that are drawn on the board. Then imagine all the user stories you have selected to work on during this Sprint are written on individual Post-It notes and stuck to the board. No new items can be added during a Sprint. Once the Sprint is over, the Scrum board will be reset before the next Sprint. The brain can process pictures 60,000 times faster than text, and because of that, a visual workflow can help keep everything transparent and easy to read.

The Scrum board shows the workflow from left to right. In *Figure 10.1*, you'll see a simple example of a Scrum board:

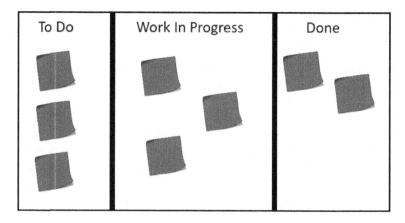

Figure 10.1

It's totally up to you how you create your swim lane categories, or how in-depth you need to make it. It's best to keep the board as simple and as easy to read as possible. The Post-It notes can have either user stories or tasks documented. It's also good to see **work in progress (WIP)** so the team keeps everything streamlined and doesn't take on too much work or multitask too much. Multitasking creates bottlenecks in the progress and slows everything down. WIP should be limited to the capacity of the team, and guess who decides the capacity? That's right, the team!

During the Sprint, the team will keep track of its progress by mapping out completed work on a **burndown chart** to help them answer the question of *How long will this project take?* Since the team determines how much work they can accomplish, and the Product Owner is refining the order of backlog items, it is easier to forecast when the work will be completed.

 We'll keep things simple for the purposes of this guide on forecasting and tracking performance. If you are interested in learning more about Scrum, you can visit the Scrum Alliance webpage at `https://www.Scrumalliance.org/`.

Let's assume the backlog has 100 stories currently listed. The team can do 20 stories a month. If things continue the way that they hope, the entire project will take five Sprints to accomplish.

Things don't always go as planned, as we all know, so a burndown chart can help show the performance trajectory of planned versus actuals, and forecast the completion of the project.

In *Figure 10.2*, you will see a basic burndown chart that shows the planned versus actual trajectory between the ideal burndown and the actual burndown. You would have the number of stories that have been completed, documented in real time, and be able to track performance. Like how we use earned value technique to compare actual performance to baselines. The team is also not going to be as precise in their estimates in the beginning of the project, and the performance will fluctuate. As the team gets a better understanding of what they are building, the more the performance will plateau and level out:

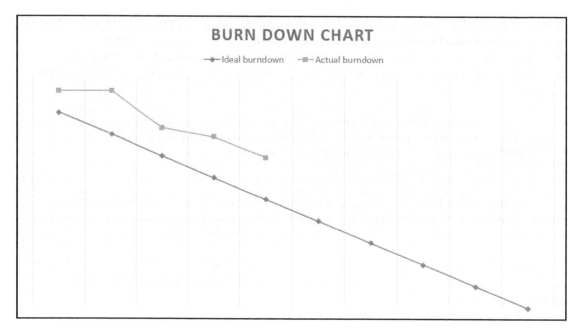

Figure 10.2

Daily Scrums

The daily Scrum is a 15-minute event for the development team to meet and create a plan for the next 24 hours. The daily Scrum can also be called a daily stand-up meeting in other agile frameworks, but is essentially the same practice. The team will be able to review work that has been accomplished since the last daily Scrum and forecast the work that can be done before the next meeting. The value of the daily Scrum is exponential. Talk about not needing other meetings! This is the only meeting that is needed because the benefits are numerous.

The daily Scrum does the following:

- Improves communication
- Eliminates the need for other meetings
- Helps identify impediments to progress
- Improves upon the development team's level of knowledge
- Acts as a key inspect-and-adapt meeting for the team to review what they are doing or not doing and adapt as needed

The daily Scrum is held at the same time and place each day to reduce complexity, and each team member answers the following questions:

- What did I do yesterday that helped to meet the Sprint goal?
- What will I do today to help meet the Sprint goal?
- Do I see any problems or impediments in my way that prevent me or the team from meeting the Sprint goal?

One of the jobs of the Scrum Master is to make sure that the team has the meeting every day, but they do not facilitate the meeting. They coach the team to keep within the 15-minute time constraint. They enforce the rule that only development team members participate in the daily Scrum, which means no pesky stakeholders interrupting. Another thing to consider if you want to try these meetings yourself is that the daily Scrum isn't about solutions to problems. It is informational only. Once the meeting wraps up, the team can work on solutions together.

The rest of the Sprint life cycle includes reviews and retrospectives.

Reviews

Reviews are held at the end of the Sprint and are comparable to the validate scope process of gaining formal acceptance of the deliverable. The customer will be testing and inspecting the results to determine whether they are working the way they would like them to and determine what they want to be worked on next.

The Scrum team and stakeholders collaborate on what was done in the Sprint and what could be done next to optimize value. Even though this sounds very formal, it is considered an informal meeting, not a status meeting. This is because the entire goal is to elicit feedback and foster collaboration between everyone involved in the project. This meeting's framework suggests the review be a four-hour meeting for one-month Sprints. For shorter Sprints, the review is usually shorter.

Who does what for the review is specific:

- The Scrum Master will ensure that the event takes place and that everyone understands its purpose.
- The Product Owner will be the one who invites the participants, because they are in the most direct contact with those who are asking for the results. The Product Owner explains to the attendees what product backlog items have been completed and what has not, as well as discussing the current product backlog.
- The team demonstrates the work accomplished to the customer and answers questions.
- The customer reviews the work and gives feedback.

Reviews may lead to a restructuring of the product backlog with newer value items, and likely completion dates are discussed based on those new items versus what is currently in the pipeline. This could be due to reviews of the current marketplace and what the potential use of the product is. Things might have changed since the last review. Everyone involved is trying to answer the question of *What is the most valuable thing to do next?*

The review isn't just about the product. It will also include reviews of the timeline, budget, potential capabilities, and the current marketplace. This helps designate priorities to the next Sprint or release. Those conversations will typically lead to a revised product backlog and help the team with planning the upcoming Sprint. As soon as the review ends, the development team will go into a retrospective meeting.

Retrospectives

The easiest way to explain **retrospectives** is that they are like lessons-learned meetings but are held by the team and for the team **only**. The goal of reflection is to look back and make changes going forward, and that is exactly what the retrospectives are for. Typically, a retrospective will last about two to three hours and happen directly after Sprint reviews, but before the next Sprint planning meeting.

The team will have in-depth discussions based on three distinct questions.

What should we:

- Stop doing?
- Start doing?
- Keep doing?

This information helps plan the next iteration and promotes continuous improvement.

There are so many benefits to the framework of Scrum, and that is why it is one of the most popular agile frameworks. It is also a far cry from the predictive project management you have reviewed throughout this guide. Remember that I mentioned that being able to tailor your projects and use what you need to be successful is currently an important skill to have? See whether a daily stand-up meeting or a retrospective at a variety of points throughout the project can help your team be more successful than they already are.

Hybrid or tailored project management

There are multiple new agile/Predictive hybrid frameworks right now. Some were designed to accommodate larger teams, some were designed to accomplish scaling to different levels of frameworks based on the product or service, and some are creations of our own that work for us. My hope is that as you read through all the best practices you have found some items that you might consider using, if you are not using them already. Perhaps some of the Scrum items caught your attention, or knowing that using the critical path method is important for schedule constraints has appealed to you. Whatever the reasons why these best practices are chosen for your projects, it's important to make sure they are practiced and understood. That can take some time, so don't worry so much about first-time execution. Continuous improvement is constant in project management, whether it be for how we do things or what things we are trying to do.

Before we go into an overview of the hybrid frameworks, please know that you will not see any of the following on the current Project+ exam. It is informational only, to give you the best overview possible of what is currently happening in the project management space, and especially in the IT industry.

There are numerous types of hybrid frameworks out there, and many are working to combat some of the constraints that agile projects present. We will go through some of those frameworks.

Types of hybrid agile frameworks

There are many reasons why hybrid agile frameworks and processes have been created. Many hybrids were created due to limitations in set predictive framework rules and best practices, and were not flexible enough for the software space. Others were created due to some restrictions on team sizes and processes in the agile environments. There are three we will cover in this guide:

- SAFe
- LeSS
- Enterprise Scrum

Scaled Agile Framework (SAFe)

SAFe stands for **Scaled Agile Framework**, and is one of many hybrid configurations that were created to address current challenges in agile frameworks. See, no matter what we use, there is always a different way to manage your unique projects. Remember that the Scrum best practice states that the team should be no larger than nine people. What if you have 100 people?

SAFe Configurations: SAFe was designed for alignment, collaboration, and delivery for large numbers of agile teams, from 50-125 or several thousand:

- **Essential SAFe**: Basic level
- **Large Solution SAFE**: Enterprise level and complex system (aerospace, defense, government)
- **Portfolio SAFe**: Enterprise for multiple solution creation
- **Full SAFe**: Large enterprise projects using hundreds to thousands of people

Elements of importance: There are several elements to consider in each configuration. All are scaled as needed.

- Metrics
- Shared services
- **Community of practice (CoP)**
- Milestones
- Roadmaps
- Vision
- System team
- Lean UX (*User eXperience*)

LeSS

Large-Scale Scrum (LeSS) was created as a way to embrace the Scrum framework, but also to make it scalable without losing the original flavor of Scrum.

LeSS levels

There are two levels of Large-Scale Scrum:

- **LeSS Level**: Up to eight teams and began in the telecom and finance industries
- **LeSS Huge**: Additional scaling elements of development added to accommodate hundreds of developers

The need for scaling became apparent and necessary due to organizational complexity in project management. Core competencies include ways to combat organizational complexity, and simpler ways of working on larger projects, without devaluing the Scrum framework. This is accomplished with **LeSS** roles, **LeSS** management, and **LeSS** organizational structures.

Enterprise Scrum

Enterprise Scrum was created to allow for faster, more efficient, and customer-driven innovation for higher profits and revenue. It also allows for scalable models and empirical project management. This set the stage for similar values and reporting structures to the original Scrum framework, but on a much larger scale.

Values of enterprise Scrum

The values of enterprise Scrum align closely with the values of Scrum, including:

- **Cultural Values**: Scrum values and elements of business analysis
- **Value List**: Value list items (such as **Product Backlog Items (PBI)**); each has a definition of ready (DOR) and done (DOD)
- **Reporting**: Burndown charts, as well as other necessary metrics and charts

Enterprise Scrum includes multiple levels of planning and improvement cycles, as well as reviews for business value and testing of the increment or results. Value list items are refined, much like backlog refinement, before the cycle continues.

The roles are like the original Scrum framework, but instead of a Product Owner, there is a business owner since the projects are enterprise-level initiatives.

This is all a *very* high-level review of *some* of the hybrid frameworks that are being used in the agile project-management space. Maybe some of the aspects of each will be something you decide to investigate further. But don't worry, they won't be on your exams. Agile is just now coming more into the forefront of project management, and humans are always looking for better ways to manage projects. *What will you do to manage your projects more effectively?*

You have taken the best first step in becoming certified in Project+. I want to congratulate you on taking this journey with me, and for bettering your skills and your career through certification. It's been my pleasure to embark on the journey with you, and let me be the very first to wish you the best of luck on your exams and all your future endeavors in the world of project management!

Questions

1. Your project work is ending and you are looking forward to meeting with your customer and showing them the result before closing the project. Which of the following is necessary before you can close out the project formally with their approval?
   - Quality control
   - Close procurement
   - Validate scope
   - Quality assurance

2. Your team has worked extremely hard on the project and you have completed all the work necessary to close out your project formally and successfully. What kind of project closure has occurred?
   - Starvation
   - Extinction
   - Integration
   - Addition

3. Which of the following project endings can best be described as an ending in which the project you are working on develops into a functional department or contributes to the ongoing operations of the organization?
   - Addition
   - Starvation
   - Extinction
   - Integration

4. Your project has been a bit behind schedule and your team has been struggling to catch up. Your sponsor is telling you that there simply are not enough resources to do the work and the team you do have is being reassigned to another project. What kind of project closing is this?
    - Starvation
    - Extinction
    - Integration
    - Addition

5. Which of the following describes a summation of the successes, the challenges of the project, and lessons learned, as well as specifics on budgetary performance, schedule performance, reviewing the scope validation process, and whether the final deliverables were accepted?
    - Lessons-learned meeting
    - Final project report
    - Retrospective
    - Review

6. What is the typical length of a Sprint in the Scrum framework?
    - Two weeks
    - One month
    - Two months
    - Three weeks

7. You are working with your team to help remove distractions from stakeholders and to coach the team on the Scrum framework. What role describes this best?
    - Project manager
    - Product Owner
    - Scrum Master
    - Development team lead

8. Which of the following are the three pillars of the Scrum framework?
    - Inspection, Sprint, and adaptation
    - Inspection, adaptation, and backlog
    - Transparency, inspection, and adaptation
    - Transparency, inspection, and communication

9. You have recently taken over a team that is practicing Scrum, and your job includes collecting all the requirements and organizing them by priority. Which of the following positions are you in?
   - Scrum Master
   - Product Owner
   - Development team
   - Project manager

10. During a Sprint planning meeting, the Product Owner is explaining all the features and functions that are necessary in the current project. They show a list of items based on priority. What is the list called?
   - Project backlog
   - Project management plan
   - Define tasks
   - Product backlog

11. You and your team have recently decided to practice some tailoring in your current project and are planning to present the requirements in a different way so they can be better understood by the team and the customer. What might be a way to present requirements rather than in list format?
   - Stories
   - Gantt chart
   - User requirements
   - User stories

12. Your team has wrapped up your project and is now in the process of closing it out. They will hold a lessons-learned meeting to discuss what went well and what may need to change for the next project. What is the equivalent to a lessons-learned meeting in the Scrum Framework?
   - Review
   - Postmortem
   - Daily Scrum
   - Retrospective

13. Ben is part of your Scrum development team and oversees updating team performance in a visual way. He will use a visual chart that tracks planned work versus actual work. What kind of chart will Ben update?
   - Gantt chart
   - Burn-up chart
   - Burn-down chart
   - Ishikawa

14. As a Scrum Master for your team, you need to make sure that the team gets together every day to discuss what they have worked on, what they will work on, and whether there are any problems with their progress. What kind of Scrum event will you hold?
    - Daily stand-up meeting
    - Scrum review meeting
    - Sprint planning meeting
    - Daily Scrum

15. Which of the following are categories of project closure? Choose all that apply.
    - Extinction
    - Add-on project
    - Integration
    - Starvation
    - Retrospective
    - Lessons learned
    - Validate scope

Assessments

Chapter 1 – Introduction to the CompTIA Project+ Exam (PK0-004)

1. Control charts.
2. Project B, because its NPV is a positive value.
3. A project initiator or sponsor.
4. Regulations are approved by a recognized body and employ rules and guidelines that should be followed.
5. It authorizes the project and the use of organizational resources to meet project requirements.
6. Organize meetings to identify and resolve misunderstandings between team members, to avoid interface problems, disintegration, and costly rework early in the project.
7. The interpersonal relationships between team members are their private issue. You should not interfere.
8. Control scope-creep completely.
9. The cost baseline will be updated, and the new baseline will be the basis for future earned value analysis.
10. Fast tracking.

Chapter 2 – Project Initiation

1. A temporary endeavor that produces a unique product service or result.
2. A group of projects managed in a coordinated fashion.
3. A group of unrelated projects and programs.
4. Functional.
5. Project-based and strong matrix.
6. Project D has a payback period of one year and an NPV of $350,000.
7. True.

8. 10.
9. The project manager is in charge of the project and the team.
10. Integration-management.
11. Constrained optimization.
12. There is an equal amount of focus on project and functional/operational work.
13. Scope-management.
14. The organization needs to change a process or product for regulatory compliance.
15. Stakeholder management.

Chapter 3 – Project Roles and Responsibilities

1. Project sponsor.
2. Coordinator.
3. PMO.
4. Procurement manager.
5. The plan, once approved, can only be changed through formal change-control. This includes the management plans and baselines.
6. Stakeholder matrix.
7. Change-control board (CCB).
8. A person or group who has requirements that must be met for the project to be considered successful.
9. Stakeholder matrix.
10. Whether you will be tracking and documenting their project performance and submitting the documentation to their functional manager for their performance reviews. How the resources will be acquired and how they will be released from project work.
11. Stakeholder-management plan, Schedule-management plan, and schedule baseline, Cost-management plan, and cost baseline.
12. Change-control board (CCB).
13. Buyer.
14. CAPM®.
15. Functional manager at the customer's organization.

Chapter 4 – Developing a Project Charter

1. Temporary and unique.
2. Initiation, planning, executing, monitoring and controlling, and closing a project or phase.
3. Development of the business case, project charter creation, identification of stakeholders.
4. To create a comprehensive project-management plan.
5. Execution.
6. The CCB.
7. After approvals, go through formal project closure for this project.
8. Overlapping.
9. Predicative projects know the full scope of work in advance and adaptive projects typically correlate with knowledge work.
10. Formally authorizes the project manager to begin project work.
11. The software and hardware used to manage communications, reporting, and performance.
12. Schedule milestones.
13. Offers more flexibility for the scope of work.
14. An agenda.
15. Confirm everyone understands the goals and objectives of the project.

Chapter 5 – Creating a Work Breakdown Structure (WBS)

1. Requirements traceability matrix.
2. Hierarchical decomposition of 100% scope of work.
3. WBS dictionary.
4. WBS, Scope statement, WBS dictionary.
5. Decomposition.
6. The code of accounts.
7. Create the scope statement.
8. Scope statement.

9. The scope statement describes what will and will not be done, and the WBS formalizes that. The scope statement **also** describes what will and will not be done, and the WBS decomposes to a level you can estimate effectively.

10. Decomposes the scope of the work to the work package level.

11. The project charter gives formal authorization to begin project work, and the scope statement clearly describes what features will and will not be produced during the project.

12. 100% scope of work as it is known today.

13. Offers more flexibility for scope of work.

14. This project's work package level is *level one*.

15. A document that describes the details for each component in the WBS.

Chapter 6 – Developing a Project Schedule

1. The schedule management plan.
2. Milestone list.
3. Sequence tasks.
4. Finish to start.
5. External.
6. Rolling wave planning.
7. Finish to start.
8. 19 days.
9. Lag time.
10. Analogous.
11. 18.3 days.
12. Fast tracking.
13. You would need to level.
14. There is not enough information to answer this question.
15. Positive float.
16. ACD.

Chapter 7 – Resource Management Planning and Communication Considerations

1. Communication and negotiation.
2. Project organizational chart.
3. RAM.
4. Attainable, consulted, informed, responsible.
5. Esteem.
6. Storming.
7. An X manager.
8. Safety.
9. Provide specific feedback and training for new skills.
10. Affiliation.
11. Money.
12. Confrontation.
13. Forcing.
14. Avoid.
15. Send out an agenda.
16. 136.

Chapter 8 – Budget and Contingency Plans for Risk

1. Three-point.
2. Training, appraisal, and prevention costs.
3. Governance gate.
4. Funding limit reconciliation.
5. The project is currently over budget.
6. Behind schedule and under budget.
7. Over budget and behind schedule.
8. BAC * % complete.

9. One thousand.
10. SWOT analysis.
11. Expected monetary value.
12. Avoid.
13. Secondary risk.
14. Qualitative.
15. Seven thousand.
16. 1.02 and 0.99.

Chapter 9 – Monitoring and Controlling Project Work

1. Validate scope.
2. Pareto diagram.
3. Plan, do, check, act.
4. Scope creep.
5. Corrective action.
6. Create a solution, such as fast tracking, and process a change request.
7. Fixed price.
8. *"Sorry, Doug, I know you'll get your work done and make your incentives easily, but that would be a breach of contract, and I can't pay you early. I'm really sorry about that!"*
9. Make or buy analysis.
10. PSOW.
11. Sole source.
12. Service Level Agreements (SLA).
13. Waiver.
14. Procurement audit.
15. Internal reorganization.

Chapter 10 – Formal Project or Phase Closure and Agile Project Management

1. Validate scope.
2. Extinction.
3. Addition.
4. Starvation.
5. Final project report.
6. One month.
7. Scrum Master.
8. Transparency, inspection, and adaptation.
9. Product owner.
10. Product backlog.
11. User stories.
12. Retrospective.
13. Burn-down chart.
14. Daily Scrum.
15. Extinction, integration, starvation.

Other Book You May Enjoy

If you enjoyed this book, you may be interested in this other book by Packt:

CompTIA A+ Certification Guide (220-901 and 220-902)

Matthew Bennett

ISBN: 978-1-78712-730-2

- Validate your skills and boost your career with CompTIA A+
- Learn all concepts raised by the A+ certification
- Understanding and installing CompTIA hardware required for CompTIA A+ 220-901
- Install and configure an Operating System on a client/desktop, covering a range of mobile and network devices and platforms
- Learn how to secure a workstation and troubleshoot any security related issues

Leave a review - let other readers know what you think

Please share your thoughts on this book with others by leaving a review on the site that you bought it from. If you purchased the book from Amazon, please leave us an honest review on this book's Amazon page. This is vital so that other potential readers can see and use your unbiased opinion to make purchasing decisions, we can understand what our customers think about our products, and our authors can see your feedback on the title that they have worked with Packt to create. It will only take a few minutes of your time, but is valuable to other potential customers, our authors, and Packt. Thank you!

Index

Made in the USA
Middletown, DE
18 February 2021